More
STORIES
OF
COMPOSERS
for young musicians

by Catherine Wolff Kendall

More STORIES OF COMPOSERS
for young musicians

by Catherine Wolff Kendall

with

- portraits
- calendar of composers' birthdays
- sources of piano and cello music
  by composers in this book
- pronunciation guide

Edwardsville, Illinois
Toadwood Publishers

ISBN 0961087811

Contents

Illustrations

A Calendar of Composers' Birthdays

January
4 - G.B. Pergolesi   (1710)
23 - M. Clementi   (1752)
27 - W.A. Mozart   (1756)
31 - F.P. Schubert   (1797)

February
3 - F. Mendelssohn   (1809)
17 - A. Corelli   (1653)
21 - K. Czerny   (1791)
23 - G.F. Handel   (1685)

March
4 - A. Vivaldi   (1678)
6 - H. Lichner   (1829)
31 - J.S. Bach   (1685)
31 - F.J. Haydn   (1732)

May
7 - P.I. Tchaikovsky   (1840)

June
8 - R. Schumann   (1810)
12 - F. Seitz   (1848)
16 - D. Popper   (1843)
19 - F.X. Chwatal   (1808)

July
4 - L.C. Daquin   (1694)

August
8 - W. Squire   (1871)
19 - G. Golterman   (1824)

September
5 - J.C. Bach   (1735)
11 - F. Kuhlau   (1786)

October
9 - C.C. Saint-Saens   (1835)
17 - S. Suzuki   (1898)
26 - D. Scarlatti   (1685)

November
6 - I.J. Paderewski   (1860)
6 - J.B.S. Breval   (1753)
14 - J.N. Hummel   (1778)
18 - C.M. von Weber   (1786)
27 - J.B. Lully   (1632)

December
4 - J.F. Burgmüller   (1806)
16 - L. van Beethoven   (1770)

dates unknown: T. Bayly (1797); Sammartini (1700 or 1701); H. Purcell (1659)
A. Vandini (1690); H. Eccles (1670); Caix d'Hervelois (1670)

JOHANN CHRISTIAN BACH

Seated by the fire, a shawl draped loosely around his shoulders, the aging, white-haired composer called out, "Johann Christian, my son, please come and help your old father read this letter. The print is too small for my dim eyes. Is it from your brother, Carl? I hope so. I want to know if King Frederick the Great was pleased with the composition that I wrote for him after my visit to his Court."

"Let me see, father," answered the thirteen year old boy. "Yes the letter is from Carl. He says that the King has received your composition, a *Musical Offering*, and he is most grateful to have such a magnificent work dedicated to him. Carl goes on to say that the King's orchestra is already rehearsing the piece for a concert at the Court. Well, father, who would not be honored to have a composition by the famous Johann Sebastian Bach?"

Christian was the youngest of the Bach sons. Like his brothers, he studied music with his father, but now that the elderly composer's eyesight was failing, the young boy was able to help his father in many ways.

When Christian was just fifteen years old, his illustrious father suffered a stroke and died. After the gathering of the Bach family from all over Europe for the funeral, Carl Philipp Emanuel said to his younger brother, "Come to Berlin, Christian, and stay with me."

So, with three claviers, and a stock of linen shirts and a little money his father had left him, Johann Christian, with his brother, Emanuel, left Leipzig. Christian's musical education continued under Emanuel's guidance. He helped him become an excellent clavier player, and gave him lessons in composition. The two brothers were often seen at the Berlin Opera House where Christian learned to appreciate and love opera.

One bright morning, Emanuel heard quick footsteps on the stairs. "Emanuel," Christian said excitedly, "a letter has just come from Milan. It is from Count Litta. He invites me to be conductor of his private orchestra. I would like to go there. It will give me the chance to compose for the Count's orchestra. What do you think I should do? I am only nineteen years old. Do you think I can do it?"

"How wonderful, Christian," Emanuel replied. "Of course you can do it! And do you know, not far from Milan in the city of Bologna, is one of the greatest music teachers in Italy—Padre Giovanni Battista Martini? It would not be too far for you to travel there to study counterpoint and harmony with him. What a wonderful opportunity for you, Christian!"

Johann Christian prepared to leave for Milan. Thanking his brother for all his care and guidance, the young musician left for his first job.

Count Litta gave great encouragement to his protegée, and for his part, Johann Christian worked diligently. He became a fine organist, and later, with the Count's help, he was appointed organist of the great Cathedral of Milan.

As Emanuel had suggested, Christian did go to Padre Martini to study. The two worked closely together, and from his teacher, Christian gained the solid musical foundation that he needed to become a fine composer.

Soon, Johann Christian's compositions began to receive a great deal of attention. The pleasing, lyrical melodies of his church music seemed to have been inspired by the operas that he had heard and enjoyed so much with his brother back in Berlin. But, as time went on, Christian began to lose interest in writing music for the church. He gave more and more attention to composing light and carefree music for the opera.

Count Litta, his patron, was not pleased. He wrote to Padre Martini, complaining that his protogée was not attending properly to his church duties.

"I must write you about Bach," he said in his letter. "Johann Christian's mind seems to be wandering away from his duties as Cathedral organist and composer. Writing operas has become first in his attentions. In just two years, he has had five operas performed!"

It seemed there was nothing that the Count or the Padre could do. The twenty-seven year old composer was determined to follow his interest in opera. When an invitation came to him from London, England, he was quick to accept. He asked the authorities at the Cathedral for a year's leave of absence to compose two operas for the King's Theatre in London. Johann Christian wanted to try his wings in a wider world of music, even though it meant he would be breaking away from the tradition of the Bach family.

Just about the same time that Johann Christian arrived in England, a new Queen had come to the English throne. She, like Bach, had been born in Germany, and she loved music very much. For the new Queen Charlotte, Johann Christian wrote a special *Ode*, which pleased her so much that she asked him to become Music Master to the Queen's household. The following year, Queen Charlotte and the whole royal court attended a performance of one of Bach's operas.

"I am reminded of the great George Frederick Handel's music," the Queen said when she heard the lofty, singing melodies of the opera. "But, I want to know, what is that new instrument I see in the orchestra?" she asked Bach after the performance.

"That is a clarinet," he explained. "It is the first time it has been used in an orchestral piece. I like the lovely, mellow sound of the instrument, and it can help the music fit the feeling of the opera story."

Although Bach's operas were not always well liked, many of the songs from the operas became favorites of the English people. Bach knew how to write music in a style that pleased them.

When Bach became Music Master to the Queen, he was greatly surprised to meet an old boyhood friend from Germany. His name was Karl Friederich Abel. He was a viola da gamba player and a composer. The two musicians were so glad to see each other again!

"Have you heard?" Abel said to Bach one day after a performance at the Court. "The Mozart family is coming to London, and will be giving a concert here this very week."

"Ah, how wonderful," exclaimed Christian. "What a privilege it will be to hear them. We must invite them to our home for a visit."

When Wolfgang's father received an invitation from Bach and Abel, he hastened to accept. The two older musicians and the eight year old Wolfgang Mozart spent many hours together, playing for one another, and talking about music. The tiny boy sat on Christian's knee in front of the clavier, and together they improvised duets. They played some of Wolfgang's own compositions. Christian made some suggestions to the young composer, and in later years, Mozart recalled with warm feelings those times he spent with Bach. He was always grateful for the help with his compositions that Johann Christian had given to him.

As time went on, Bach and Abel decided to perform together, and to organize a series of concerts. Every Wednesday afternoon, for several months in the year, people from all over London could come for these concerts where Bach and Abel's compositions, as well as compositions of other composers, were performed. The series carried on for sixteen years and became a very important part of London's musical life.

Since Bach had arrived in London, he had always been glad

JOHANN CHRISTIAN BACH

to help other musicians who were having trouble earning enough money. He would give a concert, and donate the money from the ticket sale to the troubled musician.

"I understand that our oboe-playing friend, Mr. Fischer, is in need of help," Bach told Abel. They hired the Thatched House Tavern for the concert.

"What is that on the stage?" asked someone in the audience. Everyone in the audience was taken by surprise to see a large instrument on legs, more massive than a harpsichord, but somewhat the same shape. It was a piano, and this was the first time one had been played as a solo instrument in London. Bach played a composition he had written especially for the occasion.

One day, after a concert in London, Christian had just settled for a rest, when the postman arrived with a letter from Bologna, Italy. It had been some years since Bach and Padre Martini had been together, but here was a message from the good Padre. He opened the envelope. "Let me remind you," Martini wrote, "that you promised to have a painting made of yourself that I may add to my private collection." Immediately, Bach sought out his good friend, the famous English painter, Thomas Gainsborough, who was best known for his paintings of illustrious people. It took Gainsborough two years to finish the painting of Johann Christian Bach, but at last Christian could sit at his desk to write a letter to his old friend:

"Most Reverend Father and honoured patron, I have placed in Signore Rencaglias' charge, an excellent portrait of myself by one of our best painters. He is passing thru Bologna, and no doubt, will deliver it into your hands. I beg you graciously to accept it as a small token of my heavy debt to you and pray that, when you look at it, you will give a thought to me who has the honor to be ... Your Reverence's most humble and devoted servant, Johann Christian Bach."

Gainsborough's portrait of Johann Christian Bach can still be seen in Bologna today.

Until Johann Christian was forty-six years old, he continued to compose and perform in London, and many of his compositions were included in programs given in the concert halls of that musical city. But after almost twenty years there, his popularity declined and his health failed. His housekeeper cheated him and stole his money. He was deeply in debt when he died, though the Queen helped by providing Bach's wife with enough money so that she could return to her native Italy.

On hearing of Bach's death, Wolfgang Mozart said, "It is a loss to the musical world." Although the people of London did not honor Johann Christian Bach in his later years, music-lovers all over the world remember him now as a composer of great ability and elegant style and a man of generosity and kindness.

b. Leipzig, Germany, September 5, 1735
d. London, England, January 1, 1782

JOHANN SEBASTIAN BACH

Before the stars had faded in the morning sky, Johann Sebastian jumped out of his feather bed and ran over to his sleeping brother. "Johann Jakob," he whispered, as he shook the boy, "get up. This is the day. This is Bach family day."

Each year, on this special day, the Bach relatives from all around Germany — cousins, uncles, nephews, nieces, grandparents, great aunts and uncles — gathered together to visit and make music. There were singers, trumpeters, organists, violinists, recorder players, and choirmasters. What a wonderful time they had!

Johann Sebastian had only recently begun to take violin lessons from his father. "Come, Johann, bring your violin along to our family day," the boy's father said. "You can join us in the music making. Your cousins can see how well you are playing."

There was nothing Johann Sebastian would rather do than play and listen to music. Everyone in his family did, so it was only natural that music would be the most important part of his life.

Johann Sebastian's father played violin in the castle of the Duke of Eisenach. "The duke is having some important guests today," Johann's father said as the boy was leaving for school. "I will be playing there in the beautiful garden to entertain his guests. But tonight there is a banquet at the town hall. I will be playing with the town musicians and you can come along to listen. How would you like that?"

9

"Oh, that will be splendid," answered the boy.

On Sundays, Johann Sebastian sang in the church choir where his father's cousin Christoph was organist. On other days of the week, after school, Johann often crept into the church while Christoph was practicing. "Come, Johann," Christoph would call to the small boy when he heard his footsteps on the stone stairs, "come up here in the organ loft with me while I practice." Johann spent many happy hours there.

When Johann Sebastian Bach was ten years old, a great sadness came into his life. In the same year, both his parents became ill and died, leaving him an orphan. Johann Christoph, his older brother, said, "You, Sebastian, and our brother Jakob will come to live in my home. My wife and I will try to make a good home for you." So, saying goodbye to their home and friends, Johann Sebastian and his brother Jakob left Eisenach.

In the town where they went to live, Johann Sebastian attended school near his brother's house. It was a famous school where new teaching ideas were being tried. The children were encouraged to learn by doing. Instead of being told the answers to questions, the children tried to find the answers for themselves. Johann Sebastian enjoyed this kind of school, and he learned Greek, religion, writing, arithmetic, singing, and natural science. He was especially interested in the study of religion, and when he was older and composing music, he told a friend, "All my music is written to the glory of God."

Johann Christoph continued to give his younger brother music lessons. He taught him harmony, composition, organ, and harp-sichord. "We will try this new method of playing harpsichord," Johann Christoph said during one of the lessons. "Now, curve your fingers instead of keeping them straight. In this way you can also use your thumbs as you play."

Johann Sebastian was a quick learner. When he came to his lessons, he had learned all that he had been given to study. "Please, brother, will you give me another, more difficult piece this time?" he would beg.

In a cupboard in the music room, Johann Christoph kept a book of pieces written by well-known composers. "Brother Christoph," Johann Sebastian asked one day after his lesson was finished, "would you allow me to look at that book of pieces? There is so much music that I am eager to learn."

The stern answer came back immediately. "Absolutely not," Christoph answered, "you are not ready for that book. You are too young." No amount of begging would change his mind. So one night after Johann Christoph had gone to bed, Johann Sebastian crept quietly into the music room, and reaching his small hand between the latticed panels of the locked cabinet, he pulled out the music book that his brother would not let him see. "I will copy every note in this book," he said to himself. "I am not allowed to have a candle in my room, but I can copy the book by the light of the moon." Though it took six months, he copied every note.

By the time Johann Sebastian was fifteen years old, Brother

Christoph and his wife had three children of their own, and the small house where they lived was not large enough for everyone. "Sebastian," his brother said, "it is time for us to find a school for you where you can continue your musical education. I have spoken to the Kapellmeister at the Church of St. Michael's He wants you to try for a place as a choral scholar in his school. If you are accepted, you will live there at the school, study music, and sing in the choir."

The day came for Johann Sebastian to sing for the Kappel-meister. He did very well. "You have a fine voice, Johann Sebastian, and you are an excellent sight reader. We welcome you to our school!"

Young Bach was glad to be at St. Michael's School, but it was not long before he reached the age when his clear boy soprano voice began to change, and he could no longer sing in the choir. "Johann Sebastian Bach," the Kapellmeister said, "now that you can no longer sing in the choir, we can find a place for you as a violist in our church orchestra."

The boy was happy to be able to stay at St. Michael's. He could hear so much beautiful music in the magnificent church. In the large library there, he could study church music to his heart's content. Besides, many well known composers visited St. Michael's Church, and he had the opportunity to talk and study with many of them.

One teacher who visited the school told Bach about his own great teacher, an organist and composer by the name of Johann

Adam Reinken. "Some day you must hear him play," Bohm told Bach. "Perhaps you can travel to Hamburg this summer to his concert."

When the time came, Bach had no money to go by coach to hear the concert that Reinken would play on the great organ of St. Katherine's Church. So he set out on foot for the city of Hamburg. After four days of walking, he arrived in Hamburg tired and hungry, but the moment he stepped into the church he forgot his weariness. The great music that Reinken played put every other thought from his mind. It was an experience he would never forget.

Many years later, Johann Sebastian Bach's children enjoyed telling the story of their father's trip home from Hamburg. "Father was very tired on his walk back home. His feet hurt him and he was hungry, too, but had not enough money to buy a meal at the inn. As he sat resting outside the old stone inn with the tempting smells of food coming from inside the noisy kitchen, an upstairs window suddenly flew open. Out came two fish heads and landed in Bach's lap. Picking up the heads, he found two coins inside them, enough to buy himself a dinner at the inn!"

By the time Bach was eighteen years old, he was hired to be organist at a church in Arnstadt. For nearly a hundred years members of the Bach family had played the organ there. The organ in this church was an exceptionally fine instrument, and Bach looked forward to playing new pieces he would compose for the Sunday services. Several months after he had taken the position at the church, Bach was approached by a member of the church council. With a frown on his face, he said to Bach, "Maestro, we are having many complaints about your music. Our people like the old hymns. They do not like the way you change them, with all those variations. Your job is to just keep up with the congregation's singing. You must play the same tunes all the time. And that is not the only complaint we hear. We understand the boys in the choir do not behave well for you. Besides, you spend too much time composing and not enough time training the boys."

Bach felt held down by the church authorities. He asked for a four week leave to go to a neighboring city to hear the great organist and composer, Dietrich Buxtehude. He was granted permission and left for Lubech. Bach was truly inspired by what he heard. Hour after hour he listened to Buxtehude play his organ pieces. He was enthralled by the composer's musical inventions. Never before had Bach heard such dramatic, inspiring music, with choruses and solo singers, and an orchestra with forty players.

When his four weeks were over, Bach could not bear to leave Lubech. There was so much more he wanted to hear and study. He stayed in Lubech four months, and now, inspired by Buxtehude, his compositions became even longer and more complicated. When he returned home, the church authorities once again complained. "You stayed away too long, and now that you have returned, your church music is getting more complicated and longer than ever."

What did Bach do? He would show them! He made his organ introductions to the hymn singing so short that the congregation was never ready to start singing in time!

When the authorities complained because his wife-to-be, Maria Barbara, came to the church while he was practicing to sing some of the pieces he had composed, Bach was furious. That complaint was more than Bach would stand for. "I will resign my post and seek another job," he told the authorities. "I wish to have more freedom to compose as I think right."

He did get another job, and he married Maria Barbara. His salary now was to be 85 guldens, 12 bushels of corn, 6 trusses of brushwood, and, as a bonus, 3 pounds of fish every year. The city officials even sent him a wagon to transport his furniture from Arnstadt to Mulhausen.

Bach was now twenty-two years old. He did not stay for very long in any one job. He and his wife moved from place to place seeking work, sometimes as a court musician, playing violin, sometimes as a church organist. His fame as an organist was spreading throughout Germany. Kings and noblemen invited Bach to try out new organs in their courts and palaces.

One day Bach received a letter from a friend in the court at Dresden. "You must come to Dresden," the letter said. "There is an organist from France by the name of Marchand who believes that no German musician can play as well as he. The king wishes to have a royal contest. He summons you to come."

Of course, Bach answered the king's command and appeared

at court. First, Marchand played, and he played very well indeed. Then Bach played, and the applause was thunderous.

"We shall continue the contest tomorrow," the king ordered. "Then we shall decide."

When the time came to play, Bach appeared. The audience waited for Marchand. They became impatient. Finally, a messenger was sent for him. He was nowhere to be found. It was discovered that he had left early that morning for France, afraid to compete with Bach. But Bach played one of his own compositions, and the king was so pleased with the performance that he sent him a hundred pieces of gold.

Most of the time, however, Bach and his wife had just barely enough money for their growing family. Church organists were not paid very well in those times. But Bach, a large, strong, good looking man, worked hard, and he and his family were happy together. "Come, children," he would say, "it is time for your music lesson. Today I will show you the new book I have prepared for you. It explains how to play the clavier, with lessons in harmony. And I have written pieces for you, first easy ones, then getting more difficult step by step as you advance."

And so he would work with his children, and use the books also with his other pupils. Bach was loved by his children and students, and his home was always lively with visitors and music making.

Some of the happiest days in Bach's working life were during the time he worked in the court of Prince Leopold. Writing a letter to a friend, Bach described him as "a gracious prince who loved and understood music." The prince played violin, viola da gamba, and harpsichord. "Do you have any new music for us to play tonight?" the prince would often ask, as he planned his musical evening concerts.

Bach, eager to have the prince hear his latest compositions, looked forward to those evenings. Many nights the castle was lighted until very late hours with music making, when musicians performed for the first time many of Bach's concerti, suites, and sonatas.

One day news came to the castle that George Frederick Handel would be returning to his home in Halle for a visit. Bach requested a leave to travel there to meet Handel. When he arrived, he was just one day too late. Handel had already left for England, so the two men never met.

The prince often took Bach with him on his travels. During one of these trips, Maria Barbara, Bach's wife, died. Bach was only thirty-five years old at the time.

After a few years, Bach found a position which he kept for twenty-seven years. He was made honorary conductor to the Duke of Wessenfels, and court composer to the King of Poland. It was here that he wrote most of his sacred church music.

Now Bach had married again. Anna Magdelene was the daughter of the trumpeter in the court of the Duke of Wessenfels. She had a fine singing voice and was an excellent musician. She often helped her husband write out the parts for his compositions.

JOHANN SEBASTIAN BACH

To help her learn to play the clavier, Bach prepared two music books, with pieces for teaching her to play. These books are called the Anna Magdelene Bach books.

While Bach was working in his study one sunny afternoon, there was a knock on the door. It was a messenger with a letter from his son, who was a musician in the court of King Frederick the Great. "Father," the letter read, "my employer, King Frederick the Great, often asks about my famous father. He would like very much to meet you. Can you come to the palace to pay me a visit and meet the king?"

"What do you think, Anna?" Bach asked his wife. "Shall I make the journey?" Bach was a humble man, and thought it would be an honor to be greeted by King Frederick. So it was agreed that he should go.

Every evening before supper the king had a concert in his court. Often he himself played the flute in his palace orchestra. One evening, just as the orchestra was about to play, an officer of the court handed the king a list of people who had come to the palace that day. Glancing at the list, he saw the name of Johann Sebastian Bach. He turned to the orchestra and said, "Gentlemen, old Bach has come."

Bach, who had gone to his son's rooms to rest after his journey, was called to the castle. The king greeted him with great kindness. "So, you have finally come," the king said warmly. "Let me show you around the castle. Perhaps you will play for us?"

Bach improvised upon the various Silvermann pianos in the

19

palace, as the king and the court musicians followed him from room to room. As Bach finished playing, the king exclaimed, "Only one Bach, only one Bach!"

The very next day, the king told his visitor, "We have several very fine organs in the churches in Potsdam. I would like to write a musical theme for you and have you improvise a six part fugue on these instruments."

"It would be my greatest pleasure," responded Bach. He performed this remarkable feat, much to the amazement of all who heard him.

When Bach returned to Leipzig, he composed several pieces dedicated to his new friend, King Frederick the Great.

Toward the end of his life, Bach's eyesight began to fail, weakened by the many hours spent copying music by candle light. At the age of sixty-five he died, thinking that his music was old fashioned and that no one would remember what he had written.

And forgotten it was for a time. Mozart and Beethoven had heard his music and been deeply impressed by its strength and beauty, but it was not until about a hundred years later that another composer, Felix Mendelssohn, performed Bach's *St. Matthew Passion.* Then, almost two hundred years after Bach's death, Robert Schumann suggested that a special society should publish all of Bach's compositions. It is difficult to imagine now a world without the great, inspiring music of Johann Sebastian Bach.

b. Eisenach, Germany, March 21, 1685
d. Leipzig, Germany, July 28, 1750

THOMAS HAYNES BAYLY

In the little town of Bath, in the southwestern part of England, lived young Thomas Bayly. The Avon River flowed through the center of the town, and the young boy must have spent many hours watching the water winding lazily along its way to Severn in the Bristol Channel. Many thoughts came into his mind as he listened to the tunes that the river sang while he sat along its banks. When he grew older, Thomas Bayly wrote poems and songs to express his thoughts. *Gaily the Troubadour* and *Long Long Ago* are two of his songs that have been remembered. These are the words to *Long Long Ago:*

> Tell me the tales that to me were so dear
> Long long ago, long long ago.
> Sing me the songs I delighted to hear
> Long long ago, long long ago.
> Now you are come all my grief is removed;
> Let me forget that so long you have roved.
> Let me believe that you love as you loved
> Long long ago, long ago.

Here are the words of *Gaily the Troubadour:*

> Gaily, the troubadour touched his guitar
> As he was hastening home from the war
> Singing, "From Palestine, hither I come.
> Lady love, lady love, welcome me home!"

b. Bath, England - 1797
d. London, England - 1839

21

LUDWIG VAN BEETHOVEN

The cannon on the town wall blared forth, and the band in their glittering uniforms marched through the palace gates, down the street where the Beethovens lived, and back again to the palace. Ludwig watched from the attic window. Then he ran downstairs. "I'm going to the palace, mother," the young Ludwig called out. "Grandfather said I could come. The orchestra will be playing this afternoon." Ludwig ran out the door and down the street, following the band to the gates of the palace.

Ludwig's grandfather was the master of the choir at the palace. He often invited his little grandson to visit him at the court to hear the orchestra and the choir, or to listen to the organ concerts in the chapel. Ludwig and his grandfather were very dear to one another. At home, they sang and played musical games and enjoyed each other's company.

Ludwig's father was a musician, too. He was a singer at the palace. But he did not spend much time with his son. "Where is father?" Ludwig would ask his mother as evening was coming on and they were lighting the candles. "Why doesn't he come home?"

In a sad and tired voice, his mother would answer, "He is at the tavern, sitting with his friends and spending our last few pennies on drink. If it were not for your grandfather, what would we do?"

Ludwig was very young when his grandfather died. He not only lost his best friend and a strong, guiding hand, but the

Beethoven family grew steadily poorer without Grandfather Beethoven's support.

When Ludwig was four years old, his father said, "I am teaching your two brothers to play the violin and piano. Now you are old enough to begin your lessons, too." Ludwig's brothers did not take much interest in their lessons, but with this son, the lessons were different.

"Ludwig seems to take to music naturally," Father Johann Beethoven said to his wife. "He learns easily. Do you remember the stories about young Mozart? He earned money for his family by playing concerts all over Europe. I will see to it that Ludwig practices diligently. Then he can give concerts, too."

Ludwig's father forced the boy to practice many, many long hours each day. A neighbor remembered Ludwig 'as a tiny boy, standing on a footstool in front of the clavier and weeping.'

As the boy progressed in his playing, he seemed to want to practice without his father forcing him. But Father Johann did not approve of the way that his son practiced. He wanted Ludwig to play his scales and exercises on the piano perfectly, but Ludwig had his own ideas. His fingers began to wander from his exercises, and he began making up pieces of his own. "You must not do that," Johann scolded. "You are wasting time. If you are to play concerts, you must play every note as it is written."

No amount of scolding would help. Ludwig could not stop his own ideas from coming into his head. So Johann decided to try giving his son more lessons on the violin. The same thing happened. Again, Ludwig could not make his exercises perfect. His fingers wandered into his own inventions. Johann came home one day and heard Ludwig making his own music on the violin. He burst into the room and shouted in a fit of temper, "What is that stupid stuff you are scraping at now? You know I can't stand that. Play the notes in front of you, or you will amount to nothing."

How could Johann know that his son would someday be one of the greatest composers of all time? All he knew now was that his son would not be able to earn money for his family the way Mozart had done when he was a child.

When Ludwig was eight years old, he went to study organ at the court. Then he went to the monastery in Bonn, where the monks took an interest in the young boy who wanted to know everything about music. Most of all, Ludwig wanted to know how to write music.

One of his teachers was surprised one day at his lesson when the boy came in with a piece he had written for the organ. "My goodness," the teacher exclaimed, "you cannot play that piece. Your feet cannot reach the pedals and your hands cannot stretch to play all those notes."

"But," answered Ludwig Beethoven, "I will play it when I am bigger."

Ludwig played so well that the court organist sometimes asked him to play at the chapel service. "I will be away from Bonn next Sunday, Ludwig. Will you play the church service in my place?"

Of course, Ludwig was pleased. Often he would sit down at

the great organ and begin the service with a long improvisation — a piece he would compose as he went along. The men in the court orchestra would stare in amazement at this fantastic young musician.

By the time Ludwig was eleven years old, he was accompanying at opera rehearsals and keeping the orchestra together at the performances. He became very useful in the court and soon started to receive a salary.

In order to help support the family, Ludwig left the public school when he was thirteen years old. He became organist and composer in the court, as his grandfather had been. He earned fifty florins ($63) a year. This was a big help to his family, but more important to Ludwig than the money was the chance to study the work of great composers who had lived before him.

Soon after Ludwig became court organist, a new archbishop was appointed to the court. "Beethoven," he said, "you have such an exceptional musical talent. I want to send you to Vienna to study with Mozart."

For a seventeen year old, this was quite a wonderful privilege. He thanked the archbishop for his consideration and left for Vienna.

Mozart was impressed with the young Beethoven. He heard him improvise at the harpsichord and remarked to the people around him, "This young man will make a great name for himself in the world."

Lessons with Mozart did not last long, however. After only two months in Vienna, Ludwig received a letter from his father.

"Please hurry home. Your mother is seriously ill."

Soon after he arrived in Bonn, his mother died. Now Ludwig was without anyone whom he deeply loved. With his mother gone, and his father in worsening condition, it was up to Ludwig to look after the family — his father and his two brothers. He returned to his job at the court. He not only played the organ and directed the orchestra, but he also played viola in the fine theatre orchestra. The opportunity to play in the orchestra and to listen to all the other instruments stirred in Ludwig's imagination ideas about music that he would write someday. Playing the music of Mozart, Dittersdorf, Grètry, and Martini taught him more than any lessons could. The members of the orchestra were pleased to play the pieces that Beethoven himself was beginning to compose. Happily for Ludwig, many of the orchestra players became his close friends.

Shortly after Beethoven returned to his home in Bonn, his father was sent away to a place where he could be cared for in his illness. The Beethoven home became a calmer place. Now Ludwig was able to make friends who would remain close and helpful throughout his lifetime. Some helped him find teaching jobs. Some introduced him and his compositions to important people. Others supported him with affection and understanding.

Another big change came to Beethoven's life when Franz Joseph Haydn visited Bonn and heard a performance of one of Beethoven's compositions. Haydn was a very famous composer in Vienna. "Come with me to Vienna," Haydn urged Beethoven.

LUDWIG VAN BEETHOVEN

"I will take you as a pupil."

Beethoven was glad to have this opportunity to study music with a great master, and he went to Vienna once more. This time, he would never return again to Bonn. He studied composing with Haydn, but soon discovered that the older man had his own musical ways and did not appreciate or understand Beethoven's different ideas about composing music. So, although the two men always remained good friends, Ludwig looked for other teachers to help him.

Living in Vienna was very different from living in Bonn. Vienna was truly a musical city. In Bonn, almost all music was written for the court, and performed there for just a few private guests. In Vienna, too, there was music for the court, but also music was heard in churches and theatres where many people came to hear concerts. In homes of ordinary people, musicians of all kinds gathered together to play and listen to music. Beethoven was often invited to give concerts in Vienna. He traveled to other cities of Europe as well. The name of Ludwig Beethoven was becoming well known everywhere.

Just as Beethoven was composing some of his most beautiful pieces, he realized that he was becoming deaf. He became despondent and irritable. He withdrew into himself. "My career as a teacher, conductor, and pianist will soon come to an end," he despaired. "Now I must turn only to composing."

The world of musicians recognized Beethoven as a great composer. Music publishers were always eager to publish his works, and musicians were ready to play them. A story is told that at the first rehearsal for his Seventh Symphony, the violinists refused to play a passage. "We cannot possibly play these difficult notes," they complained.

"Take your parts home and practice them, then the passages will surely go," Beethoven encouraged them.

In the days of Beethoven, the orchestra conductors did nothing but beat time. It was different, though, when Beethoven conducted. One of the violinists wrote, "The composer crouched lower and lower to tell the orchestra to play softer and softer, then he would spring into the air to show a climax. Sometimes, Beethoven would behave in strange ways toward the orchestra because he could not hear the soft passages."

In his later years, because of increasing deafness, Beethoven had more and more trouble getting along with people. He stayed by himself for long periods of time. His few visitors had to converse with him in writing. He composed fewer pieces, but the ones he did compose had far deeper musical thought than any he had composed before.

One of the last compositions that Beethoven wrote was the Ninth Choral Symphony. The performance included solo singers, a large chorus, and a large orchestra. Beethoven attended the concert, and sitting among the musicians, followed the written pages of music. When the piece ended, Beethoven was unaware of the applause for him. One of the singers reached over and tugged at his sleeve, and motioned for him to stand up. He had not heard the thunderous applause in his honor. "His turning around," the singer later said, "and the sudden conviction thereby forced on everybody that he had not done so before because he could not hear what was going on, acted like an electric shock on all present, and a volcanic explosion of sympathy and admiration followed, which was repeated again and again and seemed as if it would never end."

Beethoven, now fifty-seven years old and totally deaf, spent a summer with his younger brother at his estate in the country. On the way back to Vienna he became ill with pneumonia. During his illness, many friends came to be with Beethoven. Some people sent him gifts. One gift came from London. It was a set of forty books of the compositions of George Frederick Handel. Although Beethoven now was too weak to play the piano, he asked his friend to bring the books to his bed. "I have long wanted them," Beethoven said, "for Handel was the greatest, most skilled composer that ever lived. I can still learn from him."

Another gift arrived. It was a picture of Haydn's birthplace. Beethoven told the young man who was caring for him that day, "Look what has arrived today. It was in this home that a great man was born!"

Beethoven never recovered from his illness. Three days after he died, twenty thousand people gathered together at his funeral to say goodbye to the great musician. As he had wished to do with his music, Beethoven had "spoken to his God."

b. Bonn-on-Rhine, Germany, December 16, 1770
d. Vienna, Austria, March 26, 1827

JEAN-BAPTISTE SEBASTIAN BREVAL

or such a long time, it seemed to Jean, he had been begging his parents to let him play the cello. Now, at last, he was big enough to have an instrument of his own. The family gathered together in the music room to watch and listen as Jean drew the bow across the strings. He already knew the kind of sound he wanted to make. There were many musicians in his family, and as he was growing up, he had heard music all around him.

"Jean," his father said, "your teacher will be Maestro Jean-Baptiste Cupis. He will expect you to work hard and practice diligently."

"Yes, Father, I know. I am ready," Jean replied.

Jean's talent developed quickly. He often played for his family and friends, but his first big performance came when he was twenty-five years old and he made his debut at the famous Paris concert hall, The Concert Spirituel. On his program, he included a sonata he had composed himself. His concert was a resounding success. After that, Jean gave many brilliant solo performances of his works. For ten years, he played in the orchestra of the Concert Spirituel, then later in the Paris Opera orchestra where his brother, Stanislas, was a violinist.

Throughout Jean Breval's active life as a performer, he was also interested in teaching young cellists. Sometimes he had trouble finding beautiful pieces for his beginning students to

31

play, so he composed pieces for them himself. He also wrote a book to explain to other cellists how to become better teachers. One course of study that he wrote was to help his students practice, and to advance from their first steps on cello all the way to becoming advanced performers.

During his lifetime, Breval enjoyed performing as well as composing and teaching. Although in his early years he played in many different fine orchestras, in his later years, he preferred to compose and teach, and he passed on to many young aspiring music students the benefit of his long experience as a musician.

b. Paris, France, Novebmer 6, 1753
d. Colligis, Aisne, France, March 18, 1832

(JOHANN) FREDERICK BURGMÜLLER

May I come with you, Papa?" twelve year old Frederick begged his father. "How can I just stay at home on such an exciting day?"

"Well, I don't know. What do you think?" he asked his wife, Anne Theresa.

"Oh, please, mother, may I go?" Frederick begged again.

"If you will take care of your brother Norbert, you may go," his mother agreed. "Surely you should both be there for the opening concert. Your father has spent so many months organizing this Musical Festival, we should all be there together!"

Frederick and Norbert were proud to be at the Festival. Their father not only founded the Lower Rhine Music Festival, which is important to this day, he also composed music which was performed there.

It is no wonder that the two boys enjoyed music. As they were growing up, music was very important in their family life. "Your grandfather wanted me to be a university professor," Franz told his two sons, "but I wanted to work in the theatre, and direct plays. And I wanted to compose music, too. At first, Grandpapa tried to discourage me, but then he could see it was no use."

"We are glad you won't discourage us from music, Papa," Frederick exclaimed.

When Frederick was twenty-six years old, he moved from his home in Germany to Paris, France. His brother Norbert, remained in Germany. He was a fine composer and he was greatly admired by other musicians.

Four years after Frederick moved to Paris, he received a message that his brother had died. Robert Schumann, who had been one of Norbert's friends, wrote that "Since the early death of Schubert, nothing more deplorable has happened than that of Burgmüller."

Frederick lived in France for the rest of his life, writing small piano pieces, mostly suitable for children. His pieces, such as *Arabesque,* and *By the Limpid Stream* were musical pictures that young people still enjoy.

b. Ratisbon, Germany, Dec. 4, 1806
d. Beaulieu, Seine-et-Oise, France, Feb. 13, 1874

LOUIS CAIX d' HERVELOIS

After his lesson one afternoon, Louis' teacher said, "Louis, I have heard that there is a place for a viola da gamba player in the Duc d' Orleans' royal instrumental ensemble. Would you like me to recommend you for the job?"

After reflecting for a moment, Louis replied, "I am honored that you would think I am ready for such a position. But right now, I would rather be independent. Perhaps I can find a patron who will support my work as a composer and performer."

Indeed, Louis had no trouble finding patrons who wanted to support such a fine musician. Everyone in France enjoyed hearing him play, especially when he performed his own short dance-like pieces, with their beautiful melodies and brilliant virtuoso passages. He was such an excellent performer that a famous musician of the time, Le Blanc, honored Louis Caix d' Hervelois by referring to him as one of the three members of the *empire de la viole.*

The Caix (pronounced Kay) family contributed many fine viol players to the musical world. Francois, Louis' brother, played the bass viol. He had three children, two sons and a daughter. Louis was very fond of his little niece, Marie-Anne, who was just a baby when Louis was forty-five years old.

He was so charmed by the little girl, that he wrote a piece for viol called *La Marie-Anne de Caix*, and included it in his 5th book of pieces for bass viol. Marie-Anne and her two brothers grew up to be accomplished viol performers, and played in the court in Paris.

Louis and his wife had four children, a son and three daughters, and they, too, grew up to be viola da gambists at the French Court.

We can understand why the French people knew about the Caix family of musicans who contributed so much to the musical life of France.

b. Paris, France, c 1670
d. Paris, France, c 1760

FREDERIK FRANÇOIS CHOPIN

In a small four-room cottage, on a chilly early morning just at daybreak, Frederik Chopin was born. His mother, Justyna, his father, Nicolas, and his sister Louise lived on the estate of Count and Countess Skarbek.

Nicolas Chopin, when he was a young man of seventeen, had packed his flute, his violin, and his books, and traveled to Poland, leaving behind him his family, his friends, and the country where he was born, France. He arrive in Poland at a time when the wealthy Polish people and the nobility admired everything that was from France: French food, French clothing, French language, music, and literature. Nicolas heard that the Polish Count Skarbek was looking for a teacher for their five children. He hired Nicolas Chopin, so recently from France, to teach his children to speak and write in French, and to instruct them about French music and art.

In the course of a few years, Nicolas married Justyna, a relative of the Skarbek's who worked as housekeeper on the estate. Soon after Frederik was born, his parents began thinking of moving from the countryside to the city of Warsaw, some forty miles away.

"There is a new school opening in Warsaw," Nicolas told Justyna. "With my ability to speak and write French, and with my knowledge of French music and art, I should be able to find a job at the new Lyceum (high school)."

Frederik's father was hired at the new school, and the family moved to Warsaw. Nicolas Chopin was such a fine teacher that he soon was able to establish a boarding school of his own in a palace in the most fashionable street of Warsaw. The Skarbek children, and many other children from wealthy Polish families were sent to the Chopin school.

This house where Frederik grew up provided him with a fine education. On Thursday nights there was chamber music. There was a large room with a library full of French books. Guests - poets, painters, philosophers and musicians - were in and out of the Chopin home. Justyna always had delicious treats ready for every visitor. Home-baked bread with wild strawberry jam was the favorite. There were special days when Nicolas would call to the children, "Come, we are off to the woods," and they would hitch up the horse-drawn carriage and drive out of the city to pick wild strawberries or hunt for mushrooms.

Frederik was still very young when his parents were aware of the child's special interest in music. Justyna taught him to play the piano, and she sang for her children in her lovely, lyric voice. It was difficult at first to understand why their little son cried so when he heard beautiful music, but Justyna explained to Nicolas, "I think Frederik's tears are not of sadness, but of joy."

Soon Frederik learned to express his joy by making his own music. He would climb up on the piano stool and find melodies to satisfy his feelings.

"Will you teach me what you learned at your piano lesson?"

the four year old boy asked his sister.

"Yes, come, and I will play this piece by Bach that I have just learned."

After listening to Louise play her piece two or three times, Frederik was ready to play it himself.

"I think it is time to find a professional piano teacher for Frederick," Nicolas said to Justyna. "I will ask Prof. Albert Zywny if he will teach our son."

At the arranged time, Prof. Zywny arrived at the Chopin home. He was dressed in his yellow coat and trousers, with a yellow waistcoat and a brightly colored kerchief in the pocket. On his head was a blonde wig.

Zywny's special love was the music of Johann Sebastian Bach, and with great enthusiasm he taught Frederik many pieces by Bach. When the first part of the lesson was over, Prof. Zywny would say, "Now, Frederik, it is time for you to improvise. Here is the melody for this morning. Now see what you can do to create a beautiful composition," and with that, he played a simple folk melody on the piano. As Frederik created his pieces, his teacher wrote them down on music paper. Prof. Zywny became so interested in his young pupil that he would stop by the house every day to give Frederik a lesson. He spread news all around the city about this remarkable child, and soon Frederik was receiving invitations from palaces and wealthy families in Warsaw to perform at their social gatherings.

By the time Frederik was eight years old, he was ready to

give his first piano concert. Many important Polish families were invited to hear him play a piano concerto by a well-known composer from Vienna.

The small boy walked on to the stage dressed in his short trousers with white stockings, and with a large lace-embroidered white collar over his black velvet jacket. He played the concerto, expressing every phrase with sensitive tone and flawless technique. His audience took the young boy into their hearts.

Returning home from the concert, Frederik was met at the door by his mother. "Frederik, did you enjoy playing? What do you think the audience enjoyed most?"

"Oh, my collar, Mama," Frederik exclaimed. "They like the collar you made for me!"

Frederik spent many happy hours at the piano. He liked to play folk tunes that he heard the Polish peasants sing, and then he would expand the tunes and make them into new pieces. He improvised on melodies that he knew. Frederik's father realized that his son really needed to be trained in composing music, and he looked for the finest teacher in Warsaw.

Professor Josef Elsner became Frederik's first composition teacher. During Frederik's three years in high school, Prof. Elsner taught him the rules of composing, and they studied the music of other composers to learn what to do with musical ideas. Frederik had many new ideas of his own.

In writing to one of his friends, Frederik's teacher wrote,

FREDERIK FRANÇOIS CHOPIN

"Leave him in peace. If his method is out of the ordinary, so is his talent. What need has he of adhering rigorously to the usual rules? He follows rules of his own."

Although Prof. Elsner was not a particularly fine pianist, he did inspire his pupil with his love and understanding of music. All his life, Frederik thought of his teacher with affection and respect, and for many years he went to him for advice and direction.

One day Frederik arrived at his lesson carrying a small package. "What have you brought with you today?" Prof. Elsner asked.

"It is an invention I have made," Frederik replied. "My hands are too small to reach all the notes in the wide-stretching chords that I hear in my head. So at night I wear this hand stretcher, and hope that soon I can play all my own compositions."

"Well, Frederik, you must be careful not to injure your hands. Be patient, your hands will grow all by themselves."

During his years in high school, Frederik was a favorite among his classmates. He invented all kinds of games and jokes. They loved to watch him imitate his teachers and friends, and he drew funny pictures of them and passed them around the classroom. Frederik had many talents. When he and his sister were away on holidays, they published a home newspaper, mocking the Warsaw newspaper, with articles called "Foreign News", and "Home News". His articles were skillfully written.

Frederik was not only a friend of his school mates, but his parents' friends enjoyed him, too. A professor of natural history at the University of Warsaw invited Frederik to go to Berlin with him while he attended a conference. "You can have a wonderful time there, Frederik. There is so much to see and hear in the big city."

When he returned from the trip, Frederik's parents asked him all about it.

"Well, I heard five operas," he said. "And I saw Mendelssohn and Professor Zelter, Goethe's friend."

"Did you speak to them?" his mother asked.

"Oh, no," he answered, "I was too timid to introduce myself."

Back in Warsaw again, Frederik was ready to be composing again with Prof. Elsner. When he was nineteen years old, he graduated with distinguished awards from the Conservatory.

"Now it is time for you to visit Vienna," Prof. Elsner told Frederik. "I will give you some letters to introduce you to some musicians there. Franz Lachner might be able to arrange to have you give a performance."

Frederik thanked his teacher, and traveled to Vienna. The first thing he did was find Franz Lachner and give him his letter of introduction.

"Why, yes indeed," Franz Lachner said. "You certainly should show yourself to Vienna as a performer, not only as a composer. You do not want to make the same mistake that

Franz Schubert made. He did not perform and so people paid little attention to him."

Although Frederik never wanted to play before large audiences, he felt that he should play in Vienna to satisfy his parents and his teacher.

Notices were sent out to announce the concert, and an orchestra was gathered together. When the rehearsal time came, the orchestra members looked at the music on their stands. A hired music copier had been so careless that the musicians could hardly read the notes, and they refused to play.

"Very well, then," Frederik suggested, "if the orchestra cannot perform that piece, I will improvise a composition at the piano."

Although the audience was small, they were impressed with Chopin's brilliant playing of his *Rondo*, and they were especially pleased with the way he used peasant folk tunes in his improvisation. In a letter to his parents, Frederik told them that he had asked his friends to sit in different places in the audience so they could hear the comments that people made about his playing.

"My spies on the floor of the house declare that people were jumping up and down in their seats," he wrote. "But the general opinion is that I play too quietly or delicately. Of course they would think so, for they are accustomed to the banging of Viennese pianists."

In the audience were a number of patrons of music. The

Prince of the Imperial Court was there, and the next day Chopin received an invitation to tea at the Lichnowsky Palace. This was an important invitation and it gave Chopin the encouragement he needed. He gave a second concert, and then prepared to return to Warsaw. He said goodbye to Franz Lachner, and thanked him for all his help, and he said goodbye to his new friend, Karl Czerny, and left Vienna in high spirits.

On his return to Warsaw, he thought more about his compositions. "I could do my best work if my pieces used more of the folk music of the Polish peasants and if I would use my own special style of piano playing," he explained to his parents. He composed two piano concerti. The last movement of both pieces reminded his audiences of the dance forms and folk melodies of the countryside.

"Look, Frederik," Alfons, his friend said. "This is what they wrote about you in the newspaper."

"Chopin knows what sounds are heard in our fields and woods, he has listened to the songs of the Polish villagers. He has made it his own and has united the tunes of his native land in skillful composition and elegant execution."

These days in Warsaw were happy ones for Chopin. He spent many hours with young Polish writers, artists, and musicians who were excited with a love of their country and a desire to make it a place where new ideas could be talked about and expressed in their work. Many people looked to Chopin to be their leader. Perhaps he could make their hopes come true for a free Poland. In some pieces that Chopin composed, like his *Revolutionary Etude,* his friends could hear the enthusiasm and hope that they felt for their country.

Chopin told his friends that he was going to Vienna again for a short visit. As he was getting into the state coach to leave Warsaw, his friends gathered together to sing a cantata, sending him off with all their best wishes.

"On this second visit to Vienna," Frederik wrote to his family, "the people were not as enthusiastic as before. I have decided to leave Vienna, but where shall I go? To Italy, to London? No, I think I shall go to Paris."

On his way to Paris, when he stopped off at Stuttgart, he heard the terrible news that the Russian soldiers had captured Warsaw again. In his sadness over the plight of the Polish people, he went to the piano with pencil and paper, and composed a piece to express the despair he felt about the plight of his country. Then he continued on his way to Paris.

He did not have enough money for a carriage and horses of his own, so he traveled with fourteen other people crowded together in a large public horse-drawn carriage. It took two weeks to travel the distance to Paris, and when he arrived, he was weary and his bones ached. At the first inn he came to, he asked for a room and fell into bed, exhausted.

The next morning he was rested, and ready to start out to see this beautiful city that he had only imagined before. The music lovers of Paris had already heard about the young Polish musician, and they were waiting to hear what he could do. Chopin, in the meantime, had decided he was going to create a 'new world of music', and play in his own way, with his own style. He was twenty-two years old now, and ready to clear a path for his own music.

He gave a concert in Paris, performing his Concerto and Variations. The critics praised the young pianist, saying that they had been looking so long for new musical ideas and now, with Chopin, they had found them.

There was so much to do and see in Paris! There were so many people to meet! The city was alive with poets and painters, philosophers and musicians, who were breaking away from the old artistic ways. They wanted to express their feelings, praising nature and the glories of their country. Chopin immediately felt a kinship with these people. Along with the others, Frederik, too, was an honored guest in the homes of wealthy and aristocratic families. They, too, were excited about the new ideas being tried by the artistic people who found Paris a lively place to be.

Chopin felt comfortable fitting in with the manners and elegant style of these aristocratic families. He enjoyed going to the opera, strolling among the fashionably dressed patrons. He liked to treat his friends at the finest restaurants. He wore fine lace gloves, always spotless and cleaned at special shops. Gloves were a sign of being well dressed. He bought a walking stick and silk shirts and soft velveteen waistcoats. He sought out the finest bootmaker for patent-leather boots, and the finest tailor to make his redingote with gold buttons, his black cape lined with gray satin, and his royal blue jacket. He went to the finest perfumer, and later he bought his own carriage to take him to the homes where he gave piano lessons to children and young ladies of the wealthy establishments. All the gifted women of Paris wanted to be on friendly terms with this elegant, handsome, and delicate young man.

It seemed that everyone in Paris wanted to be a piano student of Frederik Chopin. On the days when he was scheduled to teach, he would arrive promptly at eight o'clock in the morning, dressed most tidely in his jacket of pale violet or blue, buttoned to his chin. He was ready to begin the lessons at once. If his student played well, the lesson could go on for hours, and he would call his student 'an angel'. If he was not pleased, he would sometimes become angry, wring his hands and pull his hair. At other times if his student needed help, he would patiently sit down at the other piano, and slowly play through the piece, or improvise an accompaniment for it.

Now that he was teaching more than performing, Frederik explained to his sister, "I am not fit, by my size and strength, or by my character, to be a virtuoso performer and play loud music before large audiences. I know my compositions will not sell for enough money, but many families want me for a teacher, and they pay me well. So I will teach by day, and compose during the quiet of the night."

Chopin had made up his mind that he would no longer perform to large audiences. In all his life he gave only thirty public performances. But as he retired from the stage, his fame as a composer took its place.

In his travels back to Paris, Chopin stopped off in Dresden where he met Maria, sixteen years old, a very attractive young lady and an excellent pianist. She was the daughter of Count and Countess Skarbek. Maria became Frederik's first love. He felt he had found his ideal. But Frederik was showing signs of illness, with his increasing fits of coughing, and Maria's family did not want their daughter to marry someone in such poor health.

When Maria said goodbye to Frederik for the last time, she gave him a rose, which he kept with the packet of letters she had sent him.

Because of his coughing, Chopin was advised to find a place where the climate and peaceful surroundings would be good for his health. He spent many months in Majorca, and then in Spain, where he composed with more inspiration than at any other time in his life.

On his return to Paris, he stayed by himself a great part of the time, but he continued to compose for the musical gatherings in French homes. He still taught many piano students, but his worsening health kept him away from any social life. Whenever there was a young musician in need of support, Chopin was always generous and willing to give every kind of help. Visiting musicians from Poland were especially welcome, and they appreciated the companionship that Frederik gave so freely.

In the year of 1848, Paris was restless with uneasy forbodings that a revolution would end the reign of King Louis-Philippe. Chopin gave his last concert in February, and a week later, revolution broke out. He lost his students who could no longer remain in Paris, and Chopin himself, accepted a hurried invitation from an old friend to go to England.

He played for Queen Victoria and played some concerts in public. Chopin's illness became more noticeable, but his playing was still clear and elegant, and with energy that suprised his audience. His very last concert in London was to collect money for refugees from Poland.

All the while he was in England, and in Scotland, he felt depressed and ill, and longed to be back in Paris. His friends helped him on the trip home, and though he was glad to be back once more, he was too ill to perform. A few friends stayed by him until the end of his life. He was only 39 years old. He had asked to have Mozart's *Requiem* performed at his funeral, and as Chopin, the Polish patriot would have wished, the Polish soil that he had brought with him, preserved in a silver cup, was scattered on his grave. Chopin loved his country and longed for its freedom. His music helped more than any words could to preserve his country's hopes and ideals.

b. Zelzaowa Wola nr. Warsaw, Poland, March 1, 1810
d. Paris, France, October 17, 1849

FRANZ XAVIER CHWATAL

Joseph had been practicing at the church organ all afternoon. He was annoyed! No matter which stops he pulled out, the organ would not sound the way he wanted. "Some day," he said to himself, "I will build my own organ. I will have 16 stops, and bellows that really work!"

Evening was coming on and Joseph started home past the low thatched cottages that lined the narrow streets. Smoke from the chimneys announced that it was close to suppertime.

When he reached home, he heard his older brother Franz still practicing the piano.

"What is that piece you are playing, Franz?" he asked. "I know it is not written by Mozart!"

"You're right. It is by one of our own countrymen, Jan Tomasek. He lives in Prague."

"He lives in Prague? That is surprising! I thought all our Czechoslovakian musicians had left the country and moved to Germany," Joseph said.

It was true. Many Czechoslovakian artists had gone to Germany.

"You know that the people of our country think anything that is German is better than anything that is Czechoslovakian," Franz explained. "Why, even the teachers in our schools were not allowed to teach us our own language. We had to speak German."

"I love our country, Franz," Joseph said thoughtfully. "But for me it would be best to move to Merseburg in Germany. The great organ in the Merseburg Cathedral would be a great inspiration. I could build my own organ factory, and try some of my ideas for improving the way organs are made. Would you come with me?"

"I don't know," Franz answered. "I, too, would be sad to leave our beautiful little village. But perhaps I could continue to teach piano and compose anywhere I go. I will think about it, Joseph."

Franz and Joseph discussed these plans for many months. Then, when Franz was twenty-four years old and Joseph was twenty-one, they prepared to leave Rumberg. Their travels took them over the Labe River, then over to the left bank of the Salle River. As he had dreamed for so long, Joseph set up his own organ factory, and invented some improvements in organ action. He was satisfied, but Franz was restless.

In just three years after he had been in Merseburg, Franz decided to travel North to Magdeburg.

"I am going to the city where George Telemann was born," Franz told his brother. "But we can visit each other often. The rivers and canals can take us anywhere we need to go."

For many years, Franz Chwatal lived and worked in Magdeburg. Two books of piano teaching methods and some music for male quartets, and at least 200 piano pieces were written by this musican during his lifetime.

52

b. Rumburg, Bohemia, Czechoslovakia, June 19, 1808
d. Soolbad, Elmen, Austria, June 24, 1878

MUTIUS CLEMENTI

Not a single sound could be heard inside the big stone church. Five men, sitting stiffly behind a long wooden table in the Church of San Lorenzo, waited in serious silence. All at once, the hush was broken by the quick sharp clicking of heels hastening down the marble aisle leading to the front of the church.

Muzio stopped in front of the table. He bowed deeply. The five men stared in surprise to see such a young eager face looking at them. Finally, one of the men spoke up. "What is your name, young man?"

"My name is Mutius Philippus Vincentius Franciscus Xaverius Clementi," he told the five famous organists. "My parents call me Muzio."

"And how old are you?"

"I am nine years old, sir."

"Can you imagine that you are old enough to pass our examination to become an organist of Rome?"

Muzio replied politely, "I have studied hard and I would like to try the examination."

"Very well. This is what you must do. We will show you a figured bass by Corelli, and you must compose an accompaniment on it. You may not practice it first. Then, you must transpose your accompaniment into five other keys."

Muzio took the manuscript from the judge at the head of the

table, and climbed the stairs into the organ loft. He jumped up on the high bench, and placed the page of numbers on the organ stand. After studying it for a few minutes, he began to play. The five organists at the table below could scarcely believe what they heard. They looked at each other in amazement. Muzio had carried out the exercise with the skill of a professional organist. The judges applauded. Muzio, at age nine, had passed the examination with distinction and was admitted to the coveted position of organist of Rome.

Although Muzio passed this difficult examination, he knew he needed to improve his skills, so he took organ and singing lessons, and he learned to write music, too, as all music students did at that time. His composition teacher was Gaetano Carpini. He was very strict with his pupils.

"Exercises, exercises. You must only write exercises," he ordered. "Perhaps some day you may write a beautiful piece."

But Muzio was impatient. There were so many melodies in his head that he wanted to write down on paper. He told his friends what his teacher had said.

"Well, then, Muzio, there is only one thing to do. Put those boring exercises away for a while, and write a piece for our chorus and orchestra. We will perform it for you. But just don't tell Maestro Carpini!"

The young musician could not resist his friends' suggestions. "What harm can it do?" he said. So one day, after he had finished all his exercises, Muzio began to compose an oratorio.

He did not tell his teacher, or ask for any advice.

The day came when his friends got a group together to play and sing Muzio's *Oratorio*. It was a fine work and the news of it spread among the students and teachers. When Maestro Carpini heard about it, he was dismayed to think that his student could achieve success without his help and advice.

"Why didn't you tell me?" Carpini asked Muzio. "It is a good composition, to be sure, but if you had consulted me, it would have been much better."

Muzio smiled, and replied, "Thank you, Maestro."

When Muzio Clementi was fourteen years old, he was offered a job as organist of his home Church of San Lorenzo.

"My son," Muzio's father said, "it would be a good thing for us if you would take the position at the Church of San Lorenzo. You could live here at home. I am having trouble earning enough money for our family. The Bishops of the church say that the silver vases I make for the church alter are beautiful, but the church is poor, and they cannot buy my art work. With your small salary as organist, and the little I can earn from selling my small silver figures, perhaps we can provide for our family."

Muzio agreed to take the job and he found time to continue practicing the harpsichord. But something happened to change all that.

A traveler from England came to Rome. He was looking for a musician to take home with him, someone who could provide musical entertainment at his country estate. He had heard Muzio perform and was very impressed. One afternoon, when the young organist was practicing in preparation for the Sunday services, the twenty-six year old Sir Peter Beckford slipped quietly into the church and sat down in a back pew. When Muzio finished practicing, he closed the cover over the organ keys and came down the steps. Peter Beckford was waiting.

"My name is Peter Beckford," the visitor introduced himself. "I have heard only the finest compliments about you. I would like to suggest a plan. If you will come with me to Steepleton Irwene, my estate in England, you can continue to study composition and harpsichord, and you can perform for me and my guests."

Muzio was surprised. Go to England? Leave his home and family, his city and his church? He wondered what to say.

"Please, Sir Beckford, will you come with me to my home? We must talk about this with my parents."

After a lengthy discussion with the Clementi family, Peter Beckford got up to leave. "In a few days, we will let you know what we have decided about our son," Muzio's father promised as Peter Beckford walked out the door.

"What should we do, Muzio?" his father questioned after Sir Beckford had left the house. "We are poor, and Sir Beckford has promised to pay us for your services for seven years. You can continue your musical education under his care. Perhaps we should accept his offer."

Young Muzio was not sure how he really felt, but he agreed to go.

This new life at the Beckford Estate was different from anything Muzio had ever known. The enormous home was set out in green rolling hills of the countryside, far from any city or town. In Rome, it was so different! There had been music everywhere, and the narrow streets bustled with activity. Here he missed his family, and his church, and the music that had been everywhere around him. He would be here for seven years. What would he do?

He knew he was to play the harpsichord for Sir Beckford and his friends. But he still had so much to learn! With strong determination, Muzio decided he would make the best of things, and be his own teacher. In Sir Beckford's large library there were many music manuscripts of Corelli, Scarlatti, and Handel, Johann Sebastian Bach and Carl Philipp Emanuel Bach. These would be his study books.

Muzio wrote to his parents, "I practice at the harpsichord for eight hours a day. Today I had to take some hours to entertain Sir Beckford, but tonight I will stay up late to practice, to make up for those hours lost. If there is no light to read by or fire to keep me warm, I will practice the harpsichord. If there is light enough, I will go through the scores first to learn the fingering. Then I will study them as lessons to teach myself how to write music."

For seven years, Muzio Clementi kept to a strict schedule.

Without any other musicians to encourage or teach him, he grew in skill and understanding of music.

The day came when Muzio could say goodbye to the Beckford Estate and to Sir Peter Beckford. He had completed his promised seven years and now he was twenty-two years old.

"I will go to London," he told Sir Beckford. "I am told that foreign musicians are welcome there and perhaps I can find work."

It did not take Clementi long to find a place for himself. He went directly to the Director of the fashionable opera house called King's Theatre. He had heard they needed a conductor there. In those days, the conductor of an orchestra sat at the harpsichord, playing and conducting at the same time. At last, those long hours of practice at the Beckford estate provided Muzio with the skills to fit into the musical world of London. This job gave him the chance to improve his skills even more and to refine his musical taste.

As time went on, the name of Muzio Clementi could be seen printed in more and more programs. London was a busy musical city, with many public and private concerts being given throughout the year, and Clementi was often asked to perform. Many times he played his own compositions.

"Did you hear Clementi last night?" a music critic asked his friend. "He played one of his own sonatas, and it quite amazed me. It abounds in passages peculiar and difficult. I certainly will write about it in my magazine. Clementi must have practiced those octaves for years . . . he is a most brilliant performer! Even Johann Christian Bach spoke of Clementi's playing in the highest terms, and exclaimed that he would never attempt to perform such difficult work."

Clementi enjoyed his growing success and fame, and he decided to travel in Europe to give concerts. In Paris, he was received with enthusiasm. He played before Queen Marie-Antoinette.

"My dear Monsieur Clementi," she said after his Court performance, "I think you surely must travel to Vienna to play for my brother, Emperor Joseph. If you arrive in time, you can be there to meet the Grand Duke and Duchess of Russia, and perhaps my brother will arrange to have you play for them."

Clementi was grateful for the invitation, and hurried on to Vienna. He arrived the day before Christmas, and was introduced to the Grand Duchess.

"Will you play for me?" she asked. "We will have a concert at the Court this evening."

When he arrived that evening, he was surprised to learn that Emperor Joseph had planned a piano competition as entertainment for his guests. Who would be his rival? Entering the music room, he noticed a man of elegant appearance whom he supposed was the Emperor's chamberlain. Clementi went to speak to him. After a short conversation, talking about music, Clementi discovered that he was talking to Wolfgang Amadeus Mozart. It was he, the renowned musician, who was to be his opponent in the contest!

The contest began. The Empress decided that Clementi should play first. The piano was out of tune, and some of the keys stuck. Besides, Clementi was used to playing the harpsichord, not the piano, and the sonata he wrote was written to be played on a harpsichord. Nevertheless, he played his sonata, and improvised. Then it was Mozart's turn. At the end, they sat side by side and improvised together.

Mozart wrote a letter to his father telling him about the meeting with Clementi. "Clementi plays well," he wrote, "so far as execution with the right hand goes . . . he has not a Kreuzer's worth of taste or feeling."

On the other hand, Clementi was more generous. He said to a friend, "I heard Mozart play. Until then I had never heard anyone perform with such spirit and grace."

From Vienna, Clementi continued his travels, performing on the harpsichord, composing, and teaching. He was a welcome guest wherever he went. He could speak six languages fluently, and he was a genial and witty guest. Eventually, his travels took him back to London when he was thirty-three years old. Again his name appeared on many concert programs as a composer and a performer. The newspapers wrote enthusiastic reviews of his playing. "What brilliancy of fingers, and wonderful execution."

As a piano teacher, Clementi was in great demand. Musicians who wanted to become professional pianists came to study with him. Many of his students did become well-known pianists. Others, especially young ladies, who wanted to play piano as a social accomplishment, also wanted to be taught by the great Clementi. He charged more for lessons than anyone else in London, but still people begged him to teach. Sixteen hours a day of teaching was not unusual for Clementi. The Queen asked Clementi to come to the Court to teach the two young Princesses and to play for the King to amuse him in the evenings, but he declined, explaining that he was much too busy with his work. The other reason, which he did not explain to the Queen, was that he would not be paid as much at the Court as he was paid by his own students.

One of Clementi's favorite students was the Irish lad, John Field. When John was ten years old, his father brought him to Clementi. "Will you take my boy as your apprentice? I will pay you one hundred guineas if you will keep him with you and give him his musical training. He can serve you in any way you wish. He is very talented, and a hard worker, too."

Clementi agreed to keep John Field with him. True to his father's word, John was a conscientious boy, and his exceptional talents developed rapidly.

One morning, Clementi said to John, "Come lad, let's walk over to Cheapside Road. There is something I want to show you."

When they came to 131 Cheapside, Clementi said to John, "Look up there." On the front of the building a new sign, freshly

61

MUZIO CLEMENTI

painted, read *Clementi, Banger, Hyde, Collard and Davis.*

"How wonderful, sir," John exclaimed. "Is this your new store for printing and selling music?"

"Indeed it is," answered Clementi, "and what is more, we will be building and selling pianos. I have put the money I have saved into this new business venture. You and I will take some trips, John. You can play and I will sell pianos and music. How will you like that?"

"Oh, that will be fine, sir," the boy answered. "When do we begin?"

It was some time before they could leave London. There was still a war on the continent, and travel was not safe. In the meantime, Clementi gave less and less time to composing and performing, and more and more time to his new business and to making improvements on the way pianos were made. But as soon as relative peace settled over Europe, John and Clementi went from city to city. In Paris, John played the music of Johann Sebastian Bach and was acclaimed as a young genius! Clementi enjoyed his new role as a business man.

"Pray send good stuff and let every sort of wood be well seasoned," Clementi wrote to Collard, his business partner in London. "I am in Moscow now, and Mr. Davidoff wants a Grand Pianoforte, with a tone thick and sweet. Remember," he continued, "the Russians in general possess good ears for sound. Don't forget to put in the piano case some of my sonatas, and a copy of the piano method book I wrote, *Practical Harmony*, and be sure to charge them," he added.

In the same year when Clementi was trying to make an arrangement with Ludwig van Beethoven to print his music in London, he was also making another important arrangement. The year before, in Berlin, he had met the charming and musical daughter of Johann Georg Gottfried Lehman, who was director of the chorus of the Royal Opera and music director of the Church of St. Nicolas. The young lady's name was Caroline. She was eighteen years of age; Clementi was fifty-one.

"1804 is a wonderful year for me!" exclaimed Clementi. "Beethoven will publish with our company, and Caroline will marry me!"

Caroline, Muzio, and John Field traveled together for many months. The following year, a baby boy, Carl, was born. But then sadness suddenly came into their lives. Caroline died, and left Carl and Muzio bereft. "God alone can give me strength to bear it," Muzio wrote to Collard.

Carl was left with Caroline's parents to be well cared for, but when Clementi, at the age of sixty, married again, Carl was thirteen years old, and he joined his father and new mother, Emma, in London. He and his twenty-six year old wife became parents of two boys and two girls, and with Carl, they made a happy seven. "Emma is as moderate and placid as Muzio is excitable and effervescent," one of Clementi's students wrote in his diary.

One evening, just as the Clementi family was settling down

to read in front of the fire, there was a knock on the door. "Vincent," Muzio asked his eight year old son, "please go to the door and see who it is."

Vincent returned to the sitting room with two friends, the Cramer brothers. Johann Cramer was one of Clementi's most talented pupils and his brother, Francois, was a violinist. "Good evening to you, Johann and Francois. Come, sit down. How good to see you."

As Emma served tea, the men began to talk of London, and its musical life.

"London has changed so much," Johann said. "We used to have so many concerts here, and there were so many musical organizations to perform new music."

"Yes, and so many musicians from other countries came here to England. But Napoleon's wars on the continent have stopped the composers and performers from traveling here."

"In Europe, there were many opportunities to perform my new symphonies. But in London, no group will play new music," Clementi complained. "The Concert of Ancient Music will not play any music less that twenty years old, and then they only want to play Handel's music."

"Well, perhaps we should organize a new group," Francois suggested.

With that in mind, Clementi, the Cramers and two other musicians in London organized the Philharmonic Society. Clementi's works were often performed by the group, and he conducted from the harpsichord, as he had done in earlier days.

When Clementi was seventy-eight years old, he retired from his business firm and moved his family to the countryside. His full creative life came to an end when he was eighty years old, not until he had completed putting together in three volumes, all his best compositions, in a work called *Gradus ad Parnassum.*

Clementi was buried in the place of England's best known artists, in Westminster Abbey. In his time, he was called Father of the Pianoforte and there is no piano student in the world who has not inherited his great gifts.

b. Rome, Italy, Jan. 23, 1752
d. Evesham, Worcester, England, March 10, 1832

ARCANGELO CORELLI

Arcangelo lived with his parents in a lovely shaded villa in a little town in the district of Bologna. His father, thinking it was time for his youngest son to go into the city for his education, said to Arcangelo, "Now you are thirteen years old, you must go to the city to study violin. In Bologna there is a fine teacher who is willing to have you as his student."

The young boy was an excellent student. He looked forward to serious study. After he had worked very hard for four years, his teacher said to him, "Arcangelo, you are ready for the Academia Filharmonica. You will be able to continue your violin studies and learn music composition as well."

After two years at the academy, Arcangelo prepared to take his first concert tour. He decided to go to Paris, where Jean Baptiste Lully was the favorite in the King's court. Corelli played several concerts in Paris. The people enjoyed his music, but Lully and the king did not want to have competition from other violinists. "We will not encourage this young Italian violinist to stay in Paris," they declared. They made it difficult for Corelli to find audiences to play for. So, discouraged, Corelli left France and traveled to Germany.

He was employed for a time in the services of the elector of Bavaria, and he stayed in Germany until he was twenty-eight years old. Then, longing to return to his native country, Italy, and to be back again in the sunny climate of Rome, he looked for a position in the palace of Cardinal Pietro Ottoboni.

The Cardinal was a great patron of the arts. He liked to help many painters and musicians who lived in Italy at that time, and he became Corelli's good friend and supporter. Every Monday night, in the palace of the Cardinal, a concert was given. These concerts were important events in the musical life of Rome. Many new compositions were performed. "You must play and lead one of your compositions in our next concert," the Cardinal said to Corelli. "Some important guests will be here, and I want them to hear your music."

Corelli was only too happy to do as the Cardinal wished. On the following Monday night, Arcangelo performed with the palace orchestra. Among the guests was the Queen of Sweden. She became a lifelong admirer of Corelli and often invited him to her palace, where she had an orchestra of one hundred fifty musicians.

Corelli was interested not only in music, but also in painting and sculpture. Some of the most famous artists of the time were living in Rome, and he became their good friend. He amassed a fine collection of valuable paintings. Unlike many musicians of his time, Corelli was a wealthy man. "Do you notice how very simple Corelli is in his habits and dress? He goes everywhere on foot, never hiring a carriage," remarked a musician in the palace orchestra. "He likes to save his money!"

One day there was great excitement at the palace. News had come that the great George Frederick Handel, then twenty-three years old, was coming from Germany to visit Rome. "Handel will

ARCANGELO CORELLI

be here for a rehearsal and performance of a cantata he has recently composed," the Cardinal told Corelli. "You will be leader (concertmaster) of the orchestra."

Everything was made ready for the day. Music stands and chairs were set up in the large music room, large quantities of food were ordered, and all the important people of Rome were invited.

The morning came for the first rehearsal. Handel sat at the organ; Corelli, who was about thirty years older than Handel at the time, sat at the first desk in the orchestra, as leader. After a few measures of the overture, Handel stopped playing. "Let us play that again, Corelli, this time with more excitement."

The orchestra began again. "No, no" cried Handel. "This music should have fire and exuberance!" They tried again. This time, Handel became impatient with Corelli's quiet and elegant manner of playing. He grabbed Corelli's violin and played the part himself with vigor and enthusiasm.

Corelli, always a polite and amiable person, modestly replied to Handel, "But my dear Saxon, this music is in the French style, of which I have no experience." ("Ma, caro Sussone, questa musica e rella stile francaise, di ch'io non m'intendo.")

At another rehearsal, it was obvious that Handel's music was much more complicated than music that Corelli was accustomed to playing. It was necessary for Handel to show Corelli how to play in the third position!

Occasionally, Corelli traveled away from Rome. He received a message from the leading musician in Naples, another city in Italy.

"We would like to invite you to Naples to conduct a concerto that you will compose for us."

Corelli was honored to be invited by this well-known composer, Alexandro Scarlatti. He wanted to be sure that the performance of his concerto should go well. So he took with him on the trip to Naples two violinists and a cello player. But when Scarlatti's orchestra played through the opening movement of Corelli's concerto without a mistake, Correlli called out, "They can play at Naples!" ("Si svona a Napoli!")

It happened that the king was in the audience when the concerto was performed. He did not appreciate the slow movement of the concerto. He stood up and walked out of the hall.

All over Europe, though, Corelli was held in high esteem. Young students admired him as a violinist and composer, and they came to him from all over. Corelli's music was published and performed everywhere. Many people think that Arcangelo Corelli was the founder of present day methods of violin playing. He developed new bowing techniques and was the first to use double stops and chords on the violin. He also developed new methods for shifting. His violin pieces never went beyond the third position, so that his music was never fiery and full of excitement; but his writing for slow pieces was especially beautiful and dignified, and showed great understanding of the exquisite purity of tone that can come from a violin.

b. Fusignang nr. Imola, Italy, February 17, 1653
d. Rome, Italy, January 8, 1713

KARL CZERNY

Let's put Karl's cradle here by the piano while I practice this Mozart sonata," Wenzel Czerny said to his wife. "And if he will be quiet while my student is here, we can let him stay and listen to the lesson. After all, what better entertainment is there for Karl than listening to my student learning a Clementi sonatina!"

The lively child must have enjoyed his entertainment, because by the time he was three years old, he could already play little piano pieces. Karl spent many hours playing the pieces that he heard when students came to take their lessons. He could not wait until a student was out the door to jump up on the piano bench. "Listen to this, father. Will you show me if I am using the right fingers?"

When Karl was old enough to read music, his father said, "My boy, I want you to become a good sight reader, and develop good musical taste. Each day, we will read a new piece. Come, let us try this *Prelude* by Bach."

"All right, father," the boy agreed. "But first, may I play this piece I made up myself?"

By the time Karl was ten years old, he could play all the works of Mozart and Clementi from memory. His father put aside all the money he could from his scant earnings to buy music for his son. Some students who could not afford to pay for lessons, taught Karl to speak and write in different languages in exchange for piano lessons.

One evening, just as the family was sitting down to their evening coffee, a loud knock was heard at the door.

"Run to the door and see who it is," Wenzel asked his son.

"Oh, good evening, Maestro Gelinek," Karl said. "Please come in."

Maestro Gelinek, one of the finest pianists in Vienna, hurried into the kitchen. "I am sorry to come at this time, but I must tell you what has just taken place. Do you remember, Wenzel, that yesterday I told you that I had been invited to a private party for a competition with an unknown pianist?"

"Yes, Josef, I remember," Wenzel replied.

"Well, I have just come from there," he said, still feeling quite agitated. "I will never forget this day! That man must be possessed of the devil. I have never heard such playing. He improvised on a theme in such a way that even Mozart could not! Then he played one of his own compositions, wonderful and grandiose to a high degree. What difficulties and effects he achieves! I have never thought that piano playing could be like that!"

"Indeed?" Wenzel replied.

"And what is this pianist's name?" Karl asked hurriedly.

"Well, he is a short, swarthy, stubborn-looking man with bristley black hair. His name is Ludwig van Beethoven."

After not a moment's hesitation, Karl said, "Oh, father, would you take me to this wonderful musician?"

"Perhaps," answered his father. "But first, you must learn to play some of his compositions. Possibly our violinist friend, Krumpholtz, who understands Beethoven's ideas about music, can teach you how to play one of his pieces."

Young Karl learned Beethoven's *Pathetique Sonata* under Kromholtz's careful training. When the day for the meeting arrived, Karl was both fearful and excited.

It was a blustery winter morning when Karl, his father, and Krumpholtz walked from their small house on Leopoldstadt to Beethoven's house in Tiefer Grablen. They climbed up the cold marble stairs to the 6th floor, and rapped on the door. A servant opened the door. She was untidely dressed and her uncombed hair hung to her shoulders. *"Kommen sie, bitte,"* she muttered.

The three visitors walked into a chilly, bare room. Papers and clothing were scattered everywhere, and there was no empty chair except for the rickety one at the piano.

Beethoven was sitting at the piano, in his wooly dark grey jacket and matching trousers. He had not shaved for several days, which made his face seem very dark, and his hair was long and shaggy.

Beethoven got up from the piano, and greeted his guests.

"Now Karl, what will you play for me?" he asked the ten year old boy.

"I will like to play Mozart's *Concerto* in C major," Karl answered.

Karl began. Beethoven paced up and down the room.

Gradually, he stopped his pacing, and listened more carefully. Soon, he went over to stand next to Karl's chair, and began to play the orchestra melody with his left hand.

"Excellent!" Beethoven exclaimed when Karl had played the last chord. "What will you play next?"

"May I have the honor to perform your *Pathetique Sonata*?" he asked.

"Of course," Beethoven replied.

When Karl finished playing, Beethoven said to Wenzel, "This boy has talent. I will teach him myself. Send him to me several times a week, but first of all, see that he gets Emanuel Bach's book called the *True Art of Keyboard Playing* and have him bring it to his lesson. I can see he can play the clear precise style of Mozart, but it is time to teach him to play in a legato style, and how to use his thumb. Come next Tuesday."

The Czernys and Krumpholtz thanked Beethoven for the time he spent with them, and left for home. They were elated that the great Beethoven would teach young Karl.

Karl's father would never allow his son to walk alone to Beethoven's house; sometimes he had to cancel his own students' lessons to take him. Often, when they arrived at Beethoven's home, he was busy composing, and he asked them to return on another day.

At the time when Karl was a young man, it was the custom for musicians to be invited to evening *musicales*. Mozart's wife, after her husband died, often invited musicians to her home for

KARL CZERNY

evening concerts. She told Karl, "I want you to come next Thursday evening. One of Wolfgang's pupils will play. His name is Johann Hummel. He plays Wolfgang's music most beautifully." Karl was happy to meet Johann Hummel, who had been one of Mozart's pupils and understood how Mozart wanted his pieces to be played.

In Vienna, there were many music lovers. Another friend of music in Vienna was Prince Lichnowsky. He was like a brother to Beethoven. One day, he heard Czerny play from memory one of Beethoven's sonatas.

"Czerny," the Prince said to twenty-three year old Karl, "you seem to understand Beethoven's music. I would like to have you come to my home for a few hours each morning, and play from memory all Beethoven's piano music that I ask for."

Karl was glad to perform for the Prince. He was a fine musician who loved music, and he was a friendly and generous person. Every morning Karl played for him, and each month the Prince gave him a gift which Karl took to his father to try to repay him for all he had done to give Karl his musical training.

One morning, Beethoven who had not seen Karl for two years, was at the Prince's home during one of the morning sessions.

"Well," said Beethoven, "I always said that the boy had talent. But," he added smiling, "his father was not strict enough with him."

"Ah, Herr van Beethoven," replied his father good

naturedly, "he is our only child, after all."

Beethoven was so pleased with Czerny's sightreading that he gave him the Sonata in C major to play from the manuscript. From then on, Beethoven was a friend of Czerny's until the end of his life, and Czerny became proofreader for Beethoven's works when they were published.

Although Czerny played well enough to give concerts all over Europe, he was a rather shy person, and he never thought that his playing was brilliant or flashy enough to appeal to a large audience. Besides, although he could play Beethoven's music from memory and as Beethoven wanted his music performed, the general public audiences were not yet accustomed to this kind of playing. Teaching piano rather than performing was more to Czerny's liking. He had already begun teaching when he was thirteen years old and many times he substituted for his father at lessons. He learned a great deal about teaching too, when Clementi was in Vienna and invited him to observe his teaching. Many of his students became fine performers. Franz Liszt was one of the best known of them all. Beethoven entrusted Czerny with the musical education of his nephew.

As years passed, in addition to teaching, Czerny spent more and more time composing. He wrote many kinds of music for orchestra, string ensembles, piano, and chorus. He liked to arrange other composers' large works for orchestra and chorus so that they could be played on the piano. He arranged the

William Tell Overture to be played on eight pianos with two people to each piano!

Czerny is best known today by his thousands of exercises from easy to very difficult studies which provide such a thorough understanding of piano playing. Every serious piano student is a pupil of Karl Czerny.

Throughout his life, Czerny's thoughtfulness, kindess, and generous nature were well known and appreciated by everyone who knew him. Although he was rather a shy person, he befriended anyone in need. In his will, he left all that belonged to him to his housekeeper and her brother, to The Society of the Friends of Music, to The Society for the Support of Needy Musicians, The Institute for the Deaf and Dumb, and to the Monks and Nuns of Charity in Vienna. To pianists the world over, Karl Czerny left his skill and knowledge of music.

b. Vienna, Austria, February 21, 1791
d. Vienna, Austria, July 15, 1857

LOUIS-CLAUDE DAQUIN

This was an ordinary day in the court of King Louis of France. For his lunch the King had four bowls of different kinds of soup, one whole pheasant and a partridge, a large dish of salad with two slices of ham, mutton covered with a garlic gravy, an assortment of pastries and cakes, and finally a dish of fruit and hard-boiled eggs.

After his lunch, King Louis fed his dogs, and went outdoors for some fresh air. When it was time for the evening entertainment, the ladies of the court gathered in the large wood-paneled royal apartment. They were dressed in long, low-cut, heavy brocaded dresses with frills and lace on the sleeves. Their wigs, piled high on their heads, were studded with jewels. Behind the seated ladies stood the men, dressed in their wide-sleeved, knee-length embroidered coats and silk scarves. Their wigs were curly, long and flowing.

The sixty-two year old King Louis, surrounded by his courtiers, strode into the room. He sat down heavily in his chair. "And what do we have for our entertainment tonight?" he asked.

"Your Highness, may I present Louis-Claude Daquin?" (pronounced Da-as in lap-cahn) the court musician announced. "He is only six years old, but you will be surprised to hear his skill at the harpsichord."

The King looked inquisitively at the child. Louis-Claude

bowed to the King, and climbed up onto the bench at the harpsichord. First he played a piece by Francois Courperin.

"Excellent, excellent," the King called out. "Now I would like to hear a piece by Jean Baptiste Lully."

With hardly any hesitation, Louis-Claude began. His small fingers flew up and down the harpsichord keys.

"*Merci beaucoup, merci beaucoup*," the King exclaimed loudly. "Let us call our twenty-one court violins and we will all play together." The King took his flute from the case, and they played and danced until the hour grew quite late.

It was no surprise to Louis-Claude's family that their son was so precocious. His parents and grandparents were important French scholars and teachers. They were pleased with the child's musical talent, and they thought it was only natural that Louis would distinguish himself when he was eight years old by conducting a large work for chorus and orchestra in the magnificent church of Saint-Chapelle.

Louis' grandmother lived so close to the Daquin home that she could often visit and talk to Louis about the music he was composing. She, too, was a composer, and Louis could share his ideas with her. One day, when Louis had gone outside to play, she said to his parents, "Louis has a great career ahead of him. Do you know what his teacher said to me the other day? He said that Louis' learning must come from heaven, because there is little that he needs to be told."

Louis-Claude continued to work hard as he taught himself to

81

LOUIS-CLAUDE DAQUIN

master the technique of the organ pedals and keyboard. When he was only twelve years old, he was appointed as church organist at Petit St. Antoine.

Many years later, when Louis-Claude Daquin was thirty years old, he read a notice announcing an opening for an organist at the Cathedral of St. Paul. "I must try for that job," Louis told his wife and his seven-year-old son, Pierre. "The organ in the Cathedral is a joy to hear and to play."

When Daquin arrived at the Cathedral for the audition, he found that the well-known organist and composer, Jean Philippe Rameau, was also competing for the position as organist. Daquin was judged the better of the two and he was appointed organist at St. Paul. He stayed there for six years enjoying the beauty of the Cathedral and its great organ, but one evening when he came home, Daquin's wife said that a message had come from the Monks at Cordeliers (pronounced Cor-dell-ee-ay'), a monastery in Paris.

"Louis, your teacher Marchand has died," she explained. "The monks at Cordeliers ask if you would consider taking his place as organist at the monastery."

Louis Daquin agreed to accept the position. Along with his work as organist, he had time to compose music for the organ and harpsichord. His music for Christmas, the Noëls for flutes, violins, and oboes, were favorites of the French people. One of his most famous pieces for harpsichord was *Le Coucou*, which imitates the sounds of the countryside. Wherever Daquin went, he was always asked to play *Le Coucou.*

For seven years Louis and his family enjoyed the quiet, secluded life at the monastery. They probably would have stayed there if the King of France had not invited him to his Court.

"I have been invited to be organist to the new King," Daquin told his family. "Do you think we are too old for the busy hustle of Court life?" the forty-five year old musician asked with a laugh.

Once again, the Daquin family decided to move, this time to the King's court, where they remained for thirty-three years.

From the book that Daquin's son wrote about his father, and from letters that Louis himself wrote, we know how much the composer was admired in France, not only as a musician, but as a fine and gentle man as well.

b. Paris, France, July 4, 1694
d. Paris, France, June 15, 1772

HENRY ECCLES

Henry, John and Thomas hurried home from school. It was Henry's fourteenth birthday. "Henry," his older brother John said, "we have a surprise for you. Tonight, the famous young composer Henry Purcell will be performing his latest opera, *Dido and AEnaeus.* We will go together to see the first performance. Put on your best clothes, and we will be ready to go."

The three boys were excited to be going to the opera. All three boys played the violin and were already composing music of their own. Music was an everyday part of the Eccles' family life. The boys' father, Solomon, was a musician, and Solomon's father and grandfather had been musicians too.

Several years before Henry was born, his father Solomon, a music teacher, had become a Quaker. At that time, Quakers objected to the use of music in the church, and Solomon had broken all his instruments and burned his music. But when his sons were born, he decided to teach them to play the violin and to compose music.

John Eccles, the first son, became master of the king's band of music. He also was interested in writing music for plays and operas. It was ten years after that evening when the three brothers had gone to the opera house to hear Purcell's opera that John Eccles and Henry Purcell became friends. They joined together to write the music for another opera, *Don Quixote.* John also published a collection of one hundred popular songs.

Henry Eccles was two years younger than John. He also studied violin and composition with his father. When he was twenty-four years old, he joined the same king's band that his brother John directed. At that time, a band was an orchestra of violins and viols.

When Henry was forty-three years old, something happened to change the course of his life. A concert was to be given in Stationers Hall in London. The notice read this way: "A Concert for the Entertainment of the Duke d'Aumont, Ambassador Extraordinary from France, for the Benefit of Mr. Eccles, Musician to His Grace."

The duke was impressed by Henry Eccles' performance at the concert. He spoke to Henry the following day. "I will be returning to Paris in December. Will you join my entourage and come with us to Paris to be in residence at the French court?"

Henry Eccles was pleased to be invited, and happily accepted the duke's offer. He lived in Paris for the rest of his life, and during that time he wrote two sets of violin sonatas and *Twelve Solos for the Violin*.

Several years passed after Henry left for Paris. One day back in London, John Eccles, home from work at the king's court, said to his younger brother Thomas, "I have heard at the court that George Frederick Handel is returning to England. When he was here two years ago he hired an orchestra to perform his opera. Perhaps now you would be able to get a job in his orchestra."

"That is a wonderful idea," replied Thomas. "I will certainly try for a position in Handel's orchestra. It would be a great privilege to play his music." Thomas applied, and did become a violinist in George Frederick Handel's orchestra.

Five years after Handel returned to London, he wrote the *Water Music Suite* in honor of the royal family. He planned to have it performed in an unusual way. On hot summer afternoons, the king and queen would go down to the Thames River that flowed through London, step onto the royal barges, and float along the water enjoying the cool breezes. Handel's idea was to have the *Water Music* performed by his orchestra seated on other barges that would float near the royal barge.

Handel carried out his plan, and the royal family was delighted. We can guess that one member of that orchestra performing that day was Thomas Eccles himself — and perhaps even his brother was there to stand on the bank of the river and watch the performance. Did they wish that their brother Henry, far away in Paris, could have been there to hear it too?

b. London, England - 1670
d. Paris, France - 1742

GEORGE (EDWARD) GOLTERMAN

Your legs are long enough now," George's father said as he put his arm around his young son. "Come on, climb up these big stone steps into the organ loft, and stay with me while I practice this Bach *Prelude* for the Sunday church service."

George was proud to be big enough to go with his father while he practiced. It was fun to watch his father's feet run up and down the organ pedals and to hear the deep, rumbling tones that boomed from the organ pipes. No wonder, then, that when George Golterman's father asked his son what instrument he wanted to play, he said at once, "The cello!"

"I love the low, strong voice of the cello," the boy said. "I can make it sound just like the pedal tones of the organ."

George took cello lessons for many years in his home city of Hanover, but when he was approaching his twenty-third birthday, his father said to him, "George, perhaps you should consider going to Munich. It is not so far from home, and you could study composition with Maestro Lachner, and continue your cello lessons as well."

George liked this idea, and when all the arrangements had been made, he set out for Munich. First he went to see Joseph Menter, who agreed to give cello lessons to George. His next visit was to Maestro Lachner who was composer at the Court Opera in Munich.

George explained to Maestro Lachner that he would like to study composing with him. "I have been studying cello for many years," he said, "and I have always played pieces that other people have composed. Now I would like to try writing pieces of my own."

"Good," Professor Lachner said. "We will begin your lessons tomorrow!"

"Do you think I will have time to compose music when I am traveling so much and giving so many concerts?" George asked his teacher.

"If you have the desire to do it, you will find the time," the Maestro replied.

And so George Golterman decided to try his hand at writing music. He studied for a time with Maestro Lachner, and when he was twenty-seven years old he completed his first symphony, and soon after that, a cello concerto.

After five years of studying and performing in Munich, George became Kapellmeister of a theatre in Frankfurt. His job kept him very busy, but still he found time to compose. He wrote many different kinds of pieces, but people enjoyed most the music he wrote for the cello. Although Golterman's music is not often heard in concerts now, his compositions were popular with the German people of his time. Cello students today will remember George Golterman for the excellent studies he composed to help them on the way to becoming fine musicians.

89

b. Hanover, Germany, Aug. 19, 1824
d. Frankfurt-am-Main, Germany, Dec. 29, 1898

GEORGE FREDERICK HANDEL

Music is fine for amusement, but not for an occupation," said George's father as he watched his small son smile and clap his hands whenever he heard the sound of music. George's father, who had become wealthy as the barber in the duke's court, declared, "Nobody can get rich being a musician!"

Try as he would, Herr Handel could not keep music away from his growing son. In the small German town of Halle, music could be heard everywhere. Town musicians wandered through the streets performing folk music. The chords of the church organ sounded in the courtyard, and the steeple bells clamored through the windows of little George's room.

The stern words of his father could not stop George from making music. There is a story often told about George to show how eager he was to learn to play music. His father would not allow any musical instruments in their house, so when George was five years old he begged an older friend to help him carry a clavichord (a tiny piano) to the attic of the house. There he taught himself to play, and practiced in secret while his father slept or was at work at the court.

George must have been a strong-willed boy. One day when he was seven years old, his father said to him, "George, I am going to visit your stepbrother at the court of the duke. You must stay at home."

George had never met his stepbrother, who was organist at the duke's court. He implored his father, "Please let me come with you, father."

"No, you must stay here," his father insisted. "You are too young to take the far journey. You would be a nuisance on such a long trip."

But George would not take no for an answer. He watched his father leave in the horse-drawn carriage, and immediately started after him, running as fast as his short legs could go. He never would have caught up with the carriage if it had not had an accident on the rough road. Imagine his father's surprise, then, when he saw his son running breathlessly up to the stalled carriage. "Father," George called out, "now will you let me come?"

How could his father say no? Complaining and scolding, he lifted the boy into the carriage, and away they went until they came to the court of the duke.

George was glad to meet his stepbrother. After the Sunday church service in the duke's chapel, George was allowed to climb into the organ loft to try the huge keyboard where his stepbrother performed each Sunday. George was trying some of the pieces he had been practicing in the attic at home, when the duke happened to come into the church.

"Who is playing that sweet music?" the duke asked. Walking closer to the organ console, the duke saw the seven-year-old boy. He called up to the child, whom he could barely see over the railing, and said, "What is your name, son?"

"My name is George Frederick Handel," replied the boy. The

duke spoke kindly to George, telling him how much he enjoyed music. George then told the duke, "I love music too, and would like to study all about it, but my father will not allow me to spend my time that way. He says he does not want me to become a musician."

The duke was surprised to hear this. He immediately asked to speak to George's father. "You have a very talented son," he said. "I understand that you do not wish him to study music. In my opinion," the duke went on, "it would be a shame to deprive the world of such a musical genius. Your boy is more likely to succeed in a path that nature and providence seem to have chosen for him."

The duke's words made a deep impression on George's father, and he agreed to have a music teacher for his son. As George and his father left the court, the duke filled the boy's pockets with coins, saying, "If you study conscientiously, all will be well."

When George and his father returned to Halle, a teacher was immediately found who could teach the boy organ, harpsichord, violin, and oboe. He studied composition and theory with the local church organist. Wanting to satisfy his father, George also attended the university to study law. Soon, however, he was offered a position as organist at the cathedral and castle, and he left the university to spend the rest of his life with music.

How should he begin his new life? He heard about an orchestra in Hamburg where a second violinist was needed. He applied for the job and was hired. The job would pay him very little, but he decided to try it. One day, the leader of the orchestra was out of town. The musicians in the orchestra planned to play a joke on their new young member, Handel. "Come on!" they told him, "You be our leader today."

"What a joke this will be," they all thought. But imagine their amazement when Handel conducted the orchestra with even more skill than their absent leader!

For two years, Handel stayed in Hamburg, working very hard. He wrote four operas while he was there. He saved as much of his pay as he could from his meagre salary as an orchestra player. At the age of twenty-one, he decided to leave his own country and go to Italy. With high hopes, he set off on his journey across the mountains to sunny Italy. He learned to speak the language there, and wrote operas which gave great pleasure to the Italian people. In return, the people of Italy gave Handel the nickname of "the dear Saxon," because they were so fond of this young man from the part of Germany called Saxony.

One evening, Handel dressed up in a fancy costume to go to a masquerade party to which he had been invited. He wore a good disguise, and for a time nobody knew the person behind the mask. Later in the evening, he sat down at the harpsichord and began to play. The room became absolutely quiet. A famous composer, Domenico Scarlatti, happened to be one of the guests at the party. He listened for a time, then suddenly jumped up and exclaimed for all to hear, "This stranger at the harpsichord must either be the famous Saxon, or the Devil!"

To this, everyone in the room shouted, "It must be George

Frederick Handel!"

Whenever Handel's operas were performed in Italy, the opera house was filled with enthusiastic music lovers. Loud applause would come after each beautiful song, and often shouts would be heard from the audience, "Long live the good Saxon!"

Handel made many friends while he was in Italy. Among them were some visitors from England. They invited him to come to London. So, packing up his few belongings, he crossed the mountains again, stopped off to see his mother, and then crossed the channel to England. He immediately went to work to compose an opera for the English people. It was not long before friends, meeting in the street or in their homes, would be asking, "Have you heard Handel's opera?" And they were humming and whistling the tunes.

Handel was now twenty-five years old and full of enthusiasm for the English countryside and the people he met. One of his friends was Thomas Britton, who made his living by selling coal on the streets of London. He pushed his wheelbarrow full of sacks of coal from door to door. In the evenings, when his work was done, Thomas returned to his poor lodgings, changed his clothes, and waited to receive his guests in the long, low loft over his shop.

"Welcome, George," Thomas called when he saw Handel coming down the cobblestone walk. Here, in this poor man's home, where Thomas had collected all kinds of music and musical instruments, was the weekly gathering place of professional musicians and musical amateurs of every rank, both rich and poor.

Handel spent many happy hours with Thomas and his friends.

One fine summer evening, a group of people stood along the banks of the Thames River, which flowed through the city of London. They were part of a crowd gathered to watch King George and his family returning in their royal boats from a Sunday trip on the water. "There it is," called out a small boy. "That must be the King's boat, with the crimson canopy."

"Yes, but I hear the sound of music," said one man in the group. "Where is that music coming from?"

Not far from the royal barge were several other boats filled with musicians. In one of the boats, a young man stood, leading the orchestra. The King's attention was immediately drawn to the lovely sounds of violins and trumpets. "Who is the leader of that orchestra?" the King asked.

"That is George Frederick Handel, Your Majesty," replied the courtier.

"And did he compose the music we are hearing now?" the King inquired.

"Yes, he did, Your Majesty," came the answer.

King George was so pleased that he sent Handel an invitation to live at his court. "Will you come to live at the court?" the invitation read. "I would be pleased to have you give music lessons to my daughter, the young princess."

Handel accepted the invitation with pleasure. King George agreed to pay him two hundred pounds sterling each year for his teaching.

By the time Handel was forty-one, he decided to live in England the rest of his life. Sometimes he visited Germany, but he now called England his home. Queen Anne appointed Handel to be official composer to the British court. He wrote special music for her, and she was enchanted by this charming man with the German accent. Well known poets and writers of the time enjoyed his company and marveled at his musical genius.

At first Handel's life in England was secure and contented. His days and evenings were filled with work and pleasure. Each morning he spent writing in his study. At lunchtime, he met with writers and artists for good conversation. In the afternoons he would often go to St. Paul's Cathedral for organ concerts. Sometimes he performed, and when people heard that Handel was to give a concert, the cathedral would be packed with admirers. In the evenings at Queen Anne's Tavern, Handel often sat down at the harpsichord in the large timbered music room to play a concert for everyone to enjoy.

Unfortunately, this serene, pleasant life did not last. Queen Anne, his patroness, died, and the new king did not favor Handel as she had. Fortunately, the Earl of Carnarvon heard that Handel was looking for a position. "Will you come to reside in my castle and serve me as master of music?" the Earl asked Handel. "I have a fine orchestra, a well-trained chorus, and we always have an audience that will appreciate your music."

This was just what Handel needed to give him time to work and compose without having to worry about money. He accepted the invitation gratefully. In the next three years, while he resided at the castle, a big change came in Handel's style of writing music. It was as if a closed, tight bud of a flower suddenly opened into full bloom. His operas and anthems burst forth with new life. He began to write a new, exciting kind of music called the oratorio. It was written for a large orchestra, a large chorus, and solo singers. One of these oratorios was *Judas Maccabaeus.* The story came from the Bible. It was about the ancient hero, Judas Maccabaeus, who led his army against the Syrians and recaptured the temple for the Jews.

After three years at the castle, the adventurous Handel took another turn in his life. This time, the adventure proved to be a sad mistake. He left the protection of the court to try his hand at being a business man. A new opera house had opened in London, and Handel decided to go into the business part of running the establishment. He put all the money he had saved in his life into the business.

It was a miserable failure. He was so busy writing operas that he paid little attention to the business part of the venture. Besides, the English people began to get tired of his operas.

A London newspaper article commented that the English people thought that Handel's music was too serious. The writer declared that music "should relieve clever men from the trouble of thinking."

Handel's biggest problem, however, was that other composers less gifted than he were becoming jealous of his genius. They wrote articles that were bitterly critical of everything that he wrote. When a performance of a Handel opera was scheduled, they would even plan other public events to keep people away from the opera house. They would arrange other entertainment such as cock fights, card games, or other shows. Fewer and fewer people came to hear Handel's music.

GEORGE FREDERICK HANDEL

To make matters worse, publishers and performers printed and performed Handel's music without paying him a penny for his work.

Handel's money now was all gone. Yet, though he needed help himself, he gave concerts to help other poor musicians. His health began to fail. But in a sudden surge of inspiration and energy, he composed one of his greatest oratorios, *Messiah.* He wrote the entire piece in just twenty-four days. When someone asked him, "How could you write such beautiful music?" Handel replied, "While I was writing I did think I saw all heaven before me and the great God Himself."

Once again, new wealth, fame and friends came his way. But just as he was beginning to write another opera, Handel's eyesight began to dim. When he was sixty-seven years old, he became totally blind, and had to dictate the music for someone to write down.

In spite of his blindness, Handel never complained, and was a cheerful friend until the end of his seventy-four years of life. The English king honored Handel by laying his body to rest in the Poets' Corner of Westminster Abbey, where the soft light from the great stained glass window falls upon his statue. The stone statue represents Handel looking upward and holding in his hand a carved sheet of music from his oratorio *Messiah,* with the words inscribed, "I know that my Redeemer liveth."

b. Halle, Germany, February 23, 1685
d. London, England, April 14, 1759

FRANZ JOSEPH HAYDN

Goodbye, Mama. Goodbye, Papa. Goodbye, goodbye," little Franz Joseph shouted above the noise of the clattering carriage wheels. His parents, standing in front of their house at the end of the dirt lane, waved to Joseph until the carriage disappeared from sight.

"Our little Pepperl, only six years old," Mama Haydn sobbed. "Do you think Rosina will take good care of him?"

"Do not worry, my dear Anna," Mathias comforted his wife. "Our little Pepperl is a strong, happy boy. You will see. He will do well. Come, we must take baby Michael into the house. The air is chilly."

Meanwhile, Joseph and Cousin Frank, in the horse-drawn carriage, bounced their slow way along the rutted dirt road to Hainberg. It had been Cousin Frank's idea that the six year old Joseph should come to live with him, his wife Rosina, and their children.

"My dear Mathias," Cousin Frank had said to Joseph's father, "your son loves music. Everyone knows how beautifully he sings. Why, the evenings when you take out your harp and sing together with Anna Marie and your children, people who hear the music through the open door can't help but remark about Joseph's high, sweet, clear voice. And besides, how quickly he learns!"

"Yes, I know! You are right," Mathias had replied. "You

should have seen him just last week, pretending to play the violin with a wooden box under his chin and a stick for a bow. He can keep perfect time! I wonder, though, Cousin, Pepperl is so young to be leaving home."

"We will take good care of your son," Cousin Frank had promised. "Let him come with me to Hainberg. I am the school master and choirmaster in the town. I can see to it that Joseph gets a good education. He can learn about music, sing in the church choir, and find out if he can do well enough to earn his living as a musician. If not, he can come back home to you and learn to be a wheelright, like you are and your father and your grandfather were before you. Let him come with me."

After many hours of thinking about Cousin Frank's invitation, Joseph's parents agreed to let their son go. Joseph's mother, although she was sad to have him leave home, thought that perhaps Joseph would learn more in a school in the larger town.

"If Joseph has a good education, maybe he will want to become a priest," Anna Marie had said to Mathias. "That would be my greatest wish."

The ten miles to Hainberg was a full day's journey for Cousin Frank and Joseph. As the carriage came closer to Hainberg, Cousin Frank spoke up. "See, Joseph, up ahead, the stone wall on the hill? That is the wall around our town, and when we get to the top of the hill you will see the great Danube River flowing down below." Up the hill they rode, and through the town's gate.

Cousin Frank pulled the horses to a stop in front of a small house next to the courtyard of the town hall. As the two dusty travelers climbed down from the carriage, Rosina came out of the house. "Come in, come in, and welcome to our home, Joseph," she called out.

When Joseph stepped inside the house, he could not believe his eyes! His mother Anna Marie was such a tidy housekeeper and everything in their home was scrubbed and in its proper place. He could see at a glance that Rosina was just the opposite. The house was a terrible mess. And this was to be home for a boy who was brought up to believe that tidiness was a virtue!

No sooner had Cousin Frank carried Joseph's small traveling box into the house, and shown him where he was to sleep, than he said, "Now, Joseph, come with me. We will hurry over to the church. We must sweep the aisles, and ring the vesper bells before the choir and orchestra arrive for rehearsal!"

Joseph was hungry and tired after the long journey but he ran along as fast as he could on his short legs to keep up with Cousin Frank. They came to the church. It was bigger than any he had ever seen!

Joseph helped Cousin Frank with his church chores and then sat down to watch the choir and orchestra arrive for the rehearsal. The boys and men of the choir took their places. The organist sat at the keyboard of the large, fine organ. The orchestra members came in one by one - two violinists, the cellist, and the double bass player arrived first, then the horn, trumpet and drum players came after.

"All right," Cousin Frank, the choirmaster said. "Let us begin."

To the six year old boy, this was the most wonderful sound he had ever heard, with the organ, the voices, and the instruments filling the church with beautiful music! Even though Joseph was hungry and his stomach rumbled with emptiness, he sat enthralled by the music that seemed to come from every corner of the old stone church.

Before he knew it, the rehearsal was over. Cousin Frank snuffed out the candles on the music stands, locked the church doors, and the two tired travelers walked home.

"Here is some soup and bread and cheese," Rosina said when they came into the kitchen. "Hurry now, finish your supper. You must get to bed. Tomorrow is your first day at school."

Cousin Frank was the schoolmaster, as well as choirmaster in Hainberg. He had seventy school children to care for, with two assistant teachers whom he had to pay out of his own small salary. Although he worked hard to care for his growing family he never had enough money. Joseph was always hungry, and he wished that Cousin Frank could have been as generous with food as he was with flogging!

For Joseph, who had a keen interest in everything, each day was full. School lessons, his music lessons, his practice, and his duties at home and at the church, kept him busy. Besides, there were so many extra celebrations and feast days to prepare for in the town and church.

With Autumn came the festival to celebrate the harvest. Cousin Frank's church choir and orchestra marched in procession to a different church each day performing special music. On the final day, they were to march out into the fields to celebrate the bringing in of the crops.

"Pepperl, Pepperl," Cousin Frank called breathlessly to Joseph who was at the church concentrating with all his might on his violin practice. "We are in big trouble! Our drummer is sick and cannot march with us today. I know you are small and have never played drums before, but do you think you can be the drummer in the procession?"

"Of course, I will do my best." Joseph ran home. He burst into the kitchen and found a bowl the size of a drum. He tied a cloth tightly over the top and began to beat it with two wooden spoons. The flour in the bowl rose in clouds all over the boy and the kitchen furniture, but he kept up his rhythmic beating to practice for the afternoon procession.

When the time came, the parade formed. First came the Priest, the choir, the mayor and the town council, then the school children, the workers and tradespeople of the town, and finally, the town band. Last of all, to the surprise of the watching townspeople, was little Joseph, the last player in the band, his wig askew on his head, beating the drums, and having a most joyful time.

Ever since he had come to Hainberg, Joseph was learning more and more about music. In the church choir, he already could sing his part in several masses with no trouble at all. Often he sang the solo. He was learning to play the harpsichord and the violin. The Priest at church had never seen a young boy practice with such seriousness.

It was no wonder then, in the following year when Joseph was seven years old, that the Priest called Cousin Frank and Joseph to his Parish study.

"Joseph, my boy, I called you here to meet someone who has heard about your singing. He comes from the Cathedral in Vienna. He is the court composer and choirmaster. Oh, here he comes now."

George Reutter strode into the room. He smiled and greeted everyone with a warm, firm handshake. "And is this Franz Joseph Haydn?" he asked.

"Yes, sir, I am Joseph Haydn," answered the boy, wondering what this was all about.

"I hear fine things about you, Joseph. The Priest tells me what a hard worker you are, and Cousin Frank tells me how much you love music. I heard you sing the soprano solo in High Mass on Sunday. You have a fine voice."

"Thank you, sir," Joseph replied in a quiet voice.

"Here, first have some of these nice ripe cherries from this bowl. Then we will sing a few exercises, so I can hear how you can read music at first sight."

Joseph caught the cherries that Maestro Reutter tossed him. Then he took the test, and easily carried out the exercises.

"Now, Joseph, can you sing a trill?"

"I can trill on my violin, but Cousin Frank hasn't taught me to trill with my voice."

"Well, then, I will sing a trill for you. Watch closely. Then you can try it."

Joseph watched and listened. He tried it once. He tried again. Then, on the third try he produced a beautiful, clear trill.

"*Wunderbar! Bravo,*" Maestro Reutter called out. "Here, have some more cherries for a prize," he said, and then he placed a silver coin in Joseph's hand. "I want to ask your father if he will let you come to Vienna to join the choir at St. Stephen's Cathedral."

Mathias Haydn was summoned to Hainburg to talk to Maestro Reutter. "I would like to take Joseph to Vienna. Vienna is a beautiful, musical city and your son will have a fine education in the Cathedral school," he promised, "and he will sing in the famous St. Stephen's choir."

Thinking that this would be best for Joseph, Mathias gave his consent to the plan.

"We cannot take you into the school until you are eight years old," the choirmaster from Vienna told Joseph. "In the meantime, you must practice your scales. Then I will be back again to see if you have made progress."

Joseph was determined to be ready when Herr Reutter

106

returned. For the next nine months, he worked diligently. Cousin Frank was too busy to take time to help Joseph, but that made the boy all the more determined.

"I will teach myself," he declared. "I will sing the scales, and name the notes. Everyday I will work hard."

Soon after Joseph's eighth birthday, Maestro Reutter returned. When he heard Joseph sing, he was amazed at his progress. "You have done well, Joseph. In three days, we will leave for Vienna," he said. Joseph said goodbye to all his friends. He thanked Cousin Frank and Rosina for their care, he packed his small wooden box, and was ready for the trip to the great city.

On the journey from Cousin Frank's home to his new home in the Cathedral school, Joseph was full of questions about the new life he was about to begin.

"How many other boys will be at the school?" he asked Herr Reutter.

"There will be five other choirboys, a subcantor and two teachers."

"Will we have time to play games?"

"Games?" Herr Reutter burst out. "Games? There will be no time for games! You will be too busy. Each day you will take part in two choral services - one in the morning and one in the evening. You must rehearse every day and you must practice singing, violin and harpsichord. Besides, for every important occasion in the city and the church, we must be prepared to give a concert. And the Priests expect us to perform for their Latin shows. You will see, Joseph, there will be no time for games."

"Is the Cathedral as big as the church in Cousin Frank's town?"

Herr Reutter laughed. "My boy, wait until you see St. Stephens Church. Look now, even from here you can see the tall South Tower of St. Stephen's reaching up into the clouds. When you step inside the church you will feel that you are lifted into Heaven!"

Joseph was quiet for a time. He tried to imagine a church like that. After a while, he spoke up again. "Will I hear very much music in Vienna?"

"Music in Vienna? My boy, Vienna **is** music. From morning until night, you will hear the music of all the great composers. You will hear music in the church, and in the court of the Emperor and Empress, and in the homes of noblemen. You will even hear music in the streets."

"Who plays music in the streets?" Joseph asked.

"The players and singers who are poor and hungry and have no regular jobs serenade in the streets," he explained. "They get together in groups and sing and play under the people's windows to celebrate birthdays and weddings. They always hope that their listeners will throw many coins to them in thanks."

"Oh, that would be fun!" Joseph said to himself.

As the sun was almost touching the hills in the West, Herr

Reutter reined in the horses and the carriage stopped in front of the school beside St. Stephens.

"Well, here we are," Herr Reutter announced. He stepped down from the carriage and rang the big brass bell that hung at the top of the front steps. All at once, the door opened and five young faces peered out.

"Why were you not practicing?" Herr Reutter growled to the boys in a harsh voice.

"We were waiting for you, sir," one of the boys answered timidly. "We wanted to see our new classmate."

"Very well," said Herr Reutter. "Here he is. Franz Joseph Haydn, these are your new schoolmates, Karl, George, Emmanuel, Christopher, and Wilhelm. Now, show Joseph his room, and get on to bed. We have much work to do tomorrow."

The next day after a long rehearsal, Joseph said to Wilhelm, "I am so hungry. When will we have something to eat?"

"We always feel hungry here at the school, Joseph. And you can see our clothing is in tatters, too. But let me tell you a secret. If you practice hard, and sing very well, you will be invited to perform at the homes of the wealthy noblemen in Vienna. After you sing, you will be invited to the kitchen, and there you can get plenty to eat."

So on the next special outing, Joseph was invited to go along. They were going to sing at the new castle that Empress Maria Theresa was having built for herself. For this special concert, the boys sang beautifully and behaved properly almost all day. But toward late afternoon, they noticed that the workmen had left some ladders standing against the castle. The boys, restless for some fun, climbed up and down the ladders shouting and laughing. The Empress was angry when she heard the noise.

"Get down from there, you young rascals. If I see anyone up there again, there will be a sound thrashing," the Empress called out from her balcony.

Next day, Joseph, always ready for a prank, could not resist the Empress' dare. He climbed to the top of the ladder. The Empress Theresa saw him, and ordered Herr Reutter, "Give that fair haired blockhead the scolding he deserves." Poor Joseph!

Several months later, Herr Reutter called for Joseph one evening after the Vesper service in the church. "I have some news for you, Joseph," he said. "Your brother Michael is coming here to join the choir."

At first, Joseph was happy to have his brother at the school. He helped him with his lessons and comforted him when he missed his parents. Michael had an exceptionally beautiful singing voice, and he was a quick learner. He played the organ so well that he was chosen to help the cathedral organist. Soon it was plain for Joseph to see that Michael was being asked to sing the solos in church, and was getting special attention from the Emperor and Empress. Joseph, on the other hand, was coming near to his thirteenth birthday, and his singing voice was beginning to show signs of changing. He tried to hide the croaking sounds that sometimes came out, but they were becoming more and more noticeable.

Joseph was less and less useful at St. Stephen's. Perhaps now that he could no longer sing the high parts, he could have played violin in the orchestra until his lower voice became stronger. But Herr Reutter did not ask him. Anyway, Joseph knew in his heart that he wanted more than anything else to be a composer. "How can I write music when I have had no training?" he wondered. "What can I do?"

To add to Joseph's worries, Herr Reutter was making life at school more and more unhappy for the growing boy. When Joseph wrote music and wanted his teacher to help him, Herr Reutter was always too busy and laughed at Joseph's attempt to be a composer. Finally, one day Joseph, who was always playing jokes, tried out a new pair of scissors by cutting off the pigtail of the choirboy who sat in front of him in the classroom.

Herr Reutter was furious. "Joseph, you will leave this school today," the choirmaster commanded.

Poor Joseph, now seventeen years old, with nowhere to go, and no job, packed his three ragged shirts, put on his tattered coat, and went out into the November night. He wandered about the streets of Vienna, trudging from one lamplight to another. Tired and unable to go any further, he lay down on a bench to sleep.

He had not been sleeping long when a friendly voice

awakened him. "Joseph, what are you doing here?" It was Johann Michael Spangler, a singer at St. Michael's Church. Joseph explained what had happened.

"Come along to my place, Joseph. It is only a poor garret where I live with my wife and baby, but you are welcome to share what little we have."

With great relief and trying to tell Johann how grateful he was for his kindness, Joseph followed his new friend to the small attic room near St. Michael's Church. The young family made a place for Joseph under the attic eaves.

The next day Joseph walked the streets of Vienna trying to find a way to earn at least enough money to buy his food. He remembered how Herr Reutter had told him of poor musicians who serenaded on the streets of Vienna. But now it was the middle of winter, and too cold for street concerts.

Joseph's parents, hearing of their son's troubles, begged him to give up the idea of becoming a composer. "We have always wanted you to be a Priest, Joseph. Give up your struggle against hunger and cold," they urged their son.

But Joseph was determined that somehow he would find his own way with music. He thought of one plan after another to earn a little money, but he only got hungrier and hungrier. Finally, almost desperate and ready to collapse with exhaustion, and thinking that perhaps his parents' way was the only way to a good, full meal, he started off to the monastery.

Springtime was coming to Vienna. The birds were singing

and the countryside was beginning to turn a soft yellow green. As Joseph came nearer to the monastery, his heart took on new hope. With a fresh start, he changed directions, and joined other travelers who were on their way to the hilltop to worship at a shrine. After Joseph knelt in prayer at the shrine, he went to talk to the priest.

"Father Urastil," he said, "I have come from the Choir School in Vienna. May I sing here in your choir?"

"*Ach,*" the Priest answered, "too many wandering hungry boys come here asking to sing in my choir and they only sound like frogs!"

"Well," thought Jospeh, "I know what I shall do!" A plan immediately jumped into his head. He walked over to the church. As the choir marched through the church on its way to the choir loft, he joined the procession, and sat down next to the tenor soloist.

"Please let me sing your solo this morning," Joseph whispered to the singer.

"Oh, but I cannot do that," the surprised singer replied. But just as the singer was about to stand, Joseph snatched the music from his hand, stood up, and from sight sang the tenor solo. The people in the church sat up straight and stretched their necks to see who it was that was singing with such a strong and lyric voice. All the choir listened breathlessly.

After the church service, Father Urastil, the priest, told Joseph that he was sorry for what he had said about croaking frogs. "Please, Joseph," he said, "you must stay here for a while. We can provide your food and lodging if you will sing in our choir.

For a whole week, Joseph sang in the choir, and enjoyed eating three good meals a day. Not since he had left home when he was six years old could he remember the feeling of a full, satisfied stomach! At the end of the week, though, Joseph told Father Urastil that he must return to Vienna to begin his work as a composer. When Joseph and the Priest parted at the church door, Father Urastil said, "We have taken up a small collection for you, Joseph. Here are a few coins. Good luck to you, and Godspeed."

Springtime was now in full bloom when Haydn returned to Vienna. Here and there, all around the city, serenaders with their instruments and singers and actors entertained with all kinds of fare - dance suites, and parts from operas, hunting songs and popular songs. For Joseph, who had spent so many years performing only church music, all this different music was very exciting. One evening, as he stood at a street corner, listening to a group of town musicians playing the Lully *Gavotte*, the drummer recognized his friend from the Choir School.

"Joseph Haydn, come, you must join our group. You are just the person we are looking for. We need someone to compose music for us."

Haydn was pleased to be invited. He had no money left, and

besides, it would be good to have a group to perform his music.

"We need some music by next Friday," his friend explained. "Johann Joseph Kurz, the famous comedian, wants us to perform for his wife's birthday. Can you have something ready for us?"

"Indeed I can!" Haydn replied excitedly. On Friday, Joseph, with the manuscript tucked under his arm, met his friends for a short rehearsal, and then they were off to the home of Herr Kurz.

When the serenading was over, the comedian asked the musicians, "Who wrote the music that you played tonight?"

"He did," they replied, pointing to Joseph. "His name is Franz Joseph Haydn."

"Well, young man, will you come around tomorrow? I am writing a musical show and I would like you to write the music for it."

For the nineteen year old Haydn, this was the first real commission. When he completed the work, Herr Kurz was satisfied, and paid Joseph 25 ducats.

"Now I'm a rich man," Joseph laughingly told his friends. "But the truth is," he confided to them, "I am not yet a good composer. What with giving clavier lessons all day, serenading in the evening, I have little time to study, and no one to help me and teach me."

Good fortune, though, soon led Joseph Haydn on a happier path. Upon his return to Vienna, he found a place where he could live cheaply in a small attic room. He bought an old moth-eaten clavier. With a book of sonatas by Carl Phillip Emanuel Bach that the bookstore owner had given him as a gift, Joseph spent many hours late into the night. First he would play the sonatas for the joy they gave him, then he would play them for the lessons they taught him about composing.

In the very same large house where Joseph lived, on the floor below his attic room, lived a famous court poet who had two little girls in his care. One, Marianne, was a brilliant child who took singing lessons from a famous singing teacher. The teacher asked Joseph to play the harpsichord accompaniments for her at her lessons and also teach her to play the clavier. In return, Joseph could have his meals in the poet's apartment, which was a blessing for a young man who was always hungry. But what was more important for Joseph, was that Marianne's singing teacher was also a fine composer.

"I would like to ask if you would give me composition lessons," Joseph asked Niccolo Porpora. "But I have little money to pay you for teaching me."

"In that case," answered the singing teacher, "you can pay me by playing clavier for my singing students. You can shine my shoes and care for my clothing. If you do that, I will teach you."

The arrangement worked well for both the young and eager student and Maestro Porpora. The older teacher's advice about writing music was very helpful to Joseph. It was helpful, too, that he was able to introduce Joseph to many wealthy music lovers who lived in the great estates of Vienna.

"I see you are becoming a busy teacher," Porpora said to Haydn.

"Yes," replied Haydn. "Now I am giving clavier lessons and composition lessons as well. Soon I will have enough money to move into a larger apartment with heat, perhaps. With my four church jobs on Sundays, I will be able to afford violin lessons, too."

Joseph moved into his new apartment. His days were full with teaching, but at night, after serenading, he closed himself away for the thing he loved to do the best — writing music. Slowly but surely, Haydn was teaching himself the skills to become a fine composer.

One Sunday, just as he had returned from his job at the Cathedral, there was a knock on the door. It was the Baron von Furnberg, whose large town house was not far from Haydn's apartment.

"I have come by, Maestro Haydn, to ask if you would become music master to my family. This summer we will travel to my country home, and if you will bring your viola, we can play quartets. Perhaps you can write some music especially for our group."

Joseph looked forward to a quiet time in the countryside. He hoped perhaps he might have more time for composing!

At the Baron's home it was the custom, each evening following dinner, for the Baron's string quartet to gather in the music room. "Well, Joseph, do you have anything special for us to try tonight?"

"Here is my first string quartet," Haydn said. "You would honor me if you will try it."

Haydn, playing the viola, watched and listened nervously as the group played through the first movement, then the second, the third and the fourth.

"Bravo, bravo", the other players shouted as they lifted their bows.

"Joseph, you have composed a masterful quartet. You surely must write more for our group," Baron von Furnberg told Haydn.

With this encouragement, Haydn's pen was never still. In a short time he had written twelve quartets. People were beginning to talk about that 'genius, Joseph Haydn'.

Summer was drawing to an end, and the Baron was preparing to close his country estate for the winter and move back to Vienna. Just as Haydn was wondering what he would do next, the Baron said, "Haydn, I have a friend, Count Morzin, who has a castle in Bavaria. He is looking for a composer and orchestra leader. Would you be interested in serving the Count?"

The twenty-five year old Haydn assured the Baron that he would welcome such a position, and when the Count himself invited Haydn to be his composer and Kapellmeister at his castle, he eagerly accepted. This would give him the security of a place to live and time to compose.

One evening, after a concert in the castle, The Count told

Haydn that there was to be a very important wedding in Vienna. "Our future Emperor will be married, and of course, we will all be there," he explained.

Joseph Haydn was pleased to return to the busy city once more where he could see his old friends again.

The first thing he did was to meet his serenading group.

"Joseph, it is so good to see you again. I want you to meet my friend Karl Dittersdorf," said one of Haydn's serenading companions.

Joseph and Karl immediately discovered that they had many common interests. When they were not working, they spent hours together wandering the streets of Vienna listening to music, performing, and discussing what they had heard. One night, they walked by a tavern and heard some musicians inside playing a string quartet.

"Come on, Karl," said Joseph. "Let's find out what music they are playing." No sooner had they entered the room, than Haydn recognized that it was a minuet from one of his own quartets — one that he had composed. Nudging Karl and giving him a mischievous wink, Haydn blurted out to the players, "Who wrote that piece?"

"Joseph Haydn did," they replied.

"Haydn?" Joseph said, pretending disgust. "Why, who would write such a terrible piece?"

With that, the angry players jumped up, came after Haydn, ready to beat him with their instruments. It was lucky that

Dittersdorf was there; he had to protect Joseph and get him safely out the door.

Some months passed, and Haydn and Dittersdorf were walking to St. Stephen's Cathedral. "I have something to confide to you, Karl", Joseph said. "I have asked Maria Keller to be my wife, and she has consented. We will be married here in November. But I am worried that the Count will find out about it; you know he forbids his Kapellmeister to be married!"

Haydn did not worry long, however. The very next Spring the Count had to ask his musicians to leave because he had no money to pay them.

"As for you, Joseph Haydn," the Count said, "Prince Esterhazy has asked about you. Not long ago, he came to one of our evening entertainments. He heard our orchestra play your first symphony. He was most impressed with your music. You know his Kapellmeister is getting quite old and needs someone to help him with his work."

When Prince Esterhazy heard that, indeed, Haydn would be leaving Count Morzin's castle, he immediately asked him to be in charge of the music in his Palace.

The Esterhazy family was one of the greatest Hungarian noble families in all of Europe. The men were well known as soldiers, statesmen and musicians. Prince Paul Anton Esterhazy played violin and cello. At his Palace, he had a choir and orchestra and a fine collection of music.

"I would like you to take charge of all the music," Prince

Esterhazy told Haydn. "But let me caution you. My Kapellmeister is getting old and crabby and critical, and he may be difficult to get along with."

"Have no fears, your Highness," Haydn replied, remembering how he had managed to get along with Porpora, his impatient and unpleasant teacher. "I admire Maestro Werner," Haydn said, "and I can surely be patient and kind to him."

At the age of twenty-nine, Joseph Haydn was responsible for all the musical duties of the large princely household. Each morning, when the Prince had finished his breakfast, Joseph was ushered into the Prince's room to discuss the day's events.

"What are your plans for today, Joseph?" the Prince asked.

"As soon as I leave your chambers," Haydn replied, "I will rehearse the orchestra for tonight's concert. Then I will coach the six singers for tomorrow's opera. At 11:00, I will rehearse the choir for Sunday's Church Mass. Early this afternoon I will look at all the instruments and make some repairs, and later I will start composing a symphony for Saturday's entertainment. Tonight, we will have a performance of the opera which we rehearsed last week."

"And what about the uniforms, Joseph? Have you remembered to see if they need attention? I noticed at the court performance last week, that some of the cello players' powdered hair with pigtails looked a bit unkempt, and the long white stockings needed laundering. And," the Count added after a pause, "what is this I hear about an argument among the violinists?"

"Oh, I have settled that, your Highness. The musicians are cheerful again. And don't worry, when your guests come on Saturday the musicians' uniforms will be perfect, and their pigtails in place!"

"Very well, and one more thing, Haydn. I had a good idea this morning while I was having my bath. I would like you to write three symphonies for me; one will describe morning, another, afternoon and the third, night."

"All right, your Highness, I will do it just as soon as I can," and Haydn left for his rehearsal. He sighed and shook his head wondering how he could possibly do all that was expected of him.

Less than a year after Haydn took his job at the Court, Paul Anton Esterhazy died, and his position as head of the court was taken over by his brother Nikolaus. People called him Nikolaus The Magnificent because everything he did was so grand and splendid.

Now that he was head of the Esterhazy estate, Prince Nikolaus sent for his architect and builder. "Several years ago," he told them, "I visited the grandest Palace in all of Europe.. Now I must have a Palace even more splendid. I want you to build for me the most magnificent Palace that your imagination can invent. It must be away from Vienna, deep in the forest."

When his castle was built, it had 126 rooms for guests, an opera house, a marionette theatre, masterpieces of great art in the picture gallery, and a park with statues, temples and water works.

In the Prince's own rooms there were chairs and couches covered with gold cloth, clocks that played tunes on the hour and a chair that played a flute solo when anyone sat down.

This was the Palace where Haydn spent most of his time for the next twenty-five years. In the rare hours when Haydn could free himself from his duties to the Prince, he liked to wander from the Palace and talk to the ordinary folks who lived and worked in the countryside. He would sit with the people in the tavern, and listen to them talk about their families, their troubles on the farm, and the vageries of the weather. They talked about their harvest, and the prices they could get for their produce.

It was a day in June when the local butcher in the tavern said to Haydn, "My daughter will be marrying soon. Would you write some music for her wedding?"

"It would make me happy to do that," Haydn answered with a smile.

The wedding day arrived. The bride and bridegroom told Haydn that his music had made this an especially beautiful day for them.

That night, Haydn had just blown out his candle and was getting into bed, when he heard a long, low, *Moooooo* outside. He looked out the window to see what it was. There, looking in the window at him was an ox. It had garlands of flowers on its horns and a hat of ribbons on its head. This was a gift of thanks from the butcher for the minuet that Haydn had written for the wedding. Ever after, the music has been known as the Ox Minuet.

Although Haydn was very busy with his many duties, it was a time when he could improve his skill as a composer. The musicians in the Palace orchestra and choir loved their leader very much. They called him Papa Haydn and often came to him for help and advice.

One day, two of the orchestra musicians came to Haydn. "Papa Haydn", one of them said, "why is it that the Prince can have such beautiful rooms for his guests, while we must live crowded together in such a small building? Our wives and families must stay in Vienna, because there is no place for them here, and we can see them only once or twice a year. Isn't there something you can do for us?"

Haydn thought and thought what he could do. Often when he had a problem, he solved it with a joke. Finally, an idea came to him.

The next time the orchestra came together for a rehearsal, he told the men what he had planned to do as a way of explaining to Prince Nikolaus that the musicians wanted to be allowed to go to Vienna to be with their families.

"I have composed a special symphony for this Saturday night's concert," Haydn explained. "You will play together at first, but then one by one you will stop playing, blow out the candle on your music stand, take your music under your arm, and walk off the stage, until nobody is left."

Saturday night came. The Prince's guests arrived, driving up to the gates in their fine carriages, past the guard of 150 grenadiers in their blue and red coats and white trousers and black bearskin caps. They entered the great music room with the rock crystal chandeliers and the heavy gilt-framed paintings on the walls. The Prince, dressed in his uniform covered with diamonds, greeted his guests.

The orchestra was assembled on the platform. Haydn, in his uniform of crimson and gold, entered. The evening performance began. The guests listened attentively. The last piece in the program was a new symphony, which Prince Nikolaus had never heard. With a big wink and a smile to the orchestra, Haydn gave the down beat to begin their *Farewell Symphony*. According to plan, during the performance, one by one the musicians blew out their candles and left the stage.

At the end of the concert, the smiling Prince Nikolaus walked up to Haydn. "I understand," he said. "Please tell your musicians that next week we will pack our things and return for a few months to Vienna."

Of course, the orchestra musicians thanked Papa Haydn for thinking of such a clever way to tell the Prince that they wanted to go home.

Haydn, too, was always glad to return to Vienna. He could greet his old friends once more, go to concerts, meet visiting composers, and enjoy the bustle of a busy, friendly city. A special joy was being with children.

After his work was finished one afternoon, Haydn was strolling in the park when the shouts and music of a carnival attracted his attention. As he came closer, he noticed a group of ragged little children begging a peddler to let them have some noisemakers he was selling.

"I want the horn," shouted one.

"May I have the drum?" shouted another.

"How about the bird whistles?" pleaded the third.

The peddler wanted money but the children had none.

"Here," Papa Haydn said to the peddler, giving him a handful of coins. "Let the children have the toy instruments."

The children shouted with glee, and hugged the nice man who bought the noisemakers for them. "Play something for me now," Haydn asked the children.

As he stood there, enjoying their happy faces and loud noises, an idea jumped into his head. He thanked the children for their concert, bought for himself a set of the toy instruments, and with a lively step, started home.

"Where are you going in such a hurry?" a friend called out to him as he turned the corner of the street where he lived.

"I'm going home to write a toy symphony," he called back.

Imagine the surprise of his orchestra when he said, "Today I will need only two violins and a bass. Now, here are the instruments that the rest of you will play and he handed out a tin whistle, a pair of tiny cymbals, a drum, a bird-calling whistle, a cuckoo horn, and some rattles.

The musicians of the orchestra stared in wonder at their conductor. "Forget your silly seriousness," Papa Haydn laughingly scolded the men. "Music can be fun, too, you know!" Soon, everyone was laughing as they played the *Toy Symphony.*

Some of the happiest hours in Vienna were the evenings when Wolfgang Mozart invited Haydn to his house to play chamber music.. They played into the wee hours of the morning. Haydn was fascinated by the twenty-five year old Mozart, so brilliant, with quickly changing moods, while Mozart felt secure with the forty-nine year old Papa Haydn, so warm hearted, generous and steadfast.

"My father is coming to Vienna for a visit," Wolfgang Mozart told his friend. "Will you come to my house again on Wednesday? I would like to play some of my new quartets for him."

"Indeed, I will," Haydn replied.

The evening was a happy event for everyone. When they finally put their instruments in their cases, Haydn went to Mozart's father. "Your son is the greatest composer I know," he said. "I have much to learn from him."

Young Mozart, overhearing Haydn's comment, quickly replied, "But, Papa, from Joseph Haydn I have learned how to write string quartets."

That year, written on the front page of six quartets that he had composed, Mozart inscribed the words: *Joseph Haydn gewidmet.* (Dedicated to Joseph Haydn.)

But then, holiday in Vienna would end, and the day would come to return to the Prince Esterhazy estate.

As time went on, Haydn became more and more dissatisfied

with his dreary, lonely life serving Prince Nikolaus. His fame was spreading all over Europe, and invitations were coming from everywhere. He was sixty years old, still young in spirit and longing for change and new experiences.

So, when Prince Nikolaus died and his son, who was not as interested in music as his father, took his place, the young prince said to Haydn, "In honor of my father, I will pay a yearly salary of 1400 florins, but now you are free to do whatever you wish."

Haydn expressed his gratitude to the Prince, and with hardly a backward glance, rushed off to Vienna, leaving most of his belongings behind.

During the past few years, the name of Franz Hoseph Haydn had become known to every music lover everywhere.

All at once, many offers of jobs came to Haydn from all over Europe. An invitation from the King of Naples, Italy, tempted him. He had always dreamed of going to Italy, but while he was trying to decide what to do, a stranger appeared at the door of Haydn's apartment. "My name is Johann Salomon," he announced. "I have come from London, England to fetch you. When I come back tomorrow, we will make our final plans."

"Now what shall I do?" Haydn wondered when Salomon left. "If I work for the King of Naples I will again be forced to abide by the rules of the court. Besides, I would have to compose operas, if I go there. On the other hand, in England there are large and well-trained orchestras for whom I can compose." Haydn decided to talk to Mozart about the invitation to go to London. He had already been there, so perhaps he could help him decide.

"Oh, dear Joseph," Mozart said when he heard about Salomon's invitation. "The trip is a difficult one. The boat ride across the Channel is so rough! And, Papa, you have no education for the wide world and you speak not a word of English."

"Yes, my dear Wolfgang," Haydn replied, "Perhaps you are right about the difficult journey, but though I cannot speak English, my language of music is understood all over the world."

So Haydn decided that he should go to London, although he had some misgivings. He would be leaving many of his dearest friends behind. Mozart and Haydn spent the last day together. With tears in his eyes, as they said goodbye, Mozart said, "I fear, Papa, that this will be our last goodbye." Neither of them realized then that Mozart would die before Haydn's return.

Just before Christmas, Haydn and Salomon set forth on their long journey to England. It was an awesome experience for this musician who had never before ventured more than a few miles from home.

"I remained on deck during the whole passage," he wrote to his friend Marianne in Vienna, "in order to gaze my fill at that huge monster, the ocean. When a violent wind began to blow, I saw the boisterous waves rushing on. I was seized with slight alarm. Most of the passengers were ill and looked like ghosts, but I overcame it all and arrived safely to harbor without being sick. I am rested now, and occupied in looking at this mighty and vast town of London, its various beauties and marvels causing me the most profound astonishment."

At first, Haydn did have trouble understanding the English language, but he studied his English grammar books as he walked in the woods alone each morning. His new friend, Johann Salomon, went everywhere with him helping him adjust to his new life. Since Salomon was born in Germany, he could easily help him with conversation. Haydn had no time to feel like a stranger in this new country. Whenever he attended a concert, he was showered with affectionate greetings and great honors. Soon after he arrived in London, he was invited to a Court Ball and the Prince of Wales, bedecked with dazzling diamonds, greeted Haydn with great respect.

"We would be honored, Maestro Haydn, if you would come tomorrow evening to play chamber music at my home." With his newly learned English words, Haydn said thank you to the Prince.

The day for Haydn's first London concert drew near.

"Here is an article about you in the newspaper," Salomon told Haydn. "They say you are a great composer, of course, but they think you are too old to make London music lovers excited about your music. We shall show them, eh, Joseph?"

As was his way, whenever Haydn faced possible trouble, his good humor and habits of hard work came to his help. He decided that his first concert would be the finest that London had ever heard. At the rehearsals with the orchestra of forty players, he took special care to explain his musical ideas. He played important parts on his violin to show what he wanted. He encouraged the players.

Finally, the big day came. The concert was played in the same music room where Johann Christian Bach had played many years before. Ladies with big hoop skirts and men with swords at their sides came to the concert. The soloists were ushered in by sword-bearers; Salomon was concert master, playing on a Stradivarius violin that had belonged to Corelli; Haydn conducted from the harpsichord.

The cheers that went up at the close of the concert had seldom been heard in London before. The concert was a triumph for the newcomer to London. Next day, the newspapers expressed the hope that Haydn, "the first musical genius of the age" would make his home in England. This was the first time that the composer had performed to such a large and brilliant audience. "I must try harder than ever to please these people, who have been so appreciative," he told Salomon. He was so inspired by such praise that he wrote twelve of his most beautiful symphonies, which have been called the London Symphonies.

Haydn's two-year stay in London was filled with many rich experiences. He was interested in everything, and had an insatiable curiosity.

One day, he went to the horse races at Ascot, where the English people enjoyed the composer's great enthusiasm. The following day, he traveled on to Slough to see William Herschel, a poor orchestra musician who had come from Germany. He was keenly interested in the stars and the mystery of the universe. Without any help, he had built his own enormous telescope. He had polished 400 mirrors until he was satisfied. To everyone's amazement, he had recently discovered the planet Uranus. When Haydn looked through the telescope, he was awe struck by his glimpse into the vast spaces. At first, he could say nothing.

When Haydn returned to London, he carefully recorded in his diary the measurements of Herschel's huge telescope. He did not express his deep feelings in words but only added that the astronomer often had to "sit from 5 to 6 hours under the open sky in the severest weather."

Of course, Haydn could not travel all the time. There was hard work, too, with many concerts and composing new pieces for London audiences. He had pupils to teach, too. He made many new friends, received many gifts from admirers, and was awarded high honors. The honor which pleased him most was from Oxford University, where he received an honorary degree of Doctor of Music. He may have felt rather awkward in his Doctor's cherry and cream-colored silk robe, but in a letter to a friend he wrote proudly, "I only wish my Viennese friends could have seen me." Fleeting thoughts went through his mind of his early days, more than 40 years before, when he sat hungry and cold at the bare table in his attic room in Vienna, struggling to teach himself the art of writing music.

When Haydn told his friends that he must leave London, they did not want him to go. But Prince Esterhazy commanded Haydn to return for the coronation of the Emperor. Of course, he would have to go. At the last minute, Haydn went out to buy gifts to take home to his friends. He packed his trunks with scissors, needles, knives, and spectacles. Then he said his goodbyes and promised that he would be back again.

On his way home Haydn was invited by some orchestra members to attend a special breakfast party in the Austrian countryside. As he was meandering in the garden, a young man of twenty-three strode up to Haydn.

"My name is Ludwig Beethoven," he told the master composer. "Will you come with me to the drawing room so I may play for you?"

As soon as he heard the young man play, Haydn immediately knew that this was an exceedingly gifted young musician, so when Beethoven asked if he could go to Vienna to study with him, Haydn consented.

"But I am very poor," Beethoven explained. "Would you be kind enough to speak to my patron, the Prince, and ask if he would allow me the time to go to Vienna?"

The Prince was impressed by Haydn's high regard for Beethoven's talent, and he promised to provide money enough for his lessons.

With wars and revolutions rumbling in Europe, Beethoven left for Vienna sooner than expected. Lessons with Haydn began.

It was not long before Beethoven was complaining. "It seems that Haydn has his mind on returning to London. Besides, after I do all my exercises in counterpoint, Maestro Haydn does not bother to correct my mistakes." But he continued to go to Haydn for lessons, and learned a wealth of musical knowledge from him.

The two composers worked together in Vienna until it was time for Haydn to return to London. Once again, the city greeted him with warmth and affectionate respect, and again, he worked diligently to provide London with his great music. When he was not rehearsing or composing, he was out in the English countryside taking in new sights and experiences and making friends wherever he went. The Royal Family invited Haydn to many of their affairs. The Queen, especially, often requested Haydn's presence at her musicals at Buckingham House.

But Haydn was getting older, and the pressure of work was beginning to tire him. He thought of his own little house on a quiet street back home near Vienna, where he could lead a secluded life devoted to his art.

Early on a June evening, coming home after one of Queen Charlotte's musical parties, Haydn found a letter, stamped with the familiar gold seal of the Esterhazy estate. It was from Prince Nikolaus II. "It is my wish to restore music to the importance it had when my grandfather, Nikolaus the Magnificent, was the Prince of Esterhazy. Will you return to be my Kapellmeister?"

Haydn consented to return. Although life in England was

exciting and stimulating, it had also been exhausting, and the pressure of work was too much for an aging man. He knew he had much work to do, and he chose to return to a quieter life in Vienna.

As he was packing his trunks with all his music and manuscripts, and he had carefully wrapped the beautiful coconut goblet that Clementi had given him, Haydn heard some commotion outside on the street. Looking out the window, he saw a group of people gathered around a tall man carrying a large parcel. "May I come in, Joseph?" the man called out.

"Come in, come in," Haydn said as he recognized an old friend.

"I want to say goodbye, Joseph. I am sad to see you go, but on behalf of your English friends, I want to give you this gift to take with you."

Haydn took the cover off the box his friend was carrying. It was a talking parrot, green, with a spot of red on its breast and a yellow tail.

"I hope you will think kindly of us when the parrot speaks," he said, and as he left, the parrot cried out, "Come, Papa Haydn!"

Haydn came home to Vienna this second time an honored and respected man. He was Dr. Haydn now that he had received his honorary degree at Oxford. His "London" symphonies had already become popular in Vienna, and he was asked to conduct the three latest ones soon after his return.

Unfortunately, his new patron Prince was not the generous

and warm-hearted person his grandfather had been. His arrogant temper and his narrow opinions about music were annoying to the composer. It was a good thing that whenever he had any trouble with the Prince, Haydn would always go to the Princess who could make things right again.

His main duties to the Prince were to be on hand for special occasions, and to write new church masses. While he was in London, Haydn had been deeply moved by the great oratorios of George Frederick Handel. Now he, too, wanted to write a great piece for chorus, orchestra, and solo singers. For the words, he used the opening chapters of the Bible, describing how God created the world. The years that he spent writing *The Creation* were among the happiest of his life. He felt he was expressing his deep religious thanks to his Creator for a beautiful world. When he was asked to hurry, and finish the piece, he replied, "I spend much time over it because I intend it to last a long time."

"Never was I so devout as when composing *The Creation*," he said. "I knelt down every day and prayed to God to strengthen me for my work."

In April, just a month after Haydn's sixty-sixth birthday, *The Creation* was heard for the first time at the Palace of the Prince Schwarzenberg. Haydn conducted. There was a profound silence in the audience, a feeling of religious respect. The performance was an overwhelming success.

All during this time, Europe was suffering from constant warfare and revolt against Kings and Princes. The Imperial High

Chancellor of Austria, Count von Sauran asked Haydn, "Will you write a national hymn to show the world the loyal devotion of our people to the kind and upright ruler of our Fatherland and to awaken pride in the hearts of all good Austrian people?"

Haydn wrote a tune which reminded the people of a Croatian folk song. It was played to the Emperor's great pleasure on his birthday, February 12, 1797. In an expression of thanks, he sent the composer a gold box with his portrait upon it. Haydn wrote to the Emperor, "Such a surprise and such a mark of favor, especially the portrait of my beloved monarch, I have never before received in acknowledgment of my poor talents."

Later, in the slow movement of the Kaiser quartet, Haydn used this same melody.

In honor of Haydn's 76th birthday, and to refresh his heart once more, a performance of *The Creation* was planned to be given at the University of Vienna. All the great artists of Vienna were there. Prince Esterhazy sent his carriage to bring the old Papa Haydn to the hall, and as he was being carried in an arm chair to a place where the princes and noble families sat, everyone in the audience stood in honor and respect. Because he was so weak, he had to leave after the first half of the concert. As he left the hall, Haydn asked the bearers of his chair to stop and turn him toward the orchestra. He lifted his hand as if to say a blessing, and left.

In his last days, Haydn liked to sit in his big armchair, dressed in his embroidered vest and coat of fine cloth and silk breeches, white stockings, buckled shoes, a ruffled shirt, white scarf, and a powdered, curled wig. When visitors came, if he was feeling well, he liked to show them his ring from the King of Prussia, the snuff boxes which were gifts of kings, his medals, and the watch that Lord Nelson gave him in exchange for the pen with which he wrote the Mass.

He liked to tell stories, too, about his younger days when he serenaded in the streets in Vienna, of his jokes and his tricks.

Papa Haydn had now grown weaker. For days, the noise of shells and shots fell on the city. On the 10th day of May in 1809, the French army of Napoleon arrived at the gates of Vienna. That afternoon, a loud knock was heard at the door of Haydn's house. The servants, in great fear, opened the door. It was an officer of the invading French Army. "I have come to visit Master Haydn," he explained. "Do not be frightened. I have come to pay my devoted respect."

Hearing the voices, Haydn called out, "Come in."

"Will you give me permission to sing a song from your *Creation*?" the officer asked. "And will you accompany me?" Suddenly, seeming revived, and clad in his nightshirt, Haydn had his servants carry him to the piano, and he played while the soldier sang with a beautiful voice. With tears in their eyes, thinking of the tragedy of men fighting each other, they embraced. The soldier went out into the street.

A few days later, getting up from his bed, he asked to be taken to the piano. He played the Austrian hymn three times, as if in a closing prayer.

Perhaps in his final days, the music of his last composition, *The Seasons*, went through his mind. After the orchestra sounds the music of the thunderstorm, the chorus sings, "Now Cease the Conflicts," and beast and man can enjoy the return of peace on earth.

FRANZ JOSEPH HAYDN

b. Rohrau, Lower Austria, March 31, 1732
d. Vienna, Austria, May 31, 1809

JOHANN HUMMEL

Frau Hummel pulled the feather quilt up under little Johann's chin and patted him gently on his curly head. "Mother," Johann asked sleepily, "is tomorrow the day when father will take me to his school to watch him conduct the King's band?"

"Yes, Johann, tomorrow is the day. But now, it's time to go to sleep."

Johann's mother kissed her son, closed the curtains, took the candle from the table, and made her way to the kitchen where her husband was waiting.

"How much like Wolfgang Mozart our little Johann is," Herr Hummel said. "He is only four years old, yet he already can read music and play the violin. And now he is teaching himself to play the piano! Do you think that some day we can move to Vienna where Johann can take lessons with Mozart?"

It was surely something to think about and hope for!

A few years later, Johannes Hummel heard that the Theatre of Vienna was looking for a conductor and violinist.

"Shall I apply for the job, my dear?" Johannes asked his wife. "Vienna is only 35 miles away, and the journey would not be too difficult."

"Oh, yes," she replied, "and if we go to Vienna, perhaps Mozart would listen to Johann play. He might even consider taking our son for a pupil!"

The Hummels decided that Johannes should try to win the job at the Theatre of Vienna. For two weeks, he visited in the beautiful city. He spoke to the director of the theatre about the job. Johannes was satisfied that this was the position he really wanted.

He returned home to his family. Johann was the first to be at the door when his father came home.

"Papa, what did they say? Will we go to Vienna?"

"Yes, Johann, we will go to Vienna. I have been invited to be the new conductor at the Theatre."

"And where will we live, Johannes?" his wife asked. "Did you find a house for our family?"

"Everything is arranged, my dear. We will leave in one month's time."

Johann was excited. He knew that he might play piano for Mozart, so he worked very hard in the month before they left for Vienna. He practiced his exercises, and learned some of Mozart's sonatas.

No sooner had the Hummel family settled in their new home, than Johannes asked for an appointment with Wolfgang Mozart. They went to his home.

"What will you play for me, young man?" the thirty year old Mozart asked eight year old Johann.

"I would like to play the Andante in A flat, the one you wrote when you were in London."

Johann sat down at the piano. He began. The trill on the first dotted half note sparkled crisp and clear. His phrases flowed, and the melodies sang. After the last chord, Johann lifted his hands slowly, stood up and bowed to Mozart.

"Bravo, bravo. Ein wunderkind!" applauded Mozart. "You must come to me again tomorrow, and we will begin lessons."

It was the custom in those days for a teacher to invite an exceptionally gifted pupil to live in his home as part of the family.

"Will you let Johann come and live with us?" Mozart asked Herr Hummel. "He is a fine, hardworking boy, and I would like to teach him, but without any fee."

Johann's parents were honored to be invited by so distinguished a musician, and they consented. Johann Hummel moved into Mozart's home. Mozart and his young pupil were often seen going about Vienna together.

When Johann was ten years old, Mozart decided it was time for the boy to make himself known to the musical world.

"I think your son is ready for a concert tour," Mozart told Herr Hummel.

Taking Mozart's advice, Johannes and Johann started out on a concert tour that lasted four years. They traveled all over Europe.

One night, after a concert in Weissenstein, Johann complained to his father. "Papa, I have a headache. One minute I am cold; the next minute I am hot. I do not feel at all well."

The next day, Johann had a high fever. A doctor was called

in. "I am afraid your son has small pox," he said. "He must be kept quiet and in a darkened room. He will not be able to give concerts for several weeks."

Fortunately, Johann recovered from the severe illness. When he had regained his strength, the two Hummels started out again on their tour, visiting Copenhagen, and Edinburgh and London, and The Hague in Holland.

The Hummels would have stayed longer in The Hague, where Johann played at the Prince's Palace every Sunday, but there was a war in Europe, and the French troops were coming closer to Holland. The two travelers thought it best to move on.

When they returned to Vienna, they were met by a joyful Frau Hummel. After a big welcome home dinner, the family sat around the table to talk about the future.

"Now that I am fifteen years old," Johann told his parents, "it is time for me to think about earning my own living. I like to perform, but in my heart I know that writing music is what I really want to do. Yet there is still so much I need to learn."

"Why don't you settle down here in Vienna, Johann?" his father suggested. "You can teach some piano students, and then devote the rest of your time to composing. And in Vienna, there are fine teachers who can help you learn what you want to know about music."

Johann did just that. During the day he taught nine or ten piano students. After supper, he went to his room to study and compose. Very often it was four o'clock in the morning before he blew out the candle to sleep for a few hours before the next busy day began.

One evening, when Johann's father returned from the theatre, he told Johann, "Can you imagine who came into the theatre today? It was Joseph Haydn. He has returned from London. I told him how happy we are to have him back in Vienna."

"Father, do you think Joseph Haydn would give me organ lessons?"

"Perhaps he would, Johann. You should ask him."

Johann went to Haydn's house on Neuer Markt, and Haydn, now sixty-four years old, agreed to teach the young Hummel. As they walked together to the church for their first lesson, Haydn warned, "Mind, young man, you must not play the organ too much. It will ruin your hands for piano playing."

Johann was becoming well known in this musical city. Wealthy families, and princes and nobles often asked him to attend the musical gatherings in their fine Viennese mansions, when composers and performers entertained and played their new compositions.

"Maestro Hummel," said the host Prince at one of these gatherings, "I want to introduce you to a pianist and composer who has just moved to our city from Bonn."

The Prince took Hummel by the arm and walked to the piano. "Johann Hummel, I want you to meet Ludwig Beethoven."

Hummel and Beethoven became good friends. Sometimes

they quarreled, but then they made up.

One day, Hummel received a letter from Beethoven who was angry because he thought that Hummel had criticized a piece he had composed. "Do not come anymore to me. You are a false fellow and the knacher take all such," Beethoven wrote.

But the next day Hummel received another letter from Beethoven. This time he addressed Hummel by his affectionate name, Nazerl. "Good friend, Nazerl," he wrote, "you are an honorable fellow. So come this afternoon to me. You will find Schuppanzigh and both of us will blow you up, thump you, and shake you, so you will have a fine time of it. Your Beethoven, also named Mehlschoberl, embraces you."

After some time, Johann Hummel at last found a secure position with one of the wealthiest and most musical families in all of Austria. Prince Nicolaus Esterhazy was in search of a musician who would live and work at the Palace. Franz Joseph Haydn, who was now seventy-two years old, was Kapellmeister and composer for Prince Nicolaus, but Haydn was spending more and more time in his own home in Vienna.

Prince Nicolaus described to Hummel what would be expected of him.

"I need someone who will direct my orchestra and chapel choir. There are one hundred members, and you would also teach the choir boys to play the piano, violin and cello. Of course, I would want you to compose for my chapel and theatre. And, in addition, I would require you to organize all of

Joseph Haydn's compositions so that in the future, musicians will know everything that he wrote."

Johann was accustomed to hard work, and in return for a salary of twelve hundred florins, and a place to live, he served the Prince well. He wrote music for his orchestra and his opera theatre and chapel, and he took care of all the duties of a music director. At the same time, he was also writing music for his father to conduct at the theatre in Vienna.

When Johann was thirty-three years old, he gave up his job with Prince Nicolaus, and moved back to Vienna. One morning when Johann was at the piano practicing one of Beethoven's new sonatas, the jangling bell at the front door startled him. It was the postman with a letter from Beethoven.

"Dec. 8, 1813. Dearly beloved Hummel! Please conduct this time the drumheads and the cannonades with your excellent conducting Field-Marshal staff—please do this: and if one day you may want me to cannonade you, I am at your service body and soul. Your friend, Beethoven."

Johann knew what Beethoven was asking him. Just last Friday, the two men had met by chance in front of St. Stephen's Church.

"Hummel, my good friend," Beethoven had said. "I have just finished composing my *Battle Symphony*. I want to give the first performance to raise money to help the wounded soldiers in the war. I will invite all the distinguished musicians in Vienna to play. Will you participate, too?"

Johann had agreed to be in the orchestra, and now this letter had come asking him to play the drums. The performance of the *Battle Symphony* brought all of Vienna to the concert hall. The people cheered Beethoven for composing this grand symphony especially to help his country in a time of trouble.

Although Johann Hummel kept busy in Vienna, he had trouble deciding the best way to spend his time. He had given up his concerts as a pianist and was spending most of his time composing. Did he want to be a pianist or a composer?

"Johann, my dear," said Elizabeth, his young wife, "do you think it is time for the world to hear you play the piano again?" She pursuaded Johann to return to the concert stage.

Elizabeth herself was a singer, and she could appreciate what people were saying about Hummel's playing. The music journals praised his performance. "Hummel's playing is clear and neat, with superb tone and delicate phrasing. He is so relaxed," one writer commented, "that his passages seem to be at a faster speed than they really are." Hummel's skill at improvising astonished his concert audiences. At one concert, the people in the audience were so amazed at hearing Hummel play double trills, that to see his fingers better, they stood on their seats!

Hummel was now forty-one years old, and in spite of his great success on the concert stage, he thought he needed a steady position in order to support his family.

"I have been offered a position as Kapellmeister at Weimar,"

JOHANN NEPOMUK HUMMEL

he told Elizabeth. "I will be in charge of the court theatre and special performances for the noble families and famous people. And, Elizabeth, you will be glad to know that for three months of the year, I will be permitted to go on concert tours."

The Hummel family was happy, peaceful, and secure at Weimar. Johann had time for practicing each day, for working in his gardens and going for walks, and for composing and teaching.

One of Hummel's favorite students was Ferdinand Hiller. After a lesson one day, Hummel said to his pupil, "I have had a letter from Vienna. Beethoven is not well. He is not expected to recover from his illness. Will you come with me to visit him?"

The two pianists set out from Weimar. During their stay in Vienna, they went to see Beethoven, to talk with him and give him comfort. Late in the afternoon on their way from Beethoven's home, they met an old friend of Hummel's.

"You must come to my house for dinner," the friend told Hummel.

When Hummel and Hiller arrived at their friend's home, they were introduced to a quiet young man by the name of Franz Schubert. After dinner, as the guests gathered in the resplendent music room, the young Schubert sat down at the piano, and the singer, Vogl, stood by his side and together they performed Schubert's songs, one after another. Many years later, Hiller wrote a letter to a friend, telling about that evening.

"Vogl was an elderly man with little voice left, but full of vigor and fire. Schubert's playing was good, but not masterful. Yet I have never heard the songs as they were performed then. They played and sang with such fervour and expression! I can still see the portly master, Hummel, with his simple sincerity, as he sat in a comfortable armchair in the big drawing room. He said little, but big tears were running down his cheeks."

The Hummels' peaceful life at Weimar was interrupted by short trips and concert performances in Europe. A new kind of music was attracting the interest of music lovers in Europe, and audiences were no longer so enthusiastic about Hummel's music. Although the younger musicians who came after Hummel took their places as favorites on the concert stage, they all knew how much they had learned from Hummel's long life as a genial and well-loved teacher, composer, and pianist.

b. Pressburg (now Bratislava), Czechoslovakia, November 14, 1778
d. Weimar, Germany, October 17, 1837

(DANIEL) FREDERICK (RUDOLPH) KUHLAU

Frederick and his mother and father were thankful that there had been no more shooting in the streets of Hanover for the past week. The city had suffered from the invasion of Napoleon's troops and no one knew when the soldiers would come again. As the family sat around the table, they said their prayers of thanks.

"Now, Frederick, it is time for you to go to bed. You have nothing to fear. It will be quiet tonight."

When Frederick was asleep, his father and mother talked together.

"My dear, our orders have come from the Duke," Herr Kuhlau said. "Our regiment will be moved from this city. Our wind band will go, too, and we are to take our families with us."

"Where are we to go?" his wife asked. "And when must we be ready to leave?"

"We are going to Luneburg, and we must be ready in three weeks. I know we are going to miss our musical life here in Hanover," he said. They thought of all the concerts they had taken Frederick to hear. Just last month they had heard a splendid performance of George Frederick Handel's *Messiah*. Going to concerts had been Frederick's happiest times. Would there be so much music in Luneburg?

The next day, Frederick's mother told her small son that the family would soon be leaving their home. "But before we go," she said, "there will be one more big parade. Of course, your father will play with the band, and we will be there to watch."

Frederick's first thoughts were about his father's shiney parade boots. When the day of the parade came, Frederick wanted to help his father get ready for the band. "May I help you polish your boots?" Frederick asked excitedly.

When the time came for the band to march by, Frederick and his mother stood outside, waiting. Soon, as if coming out of the earth, a shuddering rumble rose in Frederick's ears. He knew what it was.

"Here they come," he called out. "I hear the big drums." Closer and closer the sound came, and louder and louder. "Now I can see them!"

Around the corner came the Regimental Band. In the front of the musicians marched the bandsmen with their Turkish crescents gleaming silver in the sunlight. Next came the flutes piercing Frederick's ears with their high shrill notes. The flashing, crashing cymbals came next, and then the jangling triangles. Last of all, the drummers came brandishing their drumsticks high into the air, keeping the musicians' feet in time to their 1-2, 1-2 beat.

Frederick stamped his feet in time to the music. When his father passed by, he cheered and clapped his hands.

Suddenly Frederick stopped clapping. Ahead of his father, Frederick noticed a small puddle of muddy water just where his father would have to march. "Oh, he will step in the water with his beautiful shiney boots!" He held his hands over his eyes.

When he looked up, his mother was smiling, "It's all right," she comforted Frederick. "He stepped right over the puddle!"

Frederick's family and many of their friends in the band moved to Luneburg with the regiment. Frederick went to school with the other boys, but during his free time, he liked to leave the boys and walk to the magnificent church of St. Michael to hear the great organ, and listen to the choir and orchestra rehearsing.

"I am going to St. Michael's Church this afternoon, Mother," Frederick said. "There is a rehearsal of George Phillip Telemann's *Passion*."

When Frederick came home after the rehearsal, he said to his mother, "How beautiful the music was this afternoon. Listen, I'll play some of it for you on the piano." Frederick sat down at the piano, and from what he could remember from the rehearsal, he played for his mother. Frederick spent many of his free hours at the piano, practicing, and composing his own pieces.

When he was fourteen years old, Frederick moved again, but this time without his family. He went to Hamburg. There at Catherine Church was a learned musician and scholar who gave Frederick lessons in theory and composition, and within four years, the young pupil was giving piano recitals in Hamburg.

Once again, though, war forced Frederick to move. He had heard of other German composers who had gone to

Copenhagen, Denmark, and he decided to follow. Now he began earning a living as a pianist and a composer. One of the first concerts that Frederick gave was a performance of his own piano concerto, with the orchestra of Copenhagen's Royal Theatre. It was there he met the flutist of the Royal Orchestra.

"Could you help me?" he asked the flute player after a rehearsal. "I have written some compositions for flute, but I do not play the flute myself. I would like to know what you think of these compositions."

The flutist was very impressed with Kuhlau's work. "You write well for the flute," he said. "There are many flute players who will be glad when these pieces are published!"

Kuhlau had a busy musical life. He was appointed as a court musician, and then as chorus master of the Royal Theatre, where his own operas were often performed. Kuhlau traveled, too, and he received invitations to visit other countries.

One invitation came from Sweden. "Will you come again to Gothenburg and Stockholm?" the letter read. "The people enjoyed your playing so much when you were here before, and now we beg you to return. Also, there are many children of the Swedish nobility who would like to study piano with you." Kuhlau often visited Sweden. It was a short and pleasant boat trip across the water.

One of the composers in Europe whom Kuhlau admired more than any other was a musician living in Vienna. His name was Ludwig van Beethoven. Kuhlau journeyed to Vienna to visit the aging Beethoven. When he arrived, he was invited to a supper party where Beethoven was also a guest. The two pianists spent a lively evening together, sharing their ideas about music. When Kuhlau returned to Copenhagen, he was surprised to receive a letter from Beethoven. "To Frederick Kuhlau, Vienna," the letter began. Below was some music, written in Beethoven's own writing.

"What is this?" Kuhlau wondered. Looking closer, he saw that Beethoven had written a three-part song, with the words taken from Kuhlau's own name. All through the song, the words said, "*Kuh* nicht *lau*", over and over again. ("Cool, not warm.") The first four notes of each part were taken from the name of Bach - B A C H (B natural). At the end of the song, Beethoven wrote, "Remember now and then your most devoted, Beethoven."

Kuhlau treasured this letter from his old friend. He often played Beethoven's piano compositions on his concerts, and many ideas for his own compositions were learned from studying Beethoven's work.

Ever since his boyhood days in Hanover and Luneburg, Frederick had been especially interested in opera. He wrote several operas himself and one of his most famous was *Luhn*. The story was from an ancient Oriental fairy tale.

"This is certain to be a favorite opera for the Danish people," the director of the Royal Theatre told Kuhlau. "They will love the folk tunes they hear played by the different instruments of

155

the orchestra."

To this day, the people of Denmark go to the theatre to hear a performance of *Luhn*. What is more, they will never forget Frederick Kuhlau because it is the overture to his opera that has become a national hymn, the favorite music of the Danish national festival.

FRIEDERICK KUHLAU

b. Uelzen, nr. Hanover, Germany, September 11, 1786
d. Copenhagen, Denmark, March 12, 1832

HEINRICH LICHNER

There it is. I see it," little Heinrich called out. His mother and father came to the window. The evening star in the darkening winter sky gave the sign that it was time to sit down at the table for Christmas dinner.

"Our hearts are open to a stranger, keth or kin," the family said together, as they held hands around the table festive with candlelight and green boughs of pine.

"Is that why we leave an empty chair at the table?" Heinrich asked.

"Yes," said his mother. "If an unknown traveler should knock at our door tonight, we will welcome him in to share our Christmas dinner."

"We can be thankful this Christmas," Heinrich's father said. "Even though there are still foreign soldiers in our land, at least there is no fighting now. You cannot remember, Heinrich, but only four years ago, when you were just one year old, many of our Polish friends fought to try to chase those armies from our soil. But, come now, let us say our prayer of thanks on this Christmas day."

After the Lichner family had finished their dinner, Heinrich's father asked his son to play the piano for them. "Please play some Christmas hymns, Heinrich, and we will sing."

Heinrich's parents were delighted that their young son could play so well. Whenever they took him to hear the singing and dancing in town, or on Sundays when they went to Church, the first thing Heinrich did when he came home was run to the piano, and play the music he had heard.

"Someday the Polish people will be proud of you, Heinrich," his father said. "Kings of other countries may send their armies to take away our land and our freedom, but the musicians and artists and writers of Poland will keep our pride alive."

Heinrich listened to his father, but he was too young to understand the meaning of his words. He only knew that his father and mother were glad that he loved music.

When Heinrich was old enough to consider leaving his home town to study piano in another city, his teacher said "Someday, Heinrich, I would like to be able to send you to Professor Dehn in Berlin. He has just taken a post at the Royal Academy of Arts. Perhaps you have already heard about him. He is the one who first published the Brandenburg Concertos of Johann Sebastian Bach."

"Yes, indeed, I have heard of the Professor," Heinrich replied. "I would like very much to study with him. I will work hard to earn enough money to go to Berlin."

By the time Heinrich was 20 years old, he was ready to leave Harpersdorf. Traveling along the Oder River, he made his way to Berlin. For several years, under Professor Dehn's instruction, he made enormous progress as a musician. "Heinrich," Professor Dehn told his young student, "I think it is time for you to return to Poland to study with my friend Johann Theodor

Mosewius. He, too is very interested in the work of Johann Sebastian Bach. In fact, he has published a book all about his compositions for chorus and orchestra. Professor Mosewius is a fine teacher, and you can learn so much from him." Not long after that, Professor Dehn died, and Heinrich, now twenty nine years old, recalled his teacher's advice. He decided to return to Breslau, the city nearest to his home, to find Professor Mosewius.

Arriving in Breslau, he went immediately to the Institute of Church Music. There, at the top of the stairs on a large wooden door, was a sign *Johann Theodor Mosewius, Director.* He knocked. "Come in," announced the voice from the studio.

Heinrich was honored to meet this famous musician. He told him of his studies with Professor Dehn.

"He told me to come to you," Heinrich explained.

Professor Mosewius agreed to teach Heinrich Lichner. It was not long before he had enough confidence in his student to ask him to be the conductor of a singing society he had started many years before.

Heinrich Lichner found his place in the musical city of Breslau. He became cantor and organist at the Church of 11,000 Virgins and wrote many compositions for piano as well as for organ and chorus. As his father had predicted many years before when his son was just a small boy, Heinrich Lichner did grow up to be a fine musician and to contribute in his own way to the pride of the Polish people in their rich artistic life.

b. Harpersdorf, Silesia (Poland) March 6, 1829
d. Breslau, Poland Jan. 7, 1898

JEAN BAPTISTE LULLY

Far, far away, and many years ago in a tiny dark house in the city of Florence, Italy, lived a poor miller and his wife and their little son Giovanni. Each day, Giovanni's father wondered how there would be enough money to buy food for the family. There certainly was not enough money to send Giovanni to school. The young boy would get up each morning, put on his tattered clothes, and wander about the streets of the town with the other poor boys of his neighborhood. He had to learn to take care of himself at an early age. He was a bright little boy and loved the music he heard in the churches and in the market place where strolling players came to entertain with acrobats and singers, actors and musicians.

Giovanni spent many hours watching these strolling players and soon began to learn their trade. He learned to be an acrobat and could please the crowds with his dancing and his tricks. He could play the guitar and sing. In fact, it was Giovanni's performance at the carnival one day that started him on a new life.

As he was doing his act at a side show at the carnival, a grand looking man wearing a velvet suit with silver buttons and a large hat with a feather came striding by. He stopped to watch this boy who was such a clever entertainer. "Play another song for me," he asked.

Giovanni sang and accompanied himself on the guitar. A smile came over the man's face. He was surprised to see this ragged, dirty-faced young street boy who could play and sing and dance with such charm.

"Young man," the gentleman said, "I have been away from France fighting in a war. Before I left home, the cousin of the king of France asked me to bring home to her an intelligent young Italian. She wants a boy to be her servant and to teach her to speak Italian. Now I am on my way back to the French Court. Will you join my group and come with me?"

Giovanni accepted the invitation. His parents, not knowing any other way to care for their fourteen year old son, agreed to let him go. "Now perhaps Giovanni can have an education and enough food to eat and clothes to wear," they said.

So the grand chevalier and his entourage left for France. On the long and difficult trip, Giovanni entertained the traveling group with his clowning and singing comic songs and playing the violin.

Finally the group arrived at the court. Can you imagine how Giovanni felt when he saw the enormous stone palace, all surrounded by large, formal gardens, pools bordered with flowers, and paths lined with tall trees? Everyone, even the servants, was dressed in fine, elegant clothes. Giovanni could hardly believe that he could live in such a place as this.

The royal lady greeted the chevalier. "This is the boy from Italy whom I have brought to you," the chevalier told her. But she was not impressed with the disheveled looking young boy standing before her.

161

"This boy will be a cook's helper," she announced, and sent him off to the kitchen.

Giovanni was not discouraged. Although he was surrounded by pots and pans and did kitchen chores from morning until night, he never forgot about his music. He played his violin and sang to his kitchen friends. One of his favorite pastimes was to set poems to music. The beautiful "Au Clair de la Lune" was one of the songs he wrote for his friends.

One day the chevalier overheard Giovanni playing his violin to his friends in the kitchen. He told the royal lady, "That is a talented boy you have there working as a kitchen hand."

She had to agree. "Find this young man some proper clothes," she ordered. "Now he shall leave the kitchen and play in my private orchestra." In those days, kings and queens and royalty hired composers and musicians to write and play music for their private entertainment.

Giovanni became a virtuoso violinist. He gave great pleasure to everyone in the court. But one day he got into some mischief. He wrote a naughty song about the royal lady. When she heard about it, she angrily ordered Giovanni, "Leave my court forever."

By that time, though, many important persons in France knew about Giovanni's fine violin playing. "I will gladly pay for Giovanni's violin lessons," promised a wealthy gentleman. The King of France, King Louis XIV, was so impressed with this talented young man that he hired him to be a member of his orchestra.

Now Giovanni was nineteen years old. The king organized a group of young musicians to perform with Giovanni in the court, and he made him the "inspector" of the violins. He was chosen to compose dance music for the court ballet. The king was very pleased with his music, especially the new lively dances which were a welcome change from the slow and stately ones. The king appointed Lully to compose all the music for court entertainment.

Now that Giovanni had become a favorite of the French king, he decided it was time to change his Italian name to a French one, from Italian Giovanni to French Jean, from Lulli to Lully, and he added the middle name Baptiste. From that time on he was Jean Baptiste Lully.

King Louis allowed Jean to write any kind of music he wished. He had his own orchestra to play his pieces. In those days, orchestra musicians were in the habit of not paying attention to the conductor. Most court orchestras were of a rather poor quality. The conductor would pound on the floor to beat time, or lead from the harpsichord. The discipline was bad. But it was different in Lully's orchestra. The musicians knew that Lully had the strong support of the king. When he demanded "Quiet," they were quiet. When he called out, "Play in tune," they listened.

Lully introduced new instruments into the orchestra. He placed special emphasis on the string section. Lully's orchestra was the finest in France.

One of his great accomplishments was in composing for the opera. He had a rich imagination and exciting personality. He

JEAN BAPTISTE LULLY

could write great, soaring melodies to match the words. Do you remember how he had begun making up his own songs to guitar accompaniment when he was just a small child?

The king and court continued to heap great favors on Lully. In fact, he was so successful and wealthy that he decided that playing the violin was not grand enough for such an important person. He even refused to have a violin in his house. But there were people in the court who wanted to hear Lully play. They devised a trick. They would call a servant to come and play the violin in Lully's presence. The sounds were so horrible to Lully's ears that he would snatch the violin away from the servant and try to erase the tormenting sounds by playing the violin himself!

Lully continued to study music all his life. People from every part of Europe came to study with him at his academy. He lived to be fifty-five years old. He and his wife had three children who all became musicians, too. The poor little Italian street boy had become a wealthy and famous musician.

b. Florence, Italy, November 27, 1632
d. Paris, France, March 22, 1687

FELIX MENDELSSOHN

Shhhhh, Felix", his mother said. "Don't make a sound. Take your sister's hand. We must be ready when your father comes." Felix and Fanny clung to each other. Leah, their mother, held baby Rebecka in her arms, and watched anxiously through the window. "When the sky darkens," she whispered to her children, "your father will come with the carriage and we will try to escape."

Suddenly, through the foggy darkness, Leah saw the horse and carriage stop in front of the house. When she was sure no one was watching, she said, "Come now. Hurry." She urged the children outside. Quickly they climbed into the carriage. The driver slapped the horse's reins, and the wheels of the carriage clattered over the cobblestones.

When they came to the city gates, the French soldier on guard ordered the carriage to halt. He scowled as he flung open the door. Peering in, the soldier saw a family huddled together, dressed in tattered clothes, looking like a group of poor refugees. "All right," the soldier called to the driver. "Go on through." Luckily, the guard had not recognized the family of the wealthy banker, Abraham Mendelssohn. Through the cover of night, the horse and carriage whisked the Mendelssohn family on their way to Berlin.

Leah and Abraham sighed with relief. "Now we are safe," Abraham explained to Fanny, who was old enough to understand. "We had to leave our home in Hamburg, because Napoleon's soldiers had orders to arrest me. We are going to Berlin where we will not have to worry about Napoleon. We will stay at your grandmother's house until we can find a place of our own."

It took hardly any time at all before the Mendelssohns were content in their new surroundings. Leah's family lived in Berlin, and Abraham's brother gave him a place in the family's flourishing bank business.

In their new home, Felix, Fanny and Rebecka were busy from morning until night. Their parents taught them that they were on this earth to work and be useful, and to strive always to do better. Leah and Abraham were loving, affectionate parents who wanted the children to do their very best with all the good things they provided for them.

Instead of going to school, the children were taught at home by their parents. At first, their father taught them arithmetic and French language, and their mother taught them German literature, fine arts, and piano. When little Paul was born, though, the Mendelssohns decided to hire teachers to come to their home. One teacher came to prepare the children for their University examinations. Another came to give them piano lessons, another for violin lessons, and still another, Carl Zelter, gave the children lessons in writing music. Since Felix showed extraordinary talent for drawing and painting, an artist came to give art lessons. Even dancing and swimming lessons were part of their schooling.

Every morning except Sunday, Felix, Fanny, Rebecka and Paul were awakened at five o'clock, before the sun had risen. "It's time to get up," their father would say. "Eat your breakfast, and then it's on to your studies," and he sent each of them off with a hug and a kiss. When free time came in the middle of the morning, the children scampered out into the garden to run and play.

Sundays were special. The children gave concerts as a treat for their parents and guests. Felix and Fanny played piano duets, and sometimes Felix played the violin with Fanny accompanying him. Often, the pieces were ones that they had composed themselves. When Rebecka and Paul were older, she sang and he played cello at these Sunday concerts.

Felix was nine years old and Fanny was thirteen, when they made their first public appearance. First, Fanny played from memory twenty-four preludes of Johann Sebastian Bach. Following that, Felix walked briskly onto the stage wearing his tight-fitting jacket, cut very low at the neck, and wide trousers buttoned over it. His long, curly auburn hair fell loosely on his shoulders. He bowed deeply to the audience, and announced that the piece to be performed was one he wrote himself for two French horns and piano. "I will play the piano part," he announced. Everyone was amazed that a child of nine could write such music and play the piano with such exquisite skill.

No sooner had the family arrived home after the concert

than Leah said, "We have a surprise for Felix and Fanny. Cook has baked a Baumkuchen as a reward for your fine concert." It was a cake, baked in the shape of a tree. The next day Felix celebrated in his own way. He took out his brushes to paint pictures of his memory of the happy occasion, and he ended the day by practicing piano twice as much as usual.

Carl Zelter, the children's composition tutor, enjoyed teaching the Mendelssohn children. He knew how talented Felix was, but he was determined to keep him from "conceit and swollen-headedness." When Felix played in public, his teacher asked the listeners not to praise the boy too much.

Professor Zelter often wrote letters about Felix to his good friend, Johann Wolfgang Goethe (pronounced Geh-tuh) who was the most famous poet and writer in Germany at that time. Goethe wrote back to Zelter, "I would like very much to meet this Felix Mendelssohn. Can you bring him to visit me in Weimar (pronounced Vi-mar)?"

Immediately, Zelter spoke to Felix's parents. "May I take your son to visit the great Goethe?"

Abraham and Leah were pleased to think that such an illustrious person wanted to meet their son, and they gave their consent. When the teacher and his pupil arrived at Goethe's home after a long day's carriage ride, the seventy-two year old poet was strolling in his garden.

"Ah, young Mendelssohn," he said to the eleven year old boy. "Come inside to the piano. Make a little noise for me and awaken the winged spirits that have for so long lain slumbering in my piano."

Felix played for the elderly man. Sometimes he played pieces by Mozart and Bach, sometimes his own compositions. "I would like to hear you improvise at the piano," Goethe suggested. "Carl, give Felix a tune and see what kind of a piece he can make from it."

Zelter went to the piano and played a simple melody. "All right, now it is your turn to play," Prof. Zelter said. Felix sat down at the piano and played the melody exactly as his teacher had played it. Then gradually he changed the melody into a masterful composition.

Zelter was proud of Felix's improvisation, but he tried to hide his pride by exclaiming, "What a wild ride! It sounded as if the goblins and dragons were chasing you!" Goethe hugged Felix warmly, astounded at what the young boy could do, but being careful not to praise him too much, because Zelter had warned Goethe that too much praise can spoil an artist.

When Felix was not playing the piano, he and Goethe wrote poetry together, or the elder poet would watch as Felix sketched or painted with his water colors or played and ran in the garden with Goethe's grandchildren.

In the meantime, during his visit at Goethe's home, Felix was receiving letters of instruction from his family. "Sit properly," his father wrote, "and behave nicely, especially at dinner. Speak distinctly and suitably, and try as much as possible to express yourself to the point. I know what a good fellow you are and therefore think it hardly necessary to remind you to be good and modest — and not to forget often to think affectionately of us."

Fanny, who wished she could have gone with Felix, wrote him a letter, teasing, "After you come home if you can't repeat every word that Goethe said, I'll have nothing more to do with you!"

On the day before Felix was to return home to Berlin, Goethe pleaded with Prof. Zelter. "Won't you stay a few more days? Felix's happy spirit is such a joy to this old man's heart." Zelter agreed, and the two stayed on for all of sixteen days, and when finally it was time to leave, Goethe showered the young boy with blessings, and sent him home with a poem he had written especially for Fanny. In the weeks after Felix's visit, Goethe was lonely for the bright, happy, stimulating company of his new young friend. "Felix left behind him a memory which deserves to be forever cherished," Goethe wrote to Prof. Zelter.

When he returned home, Felix found his family busily preparing for the arrival of their Sunday guests. The Mendelssohn home had become a favorite gathering place where the great poets, philosophers, painters and musicians came for good conversation, good food, and, of course, good music. Felix had barely enough time to tell about his visit in Weimar, when his mother said, "Son, I want you and Fanny to play some of your duets for our guests. And please help

Rebecka prepare one of your songs to sing, and Paul to play one of your pieces on his cello." Felix could choose for the guests any of the pieces he had composed. He had already written many songs, trios for piano, violin, and cello, and even operas, string quartets, symphonies and concertos! When the family musicians played for these gatherings at home, the listeners felt they were in the presence of an extraordinary family.

Until Felix was 16 years old, the Mendelssohn family lived in a large house belonging to Abraham's mother. One afternoon, however, after all the Sunday guests had left, Abraham called his wife and children together. "Shall we tell the children our exciting news?" he asked Leah. She smiled and nodded her head. Abraham went on. "Not far from here, just at the edge of the city, there is a seven and a half acre park that was once the hunting preserve of King Frederick the Great. In the park is a large mansion with many rooms. One room is spacious enough even for presenting plays. But best of all, there is a summer house with tall windows looking out into a garden full of lilacs and beautiful trees. The summer house can seat two or three hundred people for our Sunday morning concerts. Repairs need to be made to the buildings, but when the workmen are finished, we will move to our new home. Now, what do you think of that?"

There was great excitement, and the children asked a hundred questions. "All right now, children, that is enough. Off with you to practice. Tomorrow we will visit the new house on Leipzigerstrasse."

The Mendelssohn's new home was like a great magnet, drawing together the important people of Berlin, and visitors from all over Europe. Felix was put in charge of the Sunday morning musicals. He planned the programs, and if he needed an orchestra to perform his new compositions, his father would hire musicians to come to the house for the day. Felix had to stand on a tall stool so as to be seen by the musicians who stood up to play. He conducted the rehearsals and performances. Sometimes, for a change, Felix would plan a morning of play-reading and music. The guests were given parts in the play so that everyone participated as actors and actresses. Those Sunday mornings became an important part of the life of Berlin, and of Felix's life, as well.

Although Abraham knew that his son had exceptional talent, he was not sure that music should be his life's work. "Felix," he said one day, "I am going on a business trip to Paris. I think you should come along. We will visit Luigi Cherubini at the Paris Conservatory. He will be able to judge your musical talent. You know, he is very hard to please."

The two left for Paris, and called on the aged musician. For Cherubini, Felix played the piano part of his own Piano Quartet. When he finished playing, the old teacher said to Abraham, "This boy is rich in talent. He will do well; he is already doing well." His words satisfied Abraham that his son indeed had great promise as a musician.

On the way home to Berlin, the Mendelssohns stopped in Weimar for a short visit with Goethe. They told him that Felix had dedicated the Piano Quartet to him.

Back once more on Leipzigerstrasse, Felix went to work with a new seriousness. For one of the Sunday musicals in the summer house, he wrote a piece that would be performed with a double string quartet - four violins, two violas, and two cellos. He wrote it as a birthday present for his beloved violin teacher, Eduard Reitz. "I cannot believe that a boy of sixteen could write such a masterpiece," his teacher exclaimed.

When he congratulated the young composer, Felix replied, "Oh, I had a wonderful time writing it!"

The warm summer evenings in the gardens of the Mendelssohn estate were a constant joy to the family and their friends. The scent of lilacs and the flowering trees created a peaceful surrounding for a composer. "I have just finished writing two piano pieces," Felix wrote to Fanny who was away on a visit, "but today I am going to start dreaming midsummer night dreams."

William Shakespeare's play, *A Midsummer Night's Dream*, was a favorite of the family. When guests came to the Mendelssohn home, they were often given a part in the play, and they would act it out under the trees in the garden. Now Felix had composed an overture called *A Midsummer Night's Dream*. It was like a picture, painted in musical sounds.

The first performance of the overture created a sensation at one of the Sunday morning musicals. News of this masterpiece spread quickly, and Felix was invited to other cities to conduct his new piece. Robert Schumann was in the audience at one of the performances, and he exclaimed that the composer had taken his "first and loftiest flight".

Felix very much wanted to write a full-scale opera. When he was thirteen years old, he had written four short operas, but now, with the encouragement of friends, he wrote a longer, more serious work. Late one April evening, the opera house in Berlin was crowded with admirers of Felix Mendelssohn.

They had come to hear his new opera. The first act went well, but as the opera went on the composer could feel the audience becoming restless. They were not pleased. Before the end of the opera, Felix left the theatre and walked out into the night. The failure of the opera upset him. It happened at just the same time that one of his best friends had died, and Felix became sad and discouraged.

"Come with us, Felix," two young friends insisted. "Come with us to the mountains, and soon you will feel better."

The trip did revive Felix. Now he was ready to go back to work, but before he did, he decided to look again at an unusual gift that his grandmother had sent him. It was a hand-copied manuscript of music by Johann Sebastian Bach, the *St. Mathew's Passion.* It was a very long composition, an oratorio, written for an orchestra and singers who would sing the words taken from the Bible. Felix spent many hours studying the music. He was excited by the idea of performing such a great masterpiece. At that time, in Germany, people thought that Bach's music was dull and boring, so that this music had not been performed in more than one hundred years.

"Do you think that people will want to hear Bach's music?" he asked Fanny.

"If you think it is beautiful," Fanny replied, "you will make other people love it, too."

Felix's mother also was excited about the idea of performing the *St. Mathew's Passion*. She invited about twelve musical friends to a rehearsal. Rebecka and Fanny helped copy enough chorus parts for each singer. The evening for the first rehearsal came. Felix sat at the piano, with the chorus standing all around where he could help them with their parts. The singing parts were difficult, but the group kept on. In some way, they could feel that this music by Bach was great and noble.

On the morning after the rehearsal, quite early, a loud knock on the door was heard in the Mendelssohn house. Paul, who was already awake, answered the knocking. It was Eduard Devrient (pronounced Dev-ree-ahn), who had sung the bass part in the rehearsal the night before.

"Where is your brother?" he asked Paul in a loud whisper.

"He is still sleeping," Paul answered.

"Well, we must awaken him!" Devrient declared impatiently.

They went to Felix's room, and shook him until he opened his eyes. "What are you doing here so early?" Felix asked, blinking.

"I must talk to you," Devrient said excitedly. "I could not sleep all night thinking about Bach's music. We must perform the *St. Mathew's Passion* for all of Berlin to hear."

"Oh, but who could conduct it? Who will sing the chorus parts? Who can play it?" Felix asked.

"You will conduct it, Felix. You are the only one who can understand the great music. And we will talk to your old teacher, Carl Zelter, about performing with the chorus at the Singakademie. After all, he is director of that school."

"Oh, Zelter would never agree to such an idea," Felix told his friend.

"But we must try," Devrient insisted.

The next day dressed in the blue jackets and yellow gloves in style at this time, the two musicians went to Professor Zelter. They knocked at the door of his studio. "Come in," Zelter called out in his loud, rough voice. The elderly teacher, surrounded by a thick cloud of smoke coming from his long pipe, sat at his dusty instrument with its double row of keys. He wore drab-colored knee breeches, and embroidered slippers over his thick woolen stockings. His quill pen was in his hand and a sheet of music paper before him.

"Well, what do you two fine fellows want at this early hour?" he asked in a kindly tone. "Come, sit down and tell me all about it."

As they agreed, Devrient did the talking. He explained that

they wished to perform Bach's *Passion*. Immediately, Zelter began to list all the problems they would encounter with such a venture. "When other people have tried this before and failed, why do you think you two young donkeys will succeed?" he bellowed.

Felix did not want to irritate his dear old teacher, and pulled at Devrient's sleeve to leave. But nothing would stop Devrient from arguing with the professor. Finally, in a last attempt to persuade him, Devrient said, "Perhaps two young people can cope with the problems, and if we succeed, it would bring honor to you, Herr Professor."

"Well," Zelter finally burst out, "you'll have nothing but trouble from the Singakademie choir, not to mention the trouble you will have with the orchestra, if you can find anyone to play for you. But go ahead. Try it!"

When Felix and Devrient were about to leave, Zelter let his kindly nature shine through. "I will say a good word for you when the time comes. Good luck go with you and we will see what becomes of it all."

Mendelssohn and Devrient were elated. The first rehearsal for the chorus was announced. One hundred fifty eight singers came. Zelter said to Felix, "You will see, these singers will drop away until you have no singers left in your chorus."

Imagine Zelter's surprise, then, when more singers came to the next rehearsal until the group was so large that they had to move to a larger concert room. Then the solo singers came to the rehearsal. They were captivated by the beauty and expressiveness of the melodies and at the dramatic power of Bach's music.

At the rehearsals, Felix accompanied and conducted at the same time. He had mastered all the details of the music from memory, and with his unbounded energy, patience, and understanding, he brought the *St. Mathew's Passion* to life for all those who sang. When the chorus had learned its part, it was time to bring in the orchestra. Amateur orchestra players came from the Berlin Philharmonic and section leaders came from the Royal Orchestra. When the orchestra members had taken their seats, Mendelssohn stood before them to explain what he was about to do.

"This may seem strange to you at first," he told them, "but I intend to conduct this concert with my back to the audience, and facing you. Also, I am going to use a baton, to make my beat easier to follow. Since I know the music from memory, I will be able to instruct you with my eyes as well as with the baton."

When it came time to begin rehearsals, it seemed that all of Berlin knew about it. For each rehearsal, the concert hall was crowded with interested music lovers. When tickets for the performance finally went on sale, they were all sold out within the first ten minutes. More than a thousand people were turned away because there was no room for them in the large hall. King Frederick Wilhelm III and his court attended the first performance, and in the following weeks several more performances were given to try to satisfy all the people who had been turned away.

"All of Germany was elated," Fanny wrote in her diary. "The concert was like a divine service in the church." Then she added, "The money from the concerts is going to be used to start two schools of needlework for girls of poor families."

Felix felt the wonder of Bach's music so intensely that he began to make plans to write his own oratorio. First, though, he had plans to take a trip through Europe. His father told Felix, "If you keep your eyes and ears open everywhere you go, there will be so much you can learn."

Felix traveled for the next three years. He sketched pictures, wrote letters, and composed music. When he arrived in London, a music magazine printed an article about the newcomer. "Another arrival in London is the young Felix Mendelssohn, son of the rich banker of Berlin, and I believe, grandson of the celebrated Jewish philosopher and elegant writer, Moses Mendelssohn. He is supposed to be one of the finest pianoforte players in London, and is supposed to be better acquainted with music than most professors of the art."

Felix, now twenty years old, did not disappoint his London audiences. He conducted his *Midsummer Night's Dream* overture, and a symphony he had composed when he was fifteen years old. He appeared, also, as piano soloist in Carl Maria von Weber's *Concertstuck*. At every concert there was thunderous applause for Mendelssohn.

London audiences opened their hearts to the charming, handsome young musician. Here in their midst was a pianist who played from memory with a brilliant and flowing style. Here was a conductor, who, although small and slender, was in complete command of his orchestra.

London musicians like those in Berlin were not accustomed to having their conductors facing them during the performance. Soon they came to see that they were instructed how to play, not only with the baton, but also with the expressive eyes and small gestures of their new conductor.

At one rehearsal of the *Symphony No. 8* of Beethoven, Mendelssohn was not satisfied with the way the orchestra was playing. Putting down his white baton, which had been especially carved for him, he said rather sarcastically to the orchestra, "I know every one of you is capable of composing a piece of your own, but just now I want to hear Beethoven's piece which I believe has some merit." The orchestra players tried again. "Beautiful," said the conductor, "but it should be softer there." Again they played. And again. Finally, delighted, Mendelssohn said, "What would I have given if Beethoven could have heard his own composition so well understood and so magnificently performed."

The days in London were filled with happy experiences for Mendelssohn. He was a guest in many of the most fashionable homes. Years ago, when Mozart and Haydn had been in

London, they were treated like hired servants. They entered the houses by the servants' back door, and ate their meals with the servants. But not so with Mendelssohn. This elegant, well-mannered young man mixed freely with the invited guests, and was treated as an equal.

Felix had only one complaint during his first stay in London. Just as he would begin to practice each morning, the Marlyebone Band, a group of street musicians, played their loud music outside his window. "Henry, Henry," he would shout to his landlord's son, "here, give them a shilling and tell them to go away!"

Toward the end of his London visit, in the few weeks left to Felix before he returned home to Berlin, he and a friend took a trip through Scotland and Wales. Felix was entranced by the wild and hilly Scotch countryside. When he visited the castle of Mary Queen of Scots, and stood among the ruins of the chapel where she had worshipped, he said to his friend, "I think I have found the beginning of my Scotch Symphony."

They traveled on through hills and moors. "We must visit one more place before we leave for home," his companion told Felix. They boarded a small ship and sailed out to a tiny island in the Hebrides where they visited a famous basalt cave. On the way back to the mainland, Felix, inspired by the sea and the cave, wrote a joyous letter to Fanny. "Here, Fanny," he wrote, "are the first twenty measures of my new overture, *Hebrides*, or *Fingal's Cave Overture*," and he carefully wrote out the notes of the beginnings of his newest composition.

At last, Felix was ready to leave for home after a glorious six-month stay in England. But one moring, riding in a carriage on a London street, there was an accident, the carriage overturned and he was thrown to the ground. He suffered an injured knee, and for two months was confined to his bed. When the people of London heard of the accident, they sent Felix gifts of flowers, books and fruit. Many friends visited him and tried to make him comfortable. Finally, with only a limp to show for his accident, he left for Berlin. In his absence from home, he had missed his sister Fanny's wedding to the painter, Wilhelm Hensel, but he was in time to help celebrate his parents' 25th anniversary. While he had been laid up in bed in London, he had written a charming, humorous operetta for the occasion called, *The Return from Abroad*. He handed out the parts of the music to all the family members.

"Here, Hensel," Felix said to his new brother-in-law, who could not sing in tune at all, "I have written a special part for you in the operetta. You need sing only one note." When the day of the performance arrived, everyone had learned his part, but poor Hensel, when it was time for him to sing his one note, he could not find the pitch. Everyone tried to help him by whistling and blowing his note to him, but still he could not find it. It was a big joke, and everyone, even Hensel, enjoyed the fun.

After a brief stay with his family, Felix was off again on

another trip. This time he stopped once more to visit his old friend, Goethe, who was now eighty-one years old. "I have invited an artist to come this afternoon to paint your portrait," Goethe told Felix, "and tonight some friends are coming to meet you." It was Goethe's greatest joy to have Felix play for him, hour after hour. He played some of own music, but more often the music of Beethoven, whom he had taught Goethe to admire.

When Felix told his friend that he must be on his way, the old man implored him, "Can't you stay a while longer?" Felix agreed to stay, but when he finally had to take leave, Goethe presented his young friend with a sheet of manuscript from his great book, *Faust*. On the first page, Goethe had written, "To my dear young friend, Felix Mendelssohn, powerfully tender master of the piano — a friendly souvenir of happy May days in 1830, signed Johann Wolfgang Goethe." The two friends embraced and said goodbye. When Felix left, neither of them knew that this would be the last time they would see each other.

Leaving Weimar, Felix traveled to the sunny southern part of Italy. As he did wherever he went, he made many new friends who enjoyed this cheerful, intelligent, thoughtful, good-natured musician who showed a keen interest in everything around him. Part of his pleasure in Italy was having plenty of time to compose, and he began work on his *Italian Symphony*.

After almost a year there, he went on to France. The conductor of the Paris Conservatory orchestra asked

Mendelssohn to perform Beethoven's *Fourth Piano Concerto* which would be on the same program with his own *A Midsummer Night's Dream* overture, and his newest symphony, *The Reformation.* "The men of the orchestra did not like my new symphony," Felix wrote home to Fanny. "They thought there was not enough melody, and that it was too serious. I am very disappointed."

But Felix did have some good times in Paris, especially with his three new musician friends. "Ferdinand Hiller, Frederick Chopin, Franz Liszt and I sit at the small cafe table on the avenue and discuss everything close to our hearts," Felix wrote home. "Chopin gave a concert last night, playing his own pieces, and the audience went wild with applause for him. I was in the front row, cheering."

When Felix said goodbye to his Paris friends, he left for his favorite country, England. This was his second visit, and he was greeted with tremendous affection. When he entered the rehearsal hall to conduct the Philharmonic orchestra, one of the players called out, "There is Mendelssohn," whereupon they all stood up and shouted and clapped their hands in a thunderous welcome.

Mendelssohn was in demand from all sides. He was in demand as a pianist. People said his fingers sang as they danced over the keyboard. As soon as Mendelssohn touches the keyboard, an English writer declared, it was as though a "pleasureable shock passed through his hearers and held them spellbound." Londoners also sought him as an organist and a conductor. They wanted to hear all the new pieces he was composing.

Felix would have stayed in England longer if he had not received a letter from home. "Felix," his father wrote, "your dear teacher, Prof. Zelter, died just a few days ago. We think he would have wanted you to take his place as director of the Singakademie. You must come home so that we might talk this over with you."

Felix did go home, and was pursuaded by his family to apply for his teacher's job, although he did not really want to stay in Berlin. Partly because he was so young and successful, and partly because of his religious background, Felix was not appointed for the job. Just about this same time, however, he was very happy to be invited to take a job in another city in Germany. He was asked to plan and direct the great music festival at Dusseldorf on the Rhine River, and then to stay on as the year-round music director.

Mendelssohn had not been in Dusseldorf long before he was sought out by the directors in one of Germany's finest musical cities, Leipzig. He was only twenty six years old, but already he had many kinds of experiences to prepare him for this challenging position as director of the orchestra there. This was a city with a great musical tradition - the city where Johann Sebastian Bach had lived.

Arriving in Leipzig, the young musician was immediately

taken to the hall where the Gewandhaus Orchestra gave its concerts. "This is our orchestra's home," the director explained to Felix. "This is the old market place where the Leipzig linen merchants used to sell their cloth. We call our orchestra the Gewandaus because it means 'clothing hall'."

Felix was glad to accept this new position. He was content to be living and working in this bustling, thriving city, with its University and many book publishers, and fairs which brought people from all over Europe to its market place. With support and encouragement from the city officials, Mendelssohn made Leipzig once again the great musical center of Germany.

The Gewandhaus Orchestra musicians were very fond of their new conductor. "Our orchestra is so different since Maestro Mendelssohn became our leader," one of the violinists told a friend. "Now we feel more alive. We play the beautiful music of Mozart and Bach and Beethoven that we have never heard before. And have you noticed," he added, "that the audiences really listen to our playing? It is a wonderful change from the noisy concert-goers we had to suffer with before."

"Yes," his friend replied, "and you must be happy, too, that the Maestro has pursuaded the city officials to raise your salaries!"

After a concert one day, Robert Schumann and his wife Clara walked home with Mendelssohn. The Schumanns lived in Leipzig, and the three musicians were good friends. "Felix," Robert Schumann said, "do you really think it is a good idea to conduct with a baton? Do you think it is right for the conductor to decide how all the musicans should play their parts?"

"My good friend," Mendelssohn replied, "if every musician in the orchestra plays his own way, how will anyone know how the composer really wanted his music to sound? Someone must decide, and the musicians must follow."

It did not take Schumann very long to understand that Mendelssohn was right. The Gewandhaus Orchestra became the finest in all Europe.

As Felix sat in his studio one afternoon studying the scores for his next concert, a knock on the door interrupted his thoughts. It was the postman bringing a letter from Frankfurt. Felix opened the envelope. "Can you come to Frankfurt for a few weeks?" the letter said. "Our conductor is ill and we need you to help our St. Cecelia Singing Society prepare a series of choral concerts." Of course, Felix was always ready to travel, and he accepted the invitation. Jouncing over the rough roads in a carriage, looking out over the open fields of the countryside, having long hours free to think and plan, were pure enjoyment to Felix.

After several weeks in Frankfurt, Felix began to mention in letters to his family, that there was a young lady in the chorus "whose presence has given me very happy days in Frankfurt at a time when I badly needed them."

The young lady's name was Cecile Jeanrenaud (pronounced Jahn-ra-no). Cecile became Felix's wife the following year. They were very happy together, and for Mendelssohn, as it had been for his father and grandfather before him, his wife and children and home became the center of his life. Although his performing and composing continued at a busy pace, and he did travel for festivals and concerts, he was happiest at home with his family.

Felix and Cecile made their home on the second floor of a large building near the town gates of Leipzig. Many visitors came there. The young couple enjoyed carrying on the Mendelssohn tradition of informal home concerts.

"My friend, Franz Liszt, the great young pianist, is coming for a visit today," Felix told Cecile. "He has just returned from Vienna. His audiences there cheered him for his superb playing. We must invite some friends to hear him."

That evening Felix and Cecile and their guests waited for the pianist to arrive. Hearing footsteps on the stairway, Felix opened the door and saw Franz Liszt standing there, dressed in a bright Hungarian costume. "Welcome, Franz," Felix said.

"Good evening to you, old friend," Liszt replied. "I have something special for you tonight," and he sat down at the piano. First he played an Hungarian folksong, and then variations on the song. Each variation was more fiery and flamboyant than the one before.

"Bravo, bravo," everyone shouted when he finished.

"Now, Felix," said Liszt, "you must play for us."

"Oh, but after your magnificent performance, I cannot play!" Felix said. But Liszt insisted.

"Well, all right," Felix agreed, "but you must promise not to be angry with me."

Felix sat down at the piano. First he repeated Liszt's Hungarian folk song. Then, note for note, exactly as Liszt had played, Felix repeated the variations, and even imitated Liszt's manner of swinging and swaying as he performed.

At the end, Liszt laughed at the joke. But he could not believe that Mendelssohn had memorized every note of the performance after hearing the piece just once. "Felix," Liszt remarked, "how could you do it? You have a phenomenal memory!" Everyone enjoyed Felix's prank.

Felix and Cecile and their growing children continued to live happily in Leipzig. Felix received invitations from all over Europe, sometimes to conduct his own compositions, sometimes to give organ recitals, sometimes to play the piano, and even to play viola in string quartets. He was loved everywhere he went, but always he was glad to return to his family in Leipzig.

One afternoon after a rehearsal with the Gewandhaus orchestra, Cecile met Felix at the door. "You will never guess who is here," she said with a smile. "Come."

"Paul," exclaimed Felix, as he embraced his brother warmly. "What a surprise! What brings my brother to Leipzig?"

"Well, Felix, our new King Wilhelm IV has sent me here to ask if you will come back to Berlin. The King has set about to make the Berlin Academy of Arts the center of music in all of

Germany. He wants to establish four separate schools, with you as the head of the music division of the Royal Academy of the Arts."

"But Paul, you know I do not want to live in Berlin. I am very happy here in Leipzig."

"I know that, Felix, but the King promises to pay you twice as much as you are paid here, and besides, Mother and Fanny long to have you close to them again."

It was very difficult for Felix to decide what to do. He and Cecile talked about it for many hours. Finally, after much letter writing back and forth between Felix and the King's emissaries, Felix agreed to go to Berlin. He explained quite clearly what he expected in the new position, but as it turned out the King did not conscientiously abide by Felix's requests.

Of course, Felix and Cecile and the children were glad to be near the family again. The Sunday morning musicals at Fanny's home were a joy to them. But his work at the Academy was filled with troubles.

The Berlin orchestra was not nearly as good as his Gewandhaus orchestra and the musicians were not as cooperative. Besides, much of Felix's time was taken up with his duties as Director of the school, instead of with composing and conducting. It was part of Mendelssohn's duties to write music that the King requested. One morning King Wilhelm called Felix to his chambers. When he arrived, the Court poet was standing near the King, reading some poetry. Felix immediately recognized the poetry. It was from Shakespeare's play, *A Midsummer Nights Dream.* "Felix," the poet said, "I have just finished translating the play from English to German. Now the King requests that you write music for the play."

Immediately, scenes from his childhood leaped to Felix's mind: the wondrous happy days in the garden of his parents' home, when he and his sisters and brother, and the family guests had often acted the parts of this play by Shakespeare. It had been seventeen years since Felix had composed the *Overture to a Midsummer Night's Dream.* Now his pen flew over the pages, writing music to describe all the scenes: the dancing fairies, the donkey, and the royal wedding, with the colorful sounds of the instruments describing every scene.

With the composition ready for performance, Felix led the orchestra in eleven rehearsals. The music immediately delighted the musicians and the audiences. There was just one problem at the first performance. A real dog was used in the play. In one scene, it took a nip of the leg of the person who was playing the part of the Lion. Backstage there was quite a commotion. It was decided that the real dog should be retired, and a stuffed dog used in its place!

In spite of a few successes such as this, Felix was not happy in Berlin and was impatient to leave. He had stayed for five years, and now he asked the King to release him from his duties.

"If you will promise to write music for me when I need it, and if you will come back for special concerts, I will grant your wish to leave," the King said.

Mendelssohn agreed to King Wilhelm's terms. He was so glad to leave that he wrote his friend Devrient, "The first step out of Berlin is the first step toward happiness!"

Released at last from his duties to the King, Mendelssohn set to work on a composition he had planned five years before. He had told his good friend, Ferdinand David (pronounced, Daaveed) who was concertmaster of the Gewandhaus orchestra, "I want to write a violin concerto for you. One in e minor is running through my head and the beginning of it never gives me a moment of peace." Felix had the concerto already worked out in his mind when he finally put the notes down on paper. He always consulted Ferdinand David about the technical problems of the violin, so that the concerto could be played beautifully. Finally, on a cold day in March, David performed the concerto to a wildly enthusiastic audience in Leipzig.

Another invitation came to Felix from England. Like Handel and Haydn before him, Felix loved to visit England where he always received a warm welcome. "I was never received anywhere with such universal kindness, and have made more music in these two months than I do elsewhere in two years," he wrote to Fanny. On his fifth visit, his wife Cecile joined him. It was the year when the twenty-three year old Victoria became Queen of England. Her husband was the German-born Prince Albert. Both the Queen and the Prince enjoyed music, and they invited Felix to Buckingham Palace.

Prince Albert told Mendelssohn, "The Queen enjoys singing your songs. Will you play the piano part for her?"

"But first we must take the parrot out of the room," the Queen said, "because he will sing louder than I do!" Mendelssohn took the cage from the room, and then sat down at the piano.

"Victoria has a lovely singing voice," Felix later wrote to his mother. "She sings quite charmingly, and in strict time and tune."

On each of his trips to England, thereafter, a visit to the Queen and Prince were of greatest pleasure to Felix. He dedicated his Scotch Symphony to the Queen, and she, in return, asked Mendelssohn, "What may I do for you to show my appreciation for your music?"

After thinking a moment, Felix asked, "Would you show me the royal children's nurseries?" The Queen thought this an unusual request, but she answered, "Of course," and for an hour, Queen Victoria was very pleased to show Felix the children's apartments, the closets and the wardrobes in the royal Palace.

Almost everything was perfect on this trip to England, but on one occasion, the musicians in the orchestra made Felix very angry. "Gentlemen," the conductor said, "we will now rehearse Schubert's Symphony in C." They began to play.

Suddenly there was laughter and complaining from the violin section. One musician said, "We cannot play this music with its strange harmonies and rhythms."

Mendelssohn was furious. He cancelled the concert, and refused to allow the orchestra to play his own *Ruy Blas* overture. In spite of this incident, Mendelssohn returned again and again to a warm welcome in England, but he was always glad when it came time to return to Leipzig and his family.

Just a few days after his homecoming, however, an unexpected letter arrived from his brother, Paul. "Dearest Felix, I am broken hearted to tell you this. Fanny is dead."

The shock was overwhelming to Felix. He and Fanny had been so close in mind and in heart. "This will be a changed world for us all now," Felix wrote to Fanny's husband.

To try to help the family recover from its sadness, they traveled together to Switzerland. Felix composed a Quartet, expressing the sorrow he felt so keenly.

A friend traveling to Switzerland stopped to see Felix and Cecile. "Come with me," Felix said to his friend. "I have discovered a beautiful little church with an organ."

Felix and his friend had to travel by boat to reach the church. When they arrived, the doors were unlocked. Mendelssohn sat down at the organ console. His friend listened while Felix played some music of Bach, and then went on to improvise on his own thoughts.

This was the last concert Felix ever played. It was not many months after that when he became ill. He died when he was only thirty-eight years old. All of the musical world was sad, but grateful, too, for all the beautiful music he had left to be enjoyed forever. In Europe and even in America, memorial concerts were given in memory of this most beloved musician, Felix Mendelssohn.

FELIX MENDELSSOHN

b. Hamburg, Germany, February 3, 1809
d. Leipzig, Germany, November 4, 1847

WOLFGANG AMADEUS MOZART

"I christen thee Johannes Chrysostomus Wolfgangus Theophilus Mozart," said the priest as he gently touched the tiny baby's head. Anna Marie Mozart, with her husband Leopold beside her, lovingly held their new baby as the priest said the blessings at the altar of the great cathedral. When the service was over, Leopold and Anna Marie wrapped the little baby warmly in his blanket and left for home through the dimly lighted snow-covered streets of Salzburg. At home, the baby's four year old sister Marian was waiting at the doorway. "Oh, here you are at last," she called out. "Can my little brother play with me now?"

Mother and father smiled. "Wolfgang is too little to play with you, Marian," Father Leopold Mozart explained, "but tonight some friends will be coming to our home to play music with us, and you can hold the baby on your lap while you listen."

"Oh, good, good," laughed Marian.

The Mozart house was often filled with sounds of music. Father Leopold Mozart was a violinist and composer. He liked to invite other musicians to his home to play some music they had just composed, or wanted to try. Leopold's wife Anna Marie loved music too. She was a quiet and cheerful woman, glad to have coffee and kuchen ready for refreshment on those evenings of music making.

Sometimes the music went on late into the night. Wolfgang and Marian tried hard to keep awake after they had been put to bed, so that they could listen to the music.

When Marian was seven years old, her father said to her one morning, "My little daughter, how would you like to begin lessons on the clavier?"

Marian jumped up in her father's lap. "I would love it, father," she exclaimed happily. So the lessons began. Marian learned quickly and enjoyed her lessons very much.

Little Wolfgang, just three years old, was never far away during his sister's lessons and her practicing. He listened to her while he played with his toys. "When may I take lessons, father?" Wolfgang asked.

"Oh, you are much too small," came the quick answer. But one day, after Marian's lesson, Wolfgang climbed up on the bench and played one of the pieces that his sister had played at her lesson.

"Good for you, Wolfgang, good for you!" his sister and father cried out in amazement.

By the time Wolfgang was four years old, he could imitate anything his sister played on the clavier. Best of all, he was beginning to compose his own pieces, and when he was five years old, Wolfgang composed two minuets which his father wrote down on paper.

Leopold Mozart was a fine violinist and enjoyed playing chamber music. One Sunday afternoon there was a knock on the door. "Come in, come in," Papa Mozart called out as he saw two of his friends from the court orchestra. One carried a violin, the other a cello.

"Would you like to play some trios this afternoon?" one of the men asked.

"Ach, that will be wonderful," answered Leopold.

"Papa, papa," cried young Wolfgang, "will you let me play the second violin part with you?"

"How can you play the second violin part, Wolfgang, when you have never had a violin lesson?" his father scolded.

"But one need not take a lesson in order to play," Wolfgang complained. He begged again to play.

"Very well," his father agreed, "but play softly so nobody can hear you."

They began to play the trio. They had gone no more than a few measures when everyone could hear that the boy was playing his part without a mistake.

"How can this be?" said the older violinist, who laid down his violin so that the young boy could play all the trios. At the end of the evening, all the group swept Wolfgang up in their arms with praise and kisses.

Leopold Mozart was an excellent violin teacher for his son. He had written five books about teaching violin. Wolfgang loved his father and wanted to please him, so they worked well together as teacher and pupil. But Leopold could see that his son had talent to compose music as well as to perform what others had composed. To Anna Marie, his wife, he said, "I see the spark of genius in our young son. I must help him with the discipline and training to develop his talents as a composer."

To be a success as a musician in the time when Mozart was growing up, it was necessary to get attention from rich and important people. Kings and queens, princes and counts, men in high places and wealthy aristocrats often gave money to musicians and other artists so that they could spend all their time creating and performing beautiful work.

Leopold wondered what he should do for Wolfgang and Marian. "We must take our children on a tour of Europe," Papa Mozart told Anna Marie. "They can play for all the great people. The world will be amazed at what they can do."

And so a trip was planned. The two children and their father traveled all over Germany and Austria. The young children charmed the noble people in the courts. Wolfgang, dressed in his fancy silk and velvet suits and a wig to cover his beautiful blond hair, would hop up in the laps of wealthy ladies and shower them with kisses. When his audience was attentive to his playing, he would show appreciation; but if people showed any lack of attention, he would frown in anger.

The concerts of the two children caused great excitement wherever they went. But for such a young child as Wolfgang the strain of travel was too much, and he became ill. The three had to return home. As soon as Wolfgang regained his strength they were off again on a more strenuous journey, this time to France.

They traveled through bad weather, they did not eat well, and they had to stay up late at night. Living conditions were wretched. Finally, though, after five months, the three Mozarts reached Paris.

When Wolfgang and Marian played their concerts the audiences were wildly enthusiastic. During their stay in Paris, Wolfgang composed two pairs of sonatas for violin and piano. He was only seven years old.

News about these amazing children spread everywhere. One evening after a concert in Paris, a messenger came to Leopold Mozart. He carried an invitation from the royal family in England. "You are cordially invited to come to London as guests of the court," the invitation read.

Although Leopold probably should have taken his children back home to Salzburg, he could not resist the invitation to go to England. So off they went on the long trip. There, unexpectedly, they met Johann Christian Bach, the youngest son of the great Johann Sebastian Bach. The older man and the young Wolfgang had good times together. In later years Wolfgang remembered with gratitude all that Bach had taught him about composing.

One day while the Mozarts were in London, Leopold told his children, "I have a special treat for you. Tonight you will hear your first opera."

They went to the concert hall, and the eight year old boy sat spellbound throughout the performance. When the curtain fell after the last act of the opera, Wolfgang asked his father, "May I meet the famous Italian singer?"

"Yes, of course," said his father. So winding their way through the crowd, they went backstage to compliment the singer on his great performance. The singer was so pleased with Wolfgang's interest and pleasure in the opera that he invited the Mozarts to visit him the following day. He gave Wolfgang some singing lessons.

It was then that the eight year old Wolfgang expressed a wish, "Some day I, too, will write music for an opera."

After fifteen months in London, Leopold Mozart and his two children left England. On their way back to their home in Salzburg they stopped in Holland, where the Dutch people were very kind to them. One morning Papa Mozart awoke with a sore throat. The doctors ordered him to have complete rest and quiet. This gave the nine year old Wolfgang time to do something he had been wanting to do for a long time. He could write a piece for an orchestra. He wrote his first symphony. Very soon after that, he composed two more symphonies.

Back in the little house in Salzburg on a chilly November afternoon, Anna Marie was sitting in front of the fire knitting when she heard a horse and carriage drive up to the door. To her great joy, there was her dear family, home after three long years of travel. Once more the happy Mozart family was reunited.

Now that he was back in Salzburg again, Wolfgang Mozart continued his musical studies. Several years passed, and Wolfgang's father decided it was time for his son to visit Italy. "Wolfgang," he said, "there is so much for you to hear and see in Italy. There are musicians and artists there from all over Europe. You should hear the music in the great cathedrals and see the fine paintings and sculpture in the art galleries." So once again bidding goodbye to his mother and sister, Wolfgang, with his father, left home.

Everywhere he went, Wolfgang Mozart astounded the noble people in the courts and cathedrals. Professional musicians could scarcely believe that this young boy could flawlessly perform concertos and sonatas he had never played or even seen before. "Let us give young Mozart a poem and let him compose a short piece or a song for it," they suggested, and then were amazed at the skill with which the young boy composed without even writing down a single note.

Once, in Rome, Mozart visited the magnificent Sistine Chapel when a concert was being given. The organ pealed forth, the voices of the choir lifted, and young Mozart was filled with wonder at the beauty of the sound. When the music stopped, he got up from his place in the chapel and walked home in silence. He went to his room and from memory he wrote down on paper every note of the music he had heard that afternoon.

There was a rule of the Sistine Chapel that no one but the musicians of the chapel could have copies of the music performed there. Many people had tried to write it from memory, but all had failed.

"I have heard that young Mozart has performed a remarkable musical feat," the Pope said when he heard that Wolfgang had been able to remember every note he had heard and had written down the entire composition. Instead of punishing him for disobeying the rule, the Pope bestowed a great honor by making Wolfgang Mozart a Knight of the Golden Spur. That was one of the highest honors anyone could receive from the church. He wore the beautiful golden medallion with pride.

After Wolfgang had been in Italy for a year, when he was fourteen years old, he had his first opera performed. "How does that young German boy think that he can write an opera to please the people of Italy?" some Italian composers asked jealously. "We will set the orchestra and singers against him," they plotted. But when the orchestral musicians and chorus and soloists began to rehearse Mozart's opera, they were overjoyed and inspired by the beauty of the music. Audiences greeted his opera with cheers and ovations.

When Wolfgang was sixteen years old he returned to his home in Salzburg once more. He was glad to be home with the Mozart family and their friends. He liked games and dancing and playing tricks and making jokes, but it was time for a sixteen year old young man to think seriously of earning a living. "Papa," he said, "you are a musician in the court here. Now don't you think I must leave Salzburg and find my own way in the world?"

"No, no," replied Papa Mozart, "you are not prepared to care for yourself. Your mother will go with you to Paris."

So, against her will, Wolfgang's mother left home to go with him. Although Wolfgang was now twenty-one years of age, a fine performer on the violin, piano and organ, and a composer of great skill, he could not find a permanent job. During their stay in Paris, Mozart's mother died, and Wolfgang, with sadness in his heart, returned to Salzburg.

Still he could find no permanent position. He left for Vienna, where he lived with friends and composed music of all kinds. When he was twenty-six years old he married. He and his wife were always poor. Often people did not pay Mozart for his work. Some cheated him. But Mozart and his wife were happy together.

There were times when Mozart put off until the last minute some work he had been asked to do. The emperor in Vienna was

WOLFGANG AMADEUS MOZART

very fond of Mozart's music and asked him to write some pieces for a concert at the court. When the time came for Mozart to leave for the court, his wife was worried. "What will you do, Wolfgang? You do not have your piano part written."

"Never mind, my dear," he answered, "everything will be all right. You will see."

Mozart entered the concert hall. The orchestral musicians all had their parts to play, and Wolfgang carried a sheet of paper in his hand and placed it on the piano. The emperor, who was standing by, looked at the paper. There was nothing written. "But where is your part, Mozart?" he asked. Pointing to his forehead, Mozart replied, "My part is in here, Your Majesty."

When the piece had been performed, the emperor stood up and called out, "Bravo, bravo!" The audience cheered.

Papa Leopold died when Wolfgang was thirty-one years old. Wolfgang's health began to fail, but his creative energy flourished. He produced great quantities of his most beautiful music and finally, feeling that his own life was coming to an end, he composed one of his greatest compositions, the Requiem Mass to be performed in the cathedral.

On December 5, in the cold of winter, Wolfgang Mozart died. There was no money for a funeral, nor for a stone to mark the place where he was buried. But many years later, the people of Vienna built a fine monument in memory of the great musician. All people everywhere will always remember Wolfgang Amadeus Mozart because of the magnificent music he left to the world.

b. Salzburg, Austria, January 27, 1756
d. Vienna, Austria, December 5, 1791

IGNACE JAN PADEREWSKI

Through the field of ripening wheat, Ignace ran toward the farm house, his thick red-gold hair swirling above his head, his shouting breaking the early evening quiet. "You can't catch me," he shouted over his shoulder to his sister, and he burst through the back door.

His aunt was in the kitchen, preparing supper for the children. With both hands behind his back, Ignace jumped in front of her.

"Guess what I have here," he said. "One for you and one for sister."

"What can it be?" his aunt laughed.

"Pears!" he shouted. "They are rosey ripe at last." Then Ignace turned to his sister and whispered, "When the music teacher comes to give me a lesson, I can climb into the pear tree and hide!" The two children giggled and ran out of the room.

Even though Ignace's life had been troubled when he was very young, he had a strong and lively spirit. His mother had died when he was an infant and he knew her only by the stories his father told. She had been a gentle woman, with a love of music. Then, when Ignace was only three years old, and his sister was five, something happened which left a strong impression on the small boy. It was a time when the working people in Poland were trying to become free of the Russians who ruled them. One day, the Russian Cossaks rode up to the

Paderewski home. They suspected Jan Paderewski of helping the peasants. As the soldiers took Ignace's father off to prison, the small boy tried to stop them, but they struck him with their clubs. It was a frightening time for Ignace and his sister. Now, with their mother gone, and their father in prison, the two children were sent to their aunt who lived on a farm in the countryside.

From the time Ignace had been a tiny child, he liked to play the piano. First, he made up tunes with one finger; then, he played with all his fingers. His father, who had seen that his son enjoyed music, looked for a teacher for him. His first teacher was a violinist. He would stand by the piano, beating time, while the small boy and his sister, Antonina, played duets. When it was time to practice, Ignace enjoyed himself, making up his own pieces.

Now that the children lived far out in the countryside, away from towns and cities, how could they find a piano teacher? They could not think what to do.

One winter evening, just after the sun had gone down below the hill, Ignace and Antonina heard the sound of horses' hoofs in front of their farmhouse. An elderly gentleman dressed in a fur cap and coat, and high fur boots, stepped slowly from the carriage.

"Here I am," he called out in a cheerful voice. "Your father wrote to me from prison. He asked me to be your music teacher."

Because the teacher lived so far away, it took him a full-day's journey to get to the farm house. At first he would stay a day or two; but later, he would come once a month and stay for 5 or 6 days at a time. Alas, though the teacher was kind enough, he did not teach the children the proper way to play the piano. He did not show them how to put their hands on the keys or which fingers to use. Ignace could play any way he wished, and while the teacher stood by and listened, the children played just for fun, trying arrangements of operas, and duets of every kind. The best fun was improvising, making up their own songs, with Ignace playing the bass part and his sister, the treble.

All the while, in prison, Jan Paderewski was content, thinking his talented son was learning to be a fine pianist! He had also hired a French teacher to live at the house to teach the children French, Polish and Russian. Ignace quickly learned to read and write in all those languages. He learned poetry by heart, and spent many hours reading aloud to his sister and aunt.

"I will write to Daddy in prison," four year old Ignace told his aunt one morning. The letter began, "I am writing this letter all by myself. Do you know Florian has a new pair of green boots? When are you coming home?"

Happily for everyone, Ignace's second question was soon answered. The peasants from the surrounding countryside begged the authorities to set Jan free, and he was allowed to go home to his children.

Ignace continued to enjoy his music very much, playing at home, and composing his own pieces, improvising for hours at a time to entertain his father. Some people in the neighborhood heard about the talented children in the Paderewski home, and asked Jan if they could play for a charity concert to be given in a tiny neighborhood house. He was pleased, and agreed to let his children perform. For their program, they played some duets and were given some sweets as a reward. Later on, Ignace gave some recitals by himself. There were no music stores or libraries where he could get music to learn, so his concerts were the few little arrangements of operas that he knew, and *Carnival of Venice*, and for the rest of the concert, improvisations.

At the close of one concert, someone in the audience of about twenty people got up from his chair, and went to the piano. He held a towel over the keyboard and asked Ignace to play without seeing the keys. Everyone was pleased and amazed that Ignace could perform this trick, and news spread around the countryside about the amazing young pianist. A wealthy Count heard about Ignace.

"Let me take Ignace to Kieff," he asked Jan. "The boy is so musical but he has never heard a real concert, or an orchestra, or a pianist, or a violinist, or even a singer. What do you say to that, Jan?"

"Oh, that would be a wonderful experience for my son," he answered excitedly. "Thank you so much for your kindness."

The Count and Ignace left for Kieff. The boy was thrilled by all the new exciting experiences in the big city. He could hardly believe that there was such music in the world, or indeed, that the world was such a big place.

The winter journey back from Kieff was very eventful, too. As they traveled by horse and sleigh, night came on. The snow was still falling. Ignace fell asleep under the big fur robe on the floor of the sleigh. Suddenly, the horses began to whinney. Ignace awakened. He looked out from under the robe, and saw many tiny bright glowing eyes. It was a pack of wolves coming toward the sleigh. The coachman, acting quickly, took the trunks out of the small sleigh that they were pulling, put them into the big sleigh, and then set fire to the empty sleigh. The fire frightened the wolves away, and the coachman was able to get his passengers home safely.

It was about this time, when Ignace was twelve years old, that his father spoke of sending him to the conservatory in Warsaw for a real musical education. A railway was being built connecting their town to Warsaw, so Jan thought he could take his son there at last. Fortunately, in Warsaw there was a father of a family with ten children who took an interest in the young musician, and offered to have him live with them. The house was enormous, because it was also a place where pianos were made. Ignace could practice on any piano that was not in use!

Ignace's career at the Conservatory had its ups and downs. His first piano teacher was astonished at the way Ignace played.

IGNACE PADEREWSKI

He had so many bad habits. "You had better be a composer," the teacher said. "You do well in harmony, but, oh, your piano playing! You will never be a pianist, **never.**"

Ignace tried another teacher at the Conservatory, who was satisfied with Ignace's manner of playing and did not insist that he change his bad habits. For two years, Ignace continued at the Conservatory. Then, because of an argument with the director, he was expelled from the Conservatory. He had refused to attend an orchestra rehearsal which interfered with studying for his examinations!

Now what would he do? Without telling his father, Ignace and two of his friends at the Conservatory decided to earn some money by going on a tour. They had a trio: a pianist, violinist, and a cellist, and the three musicians traveled from town to town. For awhile, everything went well, but when too many troubles overtook the trio, sixteen year old Ignace went home, ashamed for what he had done. "I am sorry, father, for all the trouble I have brought to our family," he said. "Let me go back to the Conservatory and I will work hard and earn my diploma."

Ignace did just exactly as he promised. For six months he worked day and night, and finished two years of work in that short time. Jan was proud and happy at the graduation ceremonies when Ignace performed the *Piano Concerto* by Edward Grieg, and received his diploma with honors.

"We would like you to stay on as a teacher at the

Conservatory," the director said to Ignace at the close of the ceremonies.

Ignace, now twenty years old, was glad to have a secure position. He began his teaching. He also continued his studies. But in a few years, he felt he needed more education, and left his job to go to Berlin.

A whole new musical world opened up to Ignace Paderewski. He continued to compose. He took violin and cello lessons to help him understand the instruments of the orchestra. He met many fine musicians there. All the while, though, he could not find a teacher who would encourage him about his piano playing.

Finally, however, a very famous pianist in Vienna agreed to listen to Paderewski play. "Ach," Leschetizky exclaimed, "you have tone, but you have no discipline. You do not know how to work! If you wish to have me for a teacher, you must begin all over again. You will do finger exercises and Czerny studies. Then we shall see."

Under Leschetizky's guidance, Paderewski worked very hard.

While Paderewski was practicing in his cottage one afternoon, Leschetizky came to visit. He was smiling. "Paderewski," he said, "how would you like to make your first appearance in Vienna? The great singer, Pauline Lucca, is giving a charity concert, and she wants a pianist to help fill the program. Will you play?"

Paderewski thought his teacher really wanted him to play.

"Yes, I should be very glad to do it."

From then on, Paderewski felt that he surely could become a concert pianist. He learned many pieces, and played in concerts all over Europe and the United States, South America, and Australia and South Africa.

Although he traveled everywhere, Paderewski never forgot his native country. When World War I began, he became an important spokesman for the Polish people who were struggling for their independence. He became Prime Minister of Poland and Minister of Foreign Affairs, and at the end of the war, he signed the Versailles Treaty.

Again Paderewski went back to his concert tours, and to his composing. Once more, when war came to Europe, and the Nazis invaded Poland, Paderewski traveled to the United States to plead for help for his country. This was his final journey, because he died in New York before the war was over. This great musician and statesman was buried with state honors at the Arlington National Cemetary in Washington, D.C.

b. Kurlowka, Podolia, Poland, November 6, 1860
d. New York City, USA, June 19, 1941

GIOVANNI BATTISTA PERGOLESI

A s Donna Anna looked sadly at her small frail son, she said to her husband, "We must take the little one to the Church tomorrow, and ask the Priest if Giovanni can be confirmed."

It was the custom in those early times to confirm children in the Church when they were five years old, but Giovanni's parents did not expect their son to live that long. The Priest agreed to have a special service for Giovanni when he was less than two years old.

Although Giovanni was not strong, and he limped with a deformed leg, the young child had a lively spirit. At an early age, he studied violin and harmony with the priests in the local church in Jesi.

Soon, however, the priests could see that they had an unusual pupil, and they spoke to Giovanni's parents. "We have taught all we know to your son. We would like to suggest that you send him to a teacher who can help him with his musical studies. If you would like it, we will help you find a teacher for him."

Giovanni's parents were proud of their son's talents. His father was a surveyor by trade, and he was surprised that his son was gifted with musical talent. A teacher was found for Giovanni, and he progressed remarkably in his studies.

A nobleman in the Court of Jesi heard of the young prodigy in the Pergolesi family. He spoke to Giovanni's parents. "I would like to be a patron to your son, and send him to a famous conservatory in the city of Naples. There are many wonderful musicians there, and he will be surrounded by great music."

"But how can we pay his tuition?" Giovanni's father wondered.

"You have no need to worry about that," answered the nobleman. "Your son can take part in the musical performances at the conservatory and in that way he will earn enough money to pay his expenses."

The Pergolesi family had heard many stories about the exciting city of Naples. To think that Giovanni could go there for his education! Father and Mother gave their blessing to the plan, and expressed their gratitude to Giovanni's new patron.

Taking his violin and a few of his possessions, Giovanni left for Naples. At the Conservatory, his teachers gave the boy a place in the choir. He sang in many performances.

In a few years, when his voice changed to a lower range, Giovanni was given a place playing violin in the small orchestra that went out from the Conservatory to tour in the surrounding countryside. Because he played so well, Giovanni was made the leading violinist in the group.

All the while, the young musician was learning to compose music. As he approched the final year of his Conservatory education, his teacher said to him, "Giovanni Pergolesi, it is the custom at our school to have our graduating students compose a musical composition to be performed in public. Your assignment will be to write a religious opera in three acts. Our Conservatory orchestra will perform your opera."

Giovanni worked very hard, and in the summer his opera was

ready. It was performed at a Monastery near Naples.

Now that he had completed this part of his musical training, Giovanni decided to leave the Conservatory and look for work as an independent musician. Almost at once, he received a commission from an important patron who had been at the Monastery when Giovanni's first opera had been presented. This new patron asked him to write an opera especially for him.

From that time on, Giovanni Pergolesi was constantly in demand as a composer. He wrote music for the Church, or the theatre, and often for the many celebrations and festivals held in Naples, the city of music.

One year, late in November and early in December, there were frightening earthquakes in Naples. Immediately, the Archbishop of the Church elected a Saint to protect the city against any more earthquakes. He vowed to celebrate the Saint each year with a large Church festival. Of course, special music was needed. The Archbishop approached Pergolesi.

"Can you write a composition grand enough to honor our St. Emedius? This is the Saint whom we will ask to protect us from earthquakes."

Pergolesi was happy to be asked to serve the Church in this way, and he wrote a Mass for double choir. This work brought Pergolesi his first taste of fame. Two years later, he wrote an opera to celebrate the birthday of the Empress, and after that, a cello sonata dedicated to his patron who was himself an amateur cellist.

There were times when Pergolesi had many problems when he

went to rehearse an opera he had written. He would write his opera for certain singers and certain instrumental players. But at the opening rehearsal, he might discover that there were no singers for the chorus. Perhaps there would be singers who could not perform his parts, or there might be musicians who could not play the instruments he needed for his orchestra.

What could he do? Usually, he would have to rush home and in great haste write parts of the opera over again to fit the people who were there to perform. Sometimes an opera had to be rewitten for each performance!

When Pergolesi was about twenty-one years old, his operas were not being enjoyed by his audiences as much as before. "I will write another kind of music," he decided, and for the next few months he wrote three hundred sonatas for two violins and bass.

Early in 1736, when Pergolesi was only 26 years old, his health began to fail. He moved into a monastery. He wrote a few more beautiful pieces for the Church. When he died, no special service was held for him. But 50 years later, people began to give attention to his music in a way that they had not when he was living. The people said, "Let us build a special chapel on the site of the Cathedral in Naples." There a memorial stone was set to mark the place of rest of this great musician who lived such a short but fruitful life.

b. Jesi, near Ancona, Italy - January 4, 1710
d. Pozzuoli, near Naples, Italy - March 16, 1736

DAVID POPPER

One, two, three, four, five, six, seven, eight", chimed the clock in the Town Hall Square. Three-year old David, walking beside his mother and father, already knew what time it was by the Hebrew numbers on the clock.

"We had better hurry," David's mother said, "or we will be late for the Sabbath service."

This morning was like every other Saturday morning since David could remember, when the family of Angelus and Esther Popper walked through their sunless, dingy neighborhood within the wall of the Jewish ghetto, to the clock tower, then across the narrow, cobbled street to the Pinkas Synagogue. David liked the morning service. He especially looked forward to the part of the service when the Rabbi drew apart the curtains of the Ark beneath the eternal light and lifted the Torah above his head. David's father, the Cantor, chanted the prayers, and his son, singing along softly so as not to be heard, chanted along with his father. He knew the prayers well from hearing his father practicing at home.

At the close of the service, the Popper family returned to their poor home in the ghetto tenement. They sat down at the table for their cold lunch. Any work, even cooking, was forbidden on the Jewish sabbath.

"May I sing the blessing?" David asked.

"Yes, of course you may," Angelus answered. In perfect

pitch, David imitated the chant his father often sang.

David's parents knew that their son had a gift for music. When friends would come to visit, he liked to march around the room, singing into his toy trumpet, or he would improvise tunes on the piano.

One Sabbath evening, after sundown, David was entertaining the family and some guests who had stopped by for tea. "Now it is time for bed," Esther announced to the children, and after they had settled for the night, one of the visitors spoke quietly to Angelus and Esther.

"I would like to make you an offer," he said. "I will give violin lessons to David without any charge. It would be a pleasure to teach such a bright and musical child. We all know that music is one of the few professions permitted to the Jews, so don't you agree that it would be good for David to prepare himself to play in the orchestra of the king, or in the opera?"

Gratefully, David's parents accepted the generous offer of their friend and when the boy was six years old, his violin lessons began. While he spent many hours with his violin, he continued to play the piano and to make up his own pieces.

By the time David was twelve years old, he had become a fine violinist and pianist who could play from memory any music that he heard. Many an evening, friends came to the Popper's home to sing the beautiful songs of Mendelssohn, Schubert, and Schumann and other German composers. No sooner had the friends gone home than David was sitting down at the piano, playing the songs that had been sung. His parents were pleased with what David could do, but they thought it was time for him to have a broader education.

"Now that the Emperor has issued a decree allowing Jewish people the right to travel and study and work outside the ghetto walls, perhaps we should think of sending David to study at the Prague Conservatory," Angelus said to Esther.

When David's father told him of their decision to send him to school, David asked, "Do you think the professors at the Conservatory would accept me as a student?"

"Well, we will just have to see," his father answered. "In two weeks time we will go to the Conservatory for your audition."

When David arrived at the Prague Conservatory, a group of faculty were there to hear him play, and to test his ability to match tones, and to analyze the notes in complicated chords and rhythms. The teachers were impressed with David's ability.

"David," the Conservatory director said, after the examination was over, "you will be accepted at the Conservatory on one condition. You see, we have many violinists here, but very few cellists. We would like you to change from violin to cello. If you will, then George Golterman will be your teacher. As you know, he is solo cellist with the Prague opera orchestra."

David looked at his father. The slow smile that he saw in his father's face gave him the courage to agree to the arrangement. He would now be a cello student.

The schedule at the Conservatory was strenuous indeed. In addition to practicing piano and cello, David spent six days each week studying theory and composition, French language, esthetics, and literature. He played in the orchestra and in a chamber music group.

At first, Professor Golterman, his new teacher, was hesitant to give cello lessons to a violinist. But David soon proved to his teacher that he would be proud of his pupil some day.

During his theory lesson one afternoon, David was called out of class by the Conservatory director. "David," he spoke rather nervously, "Professor Golterman is ill. He was to play tonight in the opera *William Tell*. Will you substitute for him?"

David was accustomed to substituting in the orchestra, but he always was seated at the back of the cello section. This time he was being asked to sit in Golterman's place at the first desk, and to play the long, beautiful cello solo in the overture to *William Tell*.

"Did Professor Golterman himself ask to have me take his place in the orchestra tonight?" David questioned respectfully.

"Yes, he did, David. He certainly must have great confidence in you!"

That evening, when the opera orchestra members took their places in the theatre pit, they looked in surprise at David sitting in the first cellist's chair. But the surprised expressions changed to nods of approval when David drew the first long, sustained notes of the overture from his cello. The warm, rich, sweet tones caught everyone's attention, and when his solo part ended, the audience broke into wild applause, so loud, in fact, that the conductor had to put down his baton, and ask David to take a bow acknowledging the audience's pleasure.

Six years of study at the Conservatory passed quickly for David. When he graduated, he knew it was time to look for a job.

"Come to Vienna," a friend wrote to David. "There is a small concert hall here where you could give a recital. Viennese people love music and I'm sure they would enjoy hearing you play."

David accepted his friend's invitation, and late in the summer he traveled to Vienna. He gave his recital and thought he had performed well. The next day, however, when he looked in the newspaper, he was disappointed to read the music critic's comment about his playing. "David Popper is not yet ready to start a concert career," the critic suggested. "He needs more practice and preparation."

"Perhaps the critics are right," David told his parents when he returned to Prague. "I will try to get another job in an orchestra. I know there is much for me to learn. Prince Lowenberg is looking for a cellist for his court orchestra, and I will try for the position."

David, who was now eighteen years old, was accepted as second cellist in the Court orchestra. This was a fine opportunity for him to learn the great music of his time. When the first cellist of the orchestra died, David was prepared to take his place.

With this orchestral experience, David felt more confident to give solo recitals. Even in Vienna, where before he had been criticized, he now received nothing but praise when he gave a concert playing a cello concerto by Golterman, and some of his own compositions. This time when he looked in the newspaper to see what the music critics would say, he was pleased to read that the audience "witnessed a young man of nineteen, full of enthusiasm for his instrument. Sometimes he draws out the tone from his cello with immense power, sometimes with tender sweetness," the article went on. "We feel that the young artist whom we consider among the best of our time, has a great and promising future."

With this encouragement, David began to give many concerts, more and more frequently including his own compositions. His own pieces, which he played with a personal style and tone of great beauty, always brought an especially warm response from his audiences.

Music critics, writing their comments in the newspapers, sometimes carried on arguments about a performer's style, or about the merits of a new composition.

"Look at this!" David's friend, waving a newspaper, shouted above the noise of the café as they sat around the table for supper. "The music critics are still arguing about your vibrato!

Two days ago a critic wrote that you were using too much vibrato."

"Yes, I remember," David replied. "He wrote that I used an intolerable amount of vibrato. Yesterday, another critic disagreed with that. He said there was not a trace of 'intolerable vibrato'. Now what are they writing?"

"Today," his friend answered scanning the afternoon paper, "the critic replies that the ears of people who like so much vibrato must be infected by a sickness of taste, and no longer have a sense of a natural, whole tone."

David laughed. "May I see the newspaper? I think it is quite amusing the way the music critics argue back and forth about how much vibrato we should use. It makes me wonder if they ever played an instrument themselves!"

During this time, David was still employed by Prince Lowenberg to play in his Court orchestra. In his kindness, the Prince allowed David to take time away from the Court to give concerts in various cities of Europe. When the Prince died and the court orchestra was disbanded, David had already become well-known among conductors and performers as a fine cellist. Like many other musicians, he was now drawn to Vienna, one of the great music centers of Europe.

Soon after his arrival in Vienna, David Popper wrote to his parents. "I am very happy here. I have been offered the job as first cellist in the Vienna Philharmonic Orchestra. The orchestra also plays for the opera. And can you guess what pleasant surprise I had today? Clara Schumann stopped by to invite me to play in a trio with her and a violinist friend. We will play one of her husband's compositions. I can see already how much I am going to enjoy being in Vienna. But I will be home to visit you in a few weeks."

David Popper was a busy man now. Besides his job in the orchestra, he had become a member of a string quartet which gave concerts every other Sunday. Both in the quartet and in the orchestra, he encouraged performances of new music written by young composers. One day, the Vienna Philharmonic had a new symphony by Anton Bruckner placed on their music stands. As they tried their parts, the orchestral musicians became restless, and soon they put down their instruments, "We cannot play such modern music," the concertmaster complained. "It does not even sound like music!"

"Wait, wait, gentlemen," implored David Popper from his place in the cello section. He pleaded with the orchestra members to try Bruckner's piece again. "You will like the piece when you begin to learn it. To be fair, you must try it again," he added.

David was right. They did play Bruckner's piece several times, and soon their ears became accustomed to its harmonies and rhythms.

During this time when David was playing with the Vienna Philharmonic, he had become good friends with a young concert pianist, Sophie Mentor. She often joined the quartet when they needed a pianist. After a time, David and Sophie were married. While she continued to give concerts throughout Europe, David stayed in Vienna to play with the orchestra.

After one of her concert tours, Sophie said to David, "Why don't you give up your job with the orchestra so that we can travel together to give concerts?"

David hesitated. He did not want to give up the security of his good position with the orchestra, but eventually he agreed to the plan. The young couple traveled together to give concerts. When they were not traveling, David devoted most of his time to composing cello pieces.

"There is not enough good music for solo cello," David explained to Sophie. "I hope my compositions will not only be exciting and fun to play, but will also help cello students to improve their playing. My pieces will have runs and double stops, fiery ornamentation, and difficult passages that students can use to help build their technique."

"If you will play your own pieces when you give concerts," Sophie said, "cellists everywhere will want to include them on their programs."

Indeed, that is just what happened. More of David Popper's pieces than any other composer's were performed by cellists at that time. Popper's concerts were admired everywhere. After an appearance in Copenhagen, a newspaper article praised him as a cellist and a composer. "One would find it difficult to imagine the unbelievable admiration, cheers and ovations," the article read. "He was the lion of the day. We smoked Popper cigars, and read brochures about Popper which were sold on the streets."

Most of David Popper's recitals were given in the big cities of Europe. He traveled by railroad train from city to city. The trains were slow, and the small rooms were dark, with just a tiny flame from a kerosene lamp hanging from the ceiling to provide a little light. On a trip to Russia, Popper's train stopped off at a small town on the way to the city. He got off the train to go for a short walk, and to get a glass of hot tea for refreshment. A group of townspeople, when they heard who he was, sent a spokesman to greet Popper. "Would you take a little time to play a concert in our small town?" he asked. "We hear very little music here, and we would be honored to have you play for us."

Popper was deeply pleased by this request, and he agreed to go by horse and sleigh to the quiet village. As he carried his cello onto the small stage, the audience all stood and together called out in Russian, "Good evening." The greeting warmed Popper's heart, and he played an unforgetable concert for those simple, appreciative folk.

Everywhere David Popper went, he was received with warm hospitality. In Spain, the King and Queen invited him to play at the Court. First, of course, David would have to give special greetings to the royalty. As he bowed before the Queen, he heard, "Pardon me, Herr Popper, you are stepping on my foot." To David's dismay, he saw it was the King's foot he was

DAVID POPPER

stepping on. Fortunately, the King laughed, and after the concert, he presented Popper with the Crown of Carlos III and a box of fine cigars to show his appreciation for the concert.

Ever since David Popper had been twenty-one years old, he had been traveling, changing jobs, and not feeling settled down anywhere, and now, it seemed that there were many troubles between David and Sophie. They gave up their married life. Sophie continued her career as a pianist, and David accepted an invitation from the city of Budapest in Hungary.

"In recognition of your superb musicianship as a performer and composer," the invitation read, "we wish to invite you to join the faculty of the Royal Hungarian Academy of Music in Budapest."

The Academy of Music grew in importance and stature while David Popper taught there. Now, for the first time, Popper became very interested in teaching. He met with the President of the Academy, Franz Liszt, the well-known virtuoso pianist. Popper explained to Liszt some of his reasons for taking this job. He said, "I would like to be able to pass on to my students, the future generation of cellists, the technical and musical skills that I have learned over the years. But we have so few cello students at the Academy. Could we try to encourage more students to come here to this school?"

Franz Liszt agreed to seek out more students, and within ten years, there were almost more cello students than Popper had time to teach. His days were filled with teaching, composing, and performing in a quartet.

"Johannes Brahms is coming tomorrow," Popper told the others in the quartet. "He wants us to try some of his latest compositions."

The next day, Brahms appeared at the door of the Academy. He was dressed as usual in his shabby shirt and his baggy trousers. He opened the door and went directly to the studio where the quartet was rehearsing.

"*Guten Morgen,*" he bellowed. "Are my good friends ready to take on my piano quintet? You know you are my favorite group for playing my music with such flair and imagination!"

Brahms handed out the parts and sat down at the piano. With great zeal, they played the quintet and although Brahms missed many notes, the enthusiasm of the players carried them through to the end of the piece. In their excitement, the four string players stood up and cheered for Brahms, "Bravo, Bravo!"

Popper continued to travel occasionally to other cities to give recitals. During the intermission of one of his concerts, an elderly man came to him and said, "I have an old manuscript here with parts of a cello concerto sketched out. I want to give it to you. Perhaps you can discover who the composer was."

Popper thanked the man for the manuscript, and for several years he thought nothing more about it. Then one summer, he took the manuscript from his desk and seriously studied it. At last, he was ready to say that this was Franz Joseph Haydn's work - the beginning of a cello concerto. Haydn had died before he was able to finish it, but Popper worked the concerto into concert form.

When he announced his discovery, he was invited to perform the concerto with the orchestra in Frankfurt, Germany. After the first rehearsal, the principal cellist of the orchestra introduced himself to Popper. "My name is Jean Becker," he said, "I am a great admirer of your's. I appreciate very much the many wonderful pieces you have written for the cello, and I play many of them on my concerts. Now we can add this great concerto by Haydn to our repertoire." After this first meeting, Popper and Becker became fast friends.

When Popper was sixty years old, he was invited back to his home city of Prague to play one of his own cello concerti. While he was in the city, he wanted to visit the home where he lived as a child. He found that all the wretched tenements of the ghetto had been destroyed, and new buildings put up in their place. The old opera house was still there, however, and when he entered the hall many of the cellists in the orchestra, who had been students of his, stood to greet their teacher with warm affection. The rehearsal began. Popper played his concerto with a noble and sensitive tone, but soon after the cello and orchestra began to play together, Popper took his bow off the string, and asked for silence. "Gentlemen," he said, "please play a little softer. I am now an old man and cannot play so loud." The orchestra, out of respect for Popper, followed his wishes. After the intermission, with his students listening, he played one of his most beloved pieces, the *Gavotte*.

During David Popper's early years, he helped to develop a new style of cello playing. Later in his life, he was glad to see that young cellists, like Pablo Casals, were coming along with their own new ideas of bowing and shifting. "Let youth speak," he said. Although styles of cello playing would continue to change, the pieces that David Popper wrote, so full of fantasy and good humor and technical challenges, will always be ready to fill an important place in the cello repertoire for students and their teachers.

b. Prague, Czechoslovakia, June 16, 1843
d. Baden, Vienna, Austria, Aug. 7, 1913

HENRY PURCELL

Henry watched with excitement as his father flung his scarlet robe over his shoulders. "Isn't it wonderful?" Henry's mother exclaimed. "Your father will be singing this morning at the coronation of King Charles. The Royal Chapel will be splendid once more with the bright colors of Kings!"

It had been eleven years now since England had last heard music in the churches, or had seen the elegant, colorful robes and vestments for royal occasions. The King had been banished from the throne, but today a new King was to be crowned and music would again sound in the English churches.

It was April. In London the morning air was moist and warm as two-year old Henry, and his brothers Edward and Francis made their own small procession toward the Church of Westminster Abbey. They arrived early to find a good place to watch the parade with the king's violinists in their red vests, and the king's choir in their silk shirts and scarlet robes, marching into the Abbey to perform the special anthems for the crowning of King Charles.

From that day on, Henry's mother often took her son to hear the fine music in The Abbey. The great pipe organ, the band of violins, and the voices of the choir filled the church with beautiful sounds. No wonder young Henry wanted to join in!

When he was just a small boy, he liked to compose and sing his own songs. "Don't you think we should try to get a place for

Henry in the Chapel Royal choir?" Henry's father asked his wife. "He already is showing a fine talent for music."

"Yes, I do believe he is ready," she answered, although she knew that if he joined the choir he could not live at home. He would live at the Abbey with the other choir boys and have his schooling there as well.

Henry's father spoke to Henry Cooke, the choirmaster, and just after Henry's eighth birthday, he was accepted as one of the twelve children of the chapel. He was outfitted with a scarlet cloak lined with velvet, a scarlet suit and coat trimmed with silver and silk lace. He was given 3 pairs of shoes, shirts, 1 pair of silk stockings and 2 of wool, 2 hats with bands, 2 laced cuffs and 4 plain, 3 handkerchiefs, 3 pairs of gloves, and 2½ pieces of ribbon for trimming garters and shoelaces. At the choir school, he would have lessons on the flute, violin, and organ, and his schooling would be mostly writing and Latin.

Captain Cooke, as the choirmaster was called, was a fine singer, and he taught his boys well. King Charles encouraged the boys to compose their own anthems, and he allowed them to be performed in the chapel. Henry was eager to offer an anthem of his own.

One day, carrying a large parchment under his arm, Henry knocked on the door of Captain Cooke's study.

"What is it, my boy?" Captain Cooke asked.

"I have written a piece to celebrate King Charles' birthday. I have called it *Address of the children of the Chapel Royal to the*

*King, and their Master Captain Cooke, on his Majesty's
Birthday A.D. 1670."*

"Good for you, Henry. His Majesty will be delighted,"
Henry Cooke said. "We shall try it at our next rehearsal."
Indeed, the King was pleased when he heard Henry's birthday
composition, and he sent a message of thanks to the young
composer.

For six more years, Henry continued as a choir boy, but
when he was fourteen years old, his voice changed and he could
no longer sing the soprano parts in the chapel choir.

"Henry," his new choirmaster John Blow said, "when our
choir boys' voices change, they can continue to work at the
Royal Chapel. You can be an apprentice to take care of the
keyboard and wood instruments. In payment for your work,
you will be given your clothes and a small allowance." Henry
did his job well, and the next year, he was given the
responsibility of tuning the great organ in Westminster Abbey.
Besides this, he was to be paid to copy organ music for some
new anthems. He spent many long hours in a dimly lighted
room in The Abbey, writing on lined music paper the thousands
of notes in two books of organ pieces. When he did this well, he
was appointed to be composer for the king's violins, taking the
place of one of the most distinguished musicians of the time. For
these jobs, Henry received a regular salary.

Henry's father had, at one time, been a composer for violins,
and he was pleased about his son's new appointment. "You have

HENRY PURCELL

a great responsibility now, Henry. The King's band of 24 violins is first in the royal favor. Do you know that when King Charles was banished from England, he spent some time in France at the Court of Louis XIV? The French King had a band of 24 violins, and Jean Baptiste Lully was his composer. Not to be outdone, our King wants a band of violins, too, and he wants it to be just as fine as the French King's!"

"Yes, and I will do my very best," Henry promised. "We will play at all the court functions. I have been told that his Majesty wants to be entertained at meal times, too, but for that he wants light and airy pieces. He is even thinking about having the violins play a symphony in the church services at the Royal Chapel. That is something that has never been done before. It is plain to see that I will be very busy!"

"I can tell you one thing, Henry, and I know this from experience," Henry's father said. "The King likes pieces with straightforward rhythms so he can beat time with his foot!"

Not long after, he became composer to the king's violins. Henry, at the age of eighteen, was also appointed to be the organist at Westminster Abbey. At last, in addition to his salary, he was paid enough to rent a house in St. Ann's Lane. Now he could ask Frances Peters to marry him.

In spite of all his responsibilities at the Court and the Abbey, Henry Purcell found time to write music for plays in the London theatres. Often, the players were the same 24 violinists of the king's band, and he had his choice of some of the best singers in the realm. One singer had an especially deep bass voice, and Purcell liked to provide him with very low notes to show off his skill.

One day, a Royal Courtier came to Purcell. "The King will be returning in August from his summer stay at Windsor Castle," he said. "You must have a piece ready to welcome him home." And so, as he did for every such occasion, Purcell wrote a special anthem. This time he called it *Swifter Isis, Swifter Flow*, asking the river to bring the King swiftly back to London.

After the death of King Charles, and then King James, King William of Orange and Queen Mary took the throne of England. Henry Purcell's duties continued, and he obliged the Court with compositions for every occasion. For the birthday of the new Queen, who loved music very much, he set to music the splended verse, *Now Does the Glorious Day Appear.* Queen Mary was so delighted with Purcell's music, that he was officially appointed member of the king's private music, where he already had served as harpsichord player.

Sometimes Henry Purcell was asked by people outside of the Court to compose music. On King's Street in Westminster, not far from where Purcell lived, was a school belonging to Louis Maidwell.

"Will you write an ode to one of my student's poems?" he asked Purcell. Obligingly, in the space of two weeks, Purcell composed *Celestial Music* and it was given its first performance at Louis Maidwell's school.

One of Purcell's most famous pieces which is still performed is the opera *Dido and Aeneas*. He wrote it for the young ladies at Josias Priest's school in Chelsea. He was thirty years old then, and he began writing much more music for the theatre.

During the rehearsal for one of his plays, an especially gifted boy soprano was practicing a song that Purcell had written. One of the musicians began to instruct the young boy. "Do it like this, with this ornamentation," he commanded.

Purcell, with the authority of the composer, interrupted, saying, "Oh, we can let him do it his own way; he will grace it more naturally than you or I can teach him." No wonder people loved Purcell for his kind and thoughtful spirit!

On the eve of the day celebrating St. Cecelia, the Saint in whose honor he had written so many of his most beautiful pieces, Henry Purcell died at the age of thirty-six. At his wife's suggestion, he was laid to rest in the north aisle of Westminster Abbey at the foot of the organ which he had played for over fifteen years. At his funeral, all the singers and players gathered together in their finest vestments, and performed the music that Purcell had written for the queen less than a year before. A marble tablet was placed on a pillar beside his tomb. It read, "He has gone to that blessed place where only his harmony can be exceeded."

b. London, England, 1659
d. Dean's Yard, Westminster, London, England, November 21, 1695

CHARLES CAMILLE SAINT-SAENS

At the end of the narrow street where they lived, two young women sat by the well under a big linden tree. They were listening for the sound of approaching carriage wheels. Suddenly the gate opened, and two horses pulling the carriage came to a stop. Out jumped a tiny boy.

"Camille, Camille," the two women cried out as they lifted the boy into their arms. Little Camille Saint-Saens was home again at last.

Camille's father died when his son was just two months old. The boy had been frail and sickly. He and his mother and aunt had lived in a third floor flat on a dark, narrow street, where garbage was thrown out of the windows, and foul-smelling water trickled down the gutters. The air in Paris was not good for a child who had weak lungs.

"The doctor says we must send the boy to live in fresh air and sunshine," Camille's mother explained to her aunt, and so for two years, Camille lived with friends in the open countryside, away from Paris. The baby gained in health and vigor.

Home again with his mother and aunt, the little boy grew accustomed to city life. He heard sounds so different from the kinds he had heard in the countryside. From morning until night, down the Rue de Jardinet came peddlars calling out their food and wares. Strolling singers, with drums and flutes, played their tunes. Watercarriers sloshed their buckets. Old men selling brooms and old clothes shouted up to the windows of the houses lining the streets, and loudest of all, was the squeaky barrel organ, playing its tunes over and over again.

Camille was always fascinated by sounds of every kind. "Look at Camille," his mother said to her aunt. "See how he sits in front of the fire to hear the water begin to boil in the copper kettle."

In later years, Camille, himself, remembered it this way. "I waited by the kettle with a passionate curiousity for its first murmurs, its slow crescendo so full of surprises, and the appearance of a microscopic oboe note that shrilled on upward until the boiling of the water made it cease."

Camille's mother had high hopes that her little son would become a musician. She and her aunt did everything they could to give him the love and encouragement he needed. When Camille was two and one-half years old, his Aunt Charlotte thought the time had come to open the small piano in their sitting room. Camille walked up to the piano and instead of absently pounding the keys, he delicately struck one key. He listened with fascination as the sound died away, and then struck another key. "I think Camille is ready for piano lessons," Aunt Charlotte said, watching Camille care so much for every note. She taught him the names of the notes, and soon he was playing pieces written by Mozart and Haydn.

One day, the piano tuner came to the house. Camille, in the

next room, surprised the tuner by calling out the names of the notes as they were played. "Will you play a piece for me?" he asked Camille. The tiny boy jumped up on the bench and played a short piece by Mozart. The piano tuner clapped. Then Camille played the same piece, but in another key, and then another. Everyone was amazed at the boy's skill.

Soon, Camille began to compose his own pieces. "Look what I have for you," the four-year old Camille called to his mother one day. It was his first piano composition. Sometimes he composed waltzes that were too difficult for his small hands to play, so he wrote them straight onto the paper. "I will invite my friend to the house to play the pieces for me," he told his mother, "so that I can hear with my ears what I have heard only in my head."

In the same house, but in the flat below Camille's, lived an artist painter, whose daughter was a singer and a good friend of Camille's mother. Camille wanted to do something nice for the young lady. "Here is a song," Camille said. "I wrote it especially for you."

"Oh, thank you, Camille," she answered. Then she added, "Can you come to our flat this evening? The famous painter, Ingres (pronounced Anghr), is coming for a visit. He used to be a violinist in the Theatre orchestra, and he still loves music. He painted portraits of Paganini and other musicians. I know he would like to hear you play."

That evening Camille put on his best shirt, and went

downstairs. He played a piece by Mozart for Monsieur Ingres, and then dedicated to him one of his own pieces called *Adagio*.

Several weeks later, Monsieur Ingres came back for another visit. He handed Camille a small package. "What is it?" the boy asked.

"It is something I made for you to show how much I appreciated the way you played the piece by Mozart, and for the piece you composed for me."

Camille opened the box. In it was a beautiful medallion, with a profile of Mozart painted on one side. On the other side he had written, "To Monsieur Saint-Saens, a charming interpreter of the divine artist."

As a small boy, Camille was not satisfied playing pieces written for children's exercises. He wanted to practice by playing pieces of the masters, and Aunt Charlotte was careful to see that the boy played them correctly. He studied all the piano music he could find. Then he studied many scores of orchestral pieces and operas. He wrote out his exercises every day, and figured out how different pieces were put together to make them sound beautiful.

When Camille was six years old, he wrote a short ballad for a young singer whose father was a lover of music. To show how much he appreciated the song Camille had written, he gave him as a gift two handsome red volumes of the orchestral score of Mozart's opera, *Don Giovanni*. Every day Camille studied the score, until the music became a part of him. In his older years, Saint-Saens explained how important that gift had been. "Never can there have been a happier inspiration," he wrote.

When Camille was not playing the piano or composing, he was busying himself with other endeavors. He studied Latin with a tutor when he was seven and quickly mastered the language. He read the great French masterpieces. He had no teacher for science, but he set up a window box on the balcony of his home, and planted different kinds of seeds to watch the way they grew. He studied the life cycles of caterpillars and butterflies, and often went to the stone quarries with his axe, looking for fossils. He watched the moon and stars through his opera glasses, and was excited when a friend of his mother's took him to the observatory to see the moon magnified through the telescope. There was hardly anything that did not capture the boy's interest, and he was ready to learn all he could.

Camille's first concert in his own neighborhood took place when he was not yet five years old. "He is like Mozart," people exclaimed. The critics wrote about "this small yet already great pianist who played with miraculous ease and facility — and without the music in front of him . . . All this without contortions, or shaking his hair or preening himself . . . "

"We must plan a series of concerts for Camille," his teacher suggested to Madame Saint-Saens. But Camille's mother disagreed.

"No, he must study more. There is still much for him to learn."

People standing nearby, who had heard the boy playing such mature music, asked if Camille can play such music now, what music will he be playing when he is twenty? Madame Saint-Saens calmly replied, "He will be playing his own."

News of the remarkable young musician spread far. The Duchesse d'Orleans invited him to visit her Court. "Camille, what shall I do? My son, the young Count of Paris, will not practice his music," she explained. "Perhaps if he hears you, he will be more interested in practicing."

Camille was only too glad to help. He played pieces by Bach and Handel, but the young Count only banged loudly on his drums, and rode his rocking horse. But the next day, a messenger came to 3 Rue du Jardinet, with a package for Camille Saint-Saens. It was a gold watch, addressed to "The young artist and future teacher." It was gift of appreciation from the Duchesse.

Although Camille was already well known, he continued to study and work hard. When he was thirteen years old, he entered the Conservatory. This was the same school where Lully and Gossec had worked many years before. The building itself was old and dilapidated and much too small for all the students who came to study there. Inside, the walls were dingy and the paint was peeling. But Camille loved its old look and he liked to stand in the courtyard, listening to the many sounds of all the people inside practicing on their different instruments.

Camille's harmony teacher thought it would be a good idea

for his student to learn to play the organ. When he was asked to sit down before the large instrument, and try to play, he was frightened by the strange sounds that came out. The other students in the class laughed. The teacher said, "Camille, you will just sit in the class and listen. Some day you may be allowed to play."

At the end of the class time, Camille went home. "Mama," he said, "I am going to study the 48 organ pieces by Bach. Someday, the organ teacher will ask me to play, and I will be ready." For several weeks, Camille worked hard to learn the pieces by Bach.

Then the day came. As he sat in the class listening, he heard that none of the other students could play the piece the teacher asked for. "How about you, Camille? What can you do?" the organ teacher asked. To the great surprise and satisfaction of the teacher and students, Camille sat at the organ and was able to play with great skill the piece by Bach that the teacher wanted to hear.

That year, he won the silver medal at the Conservatory.

Camille Saint-Saens wanted more than anything else to become a composer. He needed to earn some money, so he took a job as organist in a church. Each day, when he had finished his work at the church, he went home to write a symphony. When he finished the composition, his teacher at the conservatory told Camille, "We will begin to rehearse your symphony next week, but we will not tell anyone that you have written it. If people know that an eighteen year old student is the composer of a symphony, they will only laugh."

The rehearsals began. Camille and his mother and a few friends sat in the rehearsal hall. In front of them were seated two famous musicians who had known Camille some years before. At the end of the rehearsal, Camille could hear them speaking. "This is remarkably beautiful music," one of them said. "The composer must be a very gifted man."

Later, they were told that it was the eighteen year-old Camille Saint-Saens who had composed the symphony. Next day, in the mail, Camille received a letter from Charles Gounod, the famous musician who had been sitting in front of him at the rehearsal.

"My Dear Camille," it read. "Yesterday I learned officially that you were the composer of the Symphony performed on Sunday. I had doubted it—but now that I doubt no longer, I would reproach myself did I not tell you what joy it gave me. You are far in advance of your years: carry on - and remember that on Sunday, 18th December 1853 you contracted the obligation of becoming a great master—Your very happy and devoted friend, Charles Gounod. Congratulations to your worthy mother. P.S. I hope to hear it again and want very much to read it."

From this performance of his first symphony, Camille Saint-Saens was indeed on his way to becoming a great master. He became good friends with many other composers. With others he had arguments. But people everywhere enjoyed his music and he travelled to many parts of the world to perform.

Camille enjoyed good times, too. He liked to go to parties just for fun, or to gather friends together for informal evenings of music making. His mother, Mme. Saint-Saens often invited musicians and painters to Monday evening receptions in her home and Camille was the one to provide fun and good spirits. Sometimes he invited friends to wear costumes and they acted out small parts of operas. Camille would sing in a high voice to act the part of women characters. These parties gave the young composer a chance to meet important people in the world of art.

On one of these Monday evenings, Camille heard a knock at the door. "Ah, Pablo, come in," he said as he welcomed a young boy carrying a violin case under his arm. "Let me introduce you to my friends. This is Pablo Sarasate. He has just won the first prize in violin at the Paris Conservatory." The thirteen year old boy bowed shyly, but later in the evening when he played his violin, he performed with brilliance and fire.

"May I speak with you for a moment?" Pablo asked Camille. "I have been playing some nice short pieces in my concerts, but I would like it so much if you could compose a violin concerto for me."

Saint-Saens was very pleased to be asked by this violin virtuoso, and in a short time he wrote the Violin Concerto in A major, dedicating it to Pablo de Sarasate. Not long afterwards, when Saint-Saens was twenty-eight years old, and Sarasate was nineteen, he wrote the *Introduction and Rondo Capriccioso* for him. Twenty years later, at another of the Monday evening parties, Sarasate performed the third violin concerto that Camille wrote for him. Over the years, the two musicians had become good friends, and Sarasate taught Camille many secrets about violin playing. This was a great help to Saint-Saens as he wrote pieces for the violin.

Saint-Saens' life was full with composing and performing. After an especially strenuous concert tour, he decided to take a rest in a small Austrian village. "I remember," he said to himself one morning, "many years ago when I taught at the Niedermeyer school, I promised my students that I would write a special piece, imitating various animals. Now I have time to do it."

Saint-Saens enjoyed writing this piece for orchestra. He called it *Carnival of the Animals*. The piece for the cello was to imitate the graceful, floating swan, and he wrote it especially for an old friend, the cellist Lebouc. The other animals he imitated with instruments were the elephant, the tortoise, fossils, roosters and hens, fish, cuckoo, rabbits and birds, a lion, a Mongolian ass, and even pianists!

There was one period in Saint-Saens' life when he was not a happy man, and he spent most of his days by himself. He found himself arguing and competing with composers who had new ideas about music. Then, when he was fifty-three, his aged mother died. She was the only person whom he deeply cared for and Saint-Saens never recovered from his loneliness. He collected all his belongings and gave them to a museum.

Then he disappeared. He travelled far away to the Canary Islands. He assumed another name and lived in quiet solitude for a time. But his peaceful existence was suddenly ended when someone discovered who Saint-Saens really was.

He returned to France, and took up his composing again. His famous opera, *Sampson and Dalila* was performed. His mailbox was filled each day with letters from people asking for musical advice, for his opinions about their compositions, or for his autograph.

One day, in the mail, an invitation came from England. "We request the honor of your presence at the celebration of the 50th year of the Cambridge University Musical Society. We wish to award to you an honorary degree at that occasion." Peter Tchaikovsky, Max Bruch, and Edward Greig were also invited and before they took the train to Cambridge, Tchaikovsky and Saint-Saens stopped off in London to play a concert of their own compositions. Saint-Saens would return many times to England where his audiences always greeted him with great enthusiasm.

Saint-Saens remained active throughout his life. Even at the age of eighty-six, in the last year of his life, he conducted rehearsals for his opera. At a concert, he played from memory the piano part of his Septet, with his fingers flying over the keyboard at a speed that the others in the group could hardly

CHARLES CAMILLE SAINT-SAENS

match. Everyday he practiced piano for two hours, practiced singing and wrote letters.

Saint-Saens often said that children should be encouraged to study the wonders of nature, and that they should be filled with a sense of beauty by surrounding them with perfect examples of art. Camille Saint-Saens has certainly contributed his own art to enrich the lives of every child.

b. Paris, France, October 9, 1835
d. Algiers, Algieria, December 16, 1921

GIOVANNI BATTISTA SAMMARTINI

First supper, then music," Alexis said as his wife carried the tureen of steaming soup to the table. The polished cypress boards gleamed in the warm light of the candles, as the family bowed their heads to give thanks for the evening meal they were about to share.

No sooner had the prayer had been offered, than Giovanni spoke up. "Father, please tell us again that story about the time you came to Italy."

Alexis enjoyed telling his sons about his early life in France where he had been an oboe player. "When I was a boy in France," he told them, "my name was Alexis Saint-Martin. When I moved to Italy, my friends had trouble pronouncing my French name, so I changed it to Sammartini to make it easier for them to say. When you were born, your mother and I gave you real Italian names. But, come, enough of that now. Let us finish our supper, and for dessert we can play some oboe music."

Giovanni and Giuseppi took oboe lessons from their father, and when they were in their teens they both took jobs in the theatre orchestra of Milan. Giuseppi was satisifed with his job, but Giovanni became restless. He wanted to write music of his own.

With encouragement from his family, Giovanni learned what he could about composing, and when he was twenty-four years old, he composed a group of five cantatas, written for singers and orchestra. The pieces were composed especially for a church in Milan to be performed at the Friday services during Lent. The congregation of the church were very pleased with Giovanni Sammartini's music. The Bishop who was taking part in the Friday church services was also impressed with the beauty of his music. He invited the young composer to visit him the next week in his Church study.

That evening, as the family gathered together again around the supper table, Giovanni said to his brother, "Giuseppi, the Bishop has asked me to visit him next week. Will you come with me?"

"Of course I will," he answered. The next week the two young men set out on foot to the center of the city where the spires of the church jutted skyward from the low houses crowded around it. The two young men carried white paper lanterns to light their way through the dark streets of Milan. Suddenly, the clatter of wheels and the pounding of horses' hooves rose up behind them.

"Watch out!" shouted Giovanni as he grabbed his brother's arm and pulled him onto the large stones that lined the narrow way.

"Oh, that was too close!" gasped Giuseppi, shaking his fist at the carriage driver as he sped away.

For a few moments, they stood still to catch their breath, and then continued on their way.

When they arrived at the church, Giuseppi waited in the

court yard while his brother went in through the small side door of the church to find the Bishop in his study. It seemed to the waiting brother like an age before Giovanni reappeared at the church door.

"Well, I thought you would never come," Giuseppi complained. "What did the Bishop say?"

"He asked me if I would accept the position as director of music of the Church. Can you guess my answer?" Giovanni said with a smile.

"You should feel proud," Giuseppi exclaimed to his brother. "Only twenty-six years old, and already you are master of music, a composer and an organist. No wonder people are calling you 'molto celebre'!"

Indeed, prominent people in Milan came to think highly of Giovanni Sammartini as an excellent church musician, well known for his composing and conducting. Music had an important place in this city of beautiful churches and cathedrals, where many composers lived, and where their new music was often heard, not only in the churches, but in the opera houses as well. Visitors to Milan were sure to ask when they could hear a performance by Sammartini. Every seat in the church would be taken on the days when he was expected to perform.

As time went on, Sammartini became known in cities all over Europe. As far away as Holland, a big celebration was being held for the one hundredth birthday of the Theatre of Amsterdam. When Antonio Vivaldi was invited there to conduct, he chose to perform one of Sammartini's symphonies. Soon even concert goers as distant from Milan as Paris and London and Vienna were listening to his music, sometimes in churches, and sometimes in the spacious courts where wealthy noblemen took pride in the private concerts they gave in their elegant music rooms. Dukes and princes would ask composers to provide music for these lavish gatherings, and the composers themselves would often be invited. Many years later, in Vienna and Salzburg, the young Wolfgang Amadeus Mozart, and the older Franz Joseph Haydn, dressed in their velvet breeches and ruffled silk shirts, attended these concerts when Sammartini's music was played.

The young Mozart had heard so much about Giovanni Sammartini, that he had expressed the hope that some day they would meet. Finally, when Mozart was fourteen years old, and Sammartini was seventy, there was a special occasion that made this possible.

The Count Carl Joseph was giving a reception at his Court for Wolfgang Mozart and his father, Leopold. Of course, Sammartini was invited. After the reception, Leopold Mozart wrote a letter to his wife at home, telling about the evening in the court of Count Joseph. "Wolfgang has given evidence of his knowledge in the presence of Maestro Sammartini," he wrote. "Sammartini and the other brilliant people there were amazed at the young boy's ability."

At the end of that year, young Mozart wrote an opera which

was performed in Milan. Many musicians and music lovers in Italy were outraged that this young boy from another country should have an opera performed in Italy. They made all manner of nasty comments. But Sammartini came to Mozart's support, and praised the young composer's work. "Sammartini is my true friend," Mozart said.

In the time when Sammartini lived in Italy, the people of his country were glad for any reason to have a big musical festival. The best composers were called upon to write music especially for the celebrations. This time, it was a birthday that was cause for the festivities. Archduke Leopold's birthday was coming soon, and the Count at the Sforza Castle asked Giovanni to write a composition worthy of this important event.

"Please come to the Castle," the Count wrote to Giovanni.

Giovanni answered the Count's request, and when they met, the Count asked his guest, "As you approached the Castle, did you notice the gently sloping grassy bank on one side of the moat? I have been thinking that this would be a fine stage for a concert, and I would like you to consider planning and conducting a series of concerts there."

The idea appealed to Sammartini, and he agreed to the unusual plan. Three times a week, enthusiastic audiences came to hear these outdoor concerts on the banks of the Castle moat.

With all this, Sammartini was a very busy man. He had his duties at the large church in Milan, where he had become leading church organist and composer. Besides, he not only was kept very busy as director of music in ten different churches in his home city, he also organized his own traveling orchestra that gave outdoor concerts in large and small towns all over Italy.

"Sammartini is the greatest of them all," people would say when they heard his orchestra play. "Listen to his fresh style - so energetic, so new, so spirited and free."

Many of Sammartini's ideas had an influence on other composers of his time. Luigi Boccherini, the cellist, admired the composer's work. The two men met for the first time at a celebration honoring the wife of the Archduke Leopold. She was visiting Milan, and many concerts were given during the festivities. Musicians from all over Italy were invited to take part. Vandini and Tartini came, Luigi Boccherini, the cellist, and his father, the double bass player came. But the guest of honor was Sammartini, for whom the Count sent a special carriage each day to transport him back and forth to the concerts. During the reception, Boccherini said to Giovanni, "It is an honor to have finally met the great Sammartini. I have learned so much from hearing your work performed. It is full of grace and vitality. Surely, the violinists can never fall asleep playing your pieces. You give them so much to do! Even the second violins have important parts to play! Now I am inspired to return to my home in Lucca to take up my composing again."

Sammartini continued with his busy schedule and his prolific composing until the end of his life. People were amazed at his vigor as his compositions continued to speak with elegant style and lyric melodies.

His plans for his seventy-fourth year listed many important concerts for the eleven churches where he was in charge of musical activities. But suddenly, on a chilly day in January, in his seventy-fourth year, Sammartini died. Three days later, in the Cathedral of Saint Ambrogio in Milan, a memorial service was sung for him, and musicians from everywhere came to play his symphonies. Sammartini was honored "not only as a member of the Congregation of Musicians, but also because he was in his musical profession a most excellent master and celebrated by a most brilliant renown."

b. Milan, Itlay, 1700 or 1701
d. Milan, Italy, Jan. 15, 1775

DOMENICO SCARLATTI

Mimo, Mimo," Flaminia called out the window to her little brother, Domenico. "Come home, Mimo. Father is here and he is ready to give us our music lesson."

Domenico could hardly hear his sister's voice over the clatter of wagon wheels, barking dogs, the songs of the vendors calling out their wares, and the shouts of the children playing in the street.

"Mimo, Mimo," Flaminia called again.

"Coming, coming," Domenico answered. He threw down the pebbles he had been collecting, and ran into the house.

"We will just have enough time before supper to practice our little opera," Domenico's father told the children. Their father, Alessandro Scarlatti, was well-known for the operas he composed for the theatre in Naples, but this little opera was a special one to celebrate the anniversary of Domenico's aunt and uncle. "They will be here tomorrow night, so we must be ready."

Ever since Domenico was a tiny baby, he had been surrounded with music. At home there was always someone singing or playing, but he also heard music in the cathedral, in the streets, and down by the wharf where the boats came in. In Naples, a city by the sea, it seemed that everyone loved music - the fishermen and the fish mongers, the merchants and the vendors, the children and their mothers and fathers, and even the wealthy nobles who lived in the palace at the top of the hill.

Everyone in the Scarlatti family, and the aunts and uncles, too, sang or played an instrument or composed music. The household was swarming constantly with musicians, poets, and painters coming to talk with Alessandro about stage designs, or the words of an opera, or the music that he was composing.

The ten children in the Scarlatti family had only to open their ears to learn about music, and as they grew old enough to help, Alessandro put them to work arranging and copying music, tuning instruments, and even accompanying at rehearsals.

By the time Domenico was sixteen years old, he was ready to try for his first job as a professional musician. "I am going for my audition at the palace next week to try for a position at the Royal Chapel," he told Flaminia. "Do you remember how many times you and I used to run down the hill to the Chapel by the water, to marvel at the beautiful alter gleaming with its bronze statues and precious stones?"

"Yes, of course I remember," Flaminia answered. "But now I can hardly believe that you might be a musician to the Royal Chapel! Can it be possible?"

As he had hoped, Domenico was appointed to be the composer and organist at the Royal Chapel where his father, Alessandro, was director of music.

"Now," Domenico told his sister, "I can enjoy the beautiful Chapel every day."

Domenico's job at the Royal Chapel required him to compose music and play the organ for the religious services. He enjoyed his work, and perhaps he would have stayed in Naples had not his father advised him, and his brothers, to leave the city. There was trouble in Naples as neighboring countries argued and fought about who should rule the city. Alessandro, who had already left Naples, thought it best for his sons to move to Venice.

Alessandro sent a message to Domenico. "Mimo," he wrote, "I will write a letter of introduction to his Royal Highness, Prince Fernando de Medici. I want you to leave Naples, and make your way to this beautiful city."

In his letter to Prince Fernando, Alessandro wrote: "This son of mine is an eagle whose wings are grown; he must not remain idle in the nest . . . He has advanced much since he was able to serve Your Highness personally three years ago."

Obeying his father's wishes, Domenico left his job in Naples and went to Venice. In that Italian city, too, the people loved music. There were many festivals and masked parties. There was music in the public squares and on the canals where the gondoliers sang their lilting melodies. Everyone, rich and poor alike, took part in the musical festivities in Venice.

Scarlatti, now twenty years old, had developed remarkable skill at the harpsichord, but being a quiet and reserved person, he never performed in public. The pieces he composed, he felt, were for private audiences.

One day, Domenico was invited to the home of a nobleman who was having an evening of music. First on the program was a well-known harpsichordist, Thomas Roseingrave. Next, a singer performed.

"Now we shall have another performance at the harpsichord," the host announced. Domenico, standing in the corner of the room, dressed in black and in a black wig, walked forward shyly and sat down at the harpsichord. He began to play. The notes and phrases surged up and down as his fingers raced over the keyboard. Everyone who listened was spellbound.

When the performance was over, Thomas Roseingrave whispered to his friend sitting beside him, "I have never heard such passages of execution and effect. I never thought such perfection was possible. Who is that young man?"

"His name is Domenico Scarlatti, Alessandro's son," his friend replied.

"Well, I must meet this young genius."

Scarlatti and Roseingrave were introduced. They soon became fast friends. Roseingrave was from England, and was the first to publish Scarlatti's harpsichord sonatas. He encouraged pianists all over England to play Scarlatti's music.

When Domenico was twenty-four years old, he moved once again. This time he went to Rome to take his father's place in the court of the Queen of Poland. The Queen had moved her court to Rome to escape the war in her own country, and when Alessandro Scarlatti decided he wanted to return to Naples, he recommended his son, Domenico, to the Queen.

In his new position in Rome, Domenico met many important composers and virtuoso performers. One of the most lively meeting places in the city was the Palace of Cardinal Pietro Otobini. He was a wealthy personage in the Catholic Church, and he held weekly chamber music recitals in the spacious music rooms of his Palace. The Cardinal owned more than a dozen harpsichords, each one of them beautifully sculptured, with cases painted inside and out by famous Italian artists. One of the harpsichords was gilded with fine gold, and had legs carved with cupids among festoons of leaves and fruit.

It was at one of Cardinal Otobini's weekly recitals that Domenico met Arcangelo Corelli, one of the finest violinists and composers in Italy, who led performances of chamber music at the Palace. At another recital, Domenico met George Frederick Handel. The Cardinal, thinking it would be a great game, arranged a competition between Handel and Scarlatti.

"You will play one piece on the organ, then another on the harpsichord," the Cardinal directed Handel. "Then Scarlatti will play, and we shall see who is the better."

"Oh," declared Scarlatti when the playing was over. "Maestro Handel is by far the better organist."

"But you, my dear Scarlatti, are by far the better harpsichordist!"

Domenico was so impressed by the way Handel could coax every sound from the organ, that he followed him all over Italy, learning from the master organist the real power of that great instrument.

From Corelli, Handel, and his father, Domenico had learned to compose music according to the strict rules of the time. For the ten years that Domenico lived in Rome, his father, Alessandro, was still the important musician of the Scarlatti family. The son moved quietly in the musical shadow of his famous father who had already composed at least one hundred and fourteen operas.

Soon, however, there would be a change in Domenico's life to make a big difference in the way he composed music.

The Pope at the Vatican in Rome sent out a decree making Portugal a separate country. Joao V became King of Portugal. He was a wealthy King because his ships sailed from Portugal, over the great ocean to the Americas, and came back loaded with gold and silver. The King, who loved music, could have anything he wanted.

"I want to hire Domenico Scarlatti as music director in my Court," the King declared, and he sent his courtier to Rome to invite the young Scarlatti to the Court in Portugal.

So it was that at the age of thirty six, Domenico moved from Italy to Portugal to begin a new life, free from the loving, but domineering influence of his father, Alessandro.

To serve the King, Scarlatti composed not only for the Chapel, but for the feasts and celebrations of the Court. One morning, when Scarlatti appeared at the royal apartments for

DOMENICO SCARLATTI

his daily appointment, the King said, "Domenico, my daughter Maria Barbara shows promise of being a gifted musician. Her great grandfather had a sincere interest in music and owned a fabulous collection of books about music. Her grandfather was a fine composer. Maria Barbara has asked many times to begin harpsichord lessons. I would like you to be her teacher."

"It would be an honor, indeed," Domenico replied.

"In addition," the King went on, "my younger brother, Don Antonio also is passionately fond of music, and wishes you to teach him."

"Again, I will be honored," Domenico answered.

Both Maria Barbara and Don Antonio became devoted pupils of Domenico Scarlatti. After three years of service to the King, Domenico made a brief trip back to Rome, and then to Naples where he visited his ailing father. Not long after, Alessandro died.

Domenico returned to the Court of the King of Portugal. Maria Barbara, the King's daughter, resumed her lessons. "Here are some new pieces I have composed for you," Domenico told his young pupil. "These will help you in your progress as a musician. If you practice them carefully each day, I will compose more pieces for you." When Maria Barbara had mastered all the difficulties of each piece, her teacher composed new ones with even more difficult challenges.

When Maria Barbara was fourteen years old, her father, the King, arranged her engagement to marry the Crown Prince of

Spain, who was eleven years old.

"To formally announce the engagement," the King told Domenico, "we shall have a celebration of the very finest. We will have fireworks, and the lighting of the whole city. You will write special music for the occasion. The marriage of my daughter and the Crown Prince will mark the joining of Portugal and Spain. Maria Barbara will move to the Spanish Court, and she has asked that you accompany her, and continue her musical education as well as providing music for the Spanish Court."

Domenico was happy at the prospect of a secure position in the Spanish Court, and so he felt ready to have his family arrange a marriage for him. His family chose Maria Caterina Gentili. Domenico was forty-three years old, and Maria was sixteen.

A new country, and a new wife marked a new beginning in Domenico's musical development. Now Scarlatti began to soak up the sights, and sounds, and customs of Spain. He was free from the domination of his father, and the strict Italian style of writing music. He composed a large number of sonatas, and his compositions became more free in harmony and rhythm. He could improvise and compose at the keyboard, trying all kinds of ideas that his fingers could discover. All the while, Maria Barbara never failed to encourage Scarlatti in his work.

"May I play my latest sonata for you?" Scarlatti asked the Queen. "I have tried new harmonies and hand-crossings in this one."

He played for the Queen. "Now may I try it?" she asked. She went over to her favorite harpsichord, the one ornately decorated in gold and red lacquer. She sat down on the velvet-covered bench, and tried the new sonata.

"Oh, I will have to practice this," she said laughing. "You are always trying so many new musical ideas! The last one I tried to play, with the arpeggios running up and down the keyboard, and the trills and leaps, I am only just beginning to master!"

During the last twenty-eight years of Domenico Scarlatti's life, living in Spain in the service of the Queen, he wrote hundreds of sonatas. He enjoyed his freedom to compose as he wished, and he called his music an "ingenious jesting with art". He could try out his ideas, with each sonata having something new to challenge the performer. His pieces still stand as a challenge to every musician, and he certainly wrote enough music to keep anyone busy for a lifetime!

b. Naples, Italy, October 26, 1685
d. Madrid, Spain, July 23, 1757

FRANZ PETER SCHUBERT

Tap, tap, tap went the tip of the cello bow on the music stand. "Ready, play," said Franz Peter's father as he and his three children practiced the first movement of a string quartet written by Wolfgang Amadeus Mozart some years before.

"We may be too poor to give our children fancy clothes or many toys to play with," declared Herr Schubert to his wife, "but we can give them the joy of music."

Herr Schubert was a schoolmaster in a small town near Vienna. It was important that his children should have musical training. Soon after Franz started school, when he was six years old, his father sent him to study with a music teacher in their small town of Lichtenthal. At the end of the first lesson, the teacher asked Franz, "Who has been your music teacher before you came to me?"

"There has been no other," answered Franz.

"Then how is it that you already know so much about music?" the teacher asked.

Franz explained, "I have a friend who works in a piano factory. He took me along to the factory to watch him work. When it was time to go home, my friend searched all around the workshop, looking for me, but he could not find me because I was busy making up tunes and exercises on the pianos in the storeroom. My friend has taken me back to the factory many times since then."

"So that is how you have learned," Franz's teacher exclaimed in amazement.

One day Franz's teacher came to Father Schubert with tears in his eyes. "I have never had such a pupil before," he said. "Whenever I want to teach Franz anything, he already knows it."

Franz had a beautiful singing voice, too. In Vienna there was a famous boys' singing school, and Franz's father wanted very much to have his son study there. Franz had often heard the boys singing in the imperial chapel of the emperor. His eyes grew big when he saw the choir boys in their uniforms, trimmed with bands of gold. "Oh, how I would love to go to that school," thought Franz, "but my father does not have enough money to send me there. I will study hard for the examination anyway, and perhaps some chance will come to me."

So when Franz Schubert was eleven years old, he traveled to Vienna to take the examination. The teachers were pleased with Franz's musical ability. "You sing well, my boy," they said. "You need not worry about paying to come to our school. Your talent deserves a scholarship."

When Franz joined the other boys at the first lesson, they laughed and pointed to his poor clothes. They whispered, "He must be a poor miller's son." But when Franz began to sing, the boys stopped their laughing and stood in silent wonder at the sweet, pure sounds that filled the chapel.

Franz also played violin in the student orchestra. He tried to find ways to be helpful at the school. He took it upon himself to care for the instruments, give out the parts, and even take care of lighting the candles. Soon he was advanced to be orchestra leader, which was the name then for concertmaster.

One day the conductor was to be out of town. "Will you conduct the orchestra while I am away?" he asked Franz. Franz enthusiastically agreed, and he felt honored to conduct the chapel orchestra.

Although the Vienna Choir School kept the students very busy with their studies, Franz always found extra time to practice piano and to join his friends to play chamber music. He was even beginning to compose his own pieces.

By the time Franz Schubert was thirteen years old, he had composed songs, piano pieces, chamber music, some quartets, and orchestral pieces. "You must show your compositions to our teacher," urged one of Franz's friends. But Franz was shy and reserved toward his teachers and did not want to show his work to them. One day, though, the chapel master saw one of Franz's compositions, and said to himself, "This boy has a special gift. He must study composition with the finest teacher."

Franz and his new teacher became fast friends. The young boy was eager to learn and had a passion for writing music. His teacher used to say, "He has already learned everything, and God has been his teacher."

But to buy music paper for writing his compositions was a luxury that Franz could not afford. Imagine his good fortune, then, when a friend came to him and said, "Franz, let me buy the

FRANZ PETER SCHUBERT
at age sixteen

music paper for you. Your gift in return will be beautiful music for the whole world."

During the years that Franz attended the Vienna Choir School, he traveled home to Lichtenthal each Sunday to be with his parents. After supper Father Schubert would announce, "It's time for music!" Franz's sister and brother would take out their violins, father would unpack his cello, and Franz his viola, and they would be off on a quartet or two before it was time for Franz to return to school.

Sometimes when Franz was tired of working so hard at school, he enjoyed playing practical jokes on his friends. Several times he was called before the chapel master for a scolding. When he was a little older, he enjoyed going to the town tavern for an evening of dancing and singing.

But all this was to come to an end. When Franz Schubert was sixteen years old, his singing voice lost its sweetness and purity, and he could no longer reach the high notes. "We can no longer use you in our chapel choir," the singing master sadly told Franz. "We are sorry, but you must leave our school."

What would Franz do now? He wanted only to compose music, but he could not earn enough money that way. "Come and teach in my school," urged his father, the schoolmaster. "You can teach the little children their ABC's, and in your spare time, you can write music."

And this is just what Franz did. For the next two years he wrote some of his most beautiful music. It was one of the busiest times of his life. After his long hours in the school room, he would sometimes go home and compose eight songs in a single day. "If only I could spend all my hours writing music," he would say to himself, "then I could put down on paper all the musical ideas that come crowding into my head."

Until this time, not many people had heard about Franz Schubert and his compositions. Perhaps they might never have known him well if it had not been for a singer friend. He admired Schubert's songs and sang them well. Whenever he gave a concert he would include several of Schubert's songs on his program. From then on, Schubert's songs became very popular in Vienna.

There is a story about the day that two of Schubert's young friends came by his little room to take him out for dinner. They threw open the door and shouted, "Come on, Franz. You have been working too hard. Let's go out for dinner."

But when they saw Franz pacing back and forth across the floor, they stopped to look in amazement. He was reading aloud from a book of poems, then rushing to the table to write, then reading again, then writing. Finally he finished composing the song. Forgetting all about dinner, one of the friends said, "Let's take the song to the café and try it with the piano there."

They listened, but could not understand the meaning of the song. So Franz said, "Come with me." They left the café and stopped by at the school of his old teacher, a professor of harmony. With the help of a tenor to sing the words, and with Franz at the piano, they performed the song. His teacher listened, and then said to all those gathered around, "If Franz does it, it must be right. His ideas come direct from Heaven."

After a few years, Schubert left the teaching job at his father's school, and with the help of a few generous friends, he was able to live a very frugal life. Fortunately, one day Schubert received a letter from Count Esterhazy. "Would you be kind enough to live at the court and serve as music teacher to my two daughters?" he wrote.

"I would be most honored," Schubert replied in his letter. He packed up his music paper, and a few shirts, and left his tiny room to take up residence at the spacious court of the count. Here in such beautiful surroundings, Schubert was inspired to a new creative period when he wrote some of his greatest music.

Gradually, Schubert's music became known to more and more people. Now his music was being published so that many people all over Europe could perform his work. Unfortunately, the publishers paid him very little. Sometimes they paid him only twenty cents for a composition. His songs and dance music became so popular that parties in the homes of wealthy people were entirely devoted to his music.

When Schubert was twenty-five years old and still very poor, he had a serious illness, but in spite of his troubles he was able to write some of his most beautiful string quartets and chamber music. Hearing of Schubert's illness, Count Esterhazy once again invited him to his summer home. "Please come to us again," he begged Franz.

The summer did Franz a world of good. His spirits and health revived. He continued to write, and when he was thirty-one years old, he gave his first and only public concert. It was both a financial and a musical success. "Now I will be able to buy a piano of my own," Schubert exclaimed in joy. But not long after, toward the end of that year, when Schubert was only thirty-one years old, he contracted typhoid fever and died.

On his tombstone these words are engraved: "The Art of Music has here entombed a rich treasure, but yet far fairer hopes."

b. Lichtenthal nr. Vienna, Austria, January 31, 1797
d. Vienna, Austria, November 19, 1828

ROBERT SCHUMANN

Father," begged young Robert Schumann, "I would like very much to study music." This youngest child of Frau and Herr Schumann was always happiest when music was being played in his church or on the street corners in the small Saxon town in Germany where he was born. So one day, when Robert was seven years old, his father said, "Let us go to St. Mary's Church. The organist there has agreed to have you as his student."

That was a joyful day in Robert's life, and soon his teacher was proud of this child who played the piano so well. Within a year he was composing dances to play for his friends. His teacher often told him, "Robert, God has given you a great talent, and very precious is such a gift. Use it well."

Robert enjoyed inventing musical games. One of his favorite games was "Guess Who This Is." "I am thinking of somebody in this room," he would say. "Now, I will go to the piano and improvise some music that describes the person I am thinking of."

Everyone in the room would try to guess which person the music described. His musical descriptions were always so good that his playmates cheered for him as they called out the correct answer.

When Robert Schumann was nine years old, he was taken to a concert given by a very fine pianist. Never before had he heard music played so beautifully. "From now on," he told himself, "I will try to become a fine musician. Each day I must try my best.

There is no other way to succeed."

Sometimes he found it difficult to practice as he should. He would rather play pretty tunes and make up his own songs than practice his lessons. One of his greatest pleasures was making music with his friends. He formed a small orchestra with two violins, two flutes, a clarinet, and two horns. He was the conductor and played the piano which his father had given him as a gift. If Robert could not find printed music that his orchestra could play, he composed some pieces himself.

Robert's two special interests were music and poetry. When he was not writing music, he was creating poetry. His father encouraged him in his work. It was a sad loss for fifteen year old Robert, then, when his father died. His mother was not convinced that music or writing poetry should be Robert's life work. "You should go to the university to study to be a lawyer," she pleaded. "You could graduate with honors and become the finest lawyer in the empire."

Because he lived with his mother and wanted to please her, Robert left for Leipzig to attend law school. His heart was not in it, though, and he spent little time studying. Most of the time he was playing piano and making music with his friends. He wrote to his mother, "I have no taste for the law. My studies are dry and irksome, but I have resolved to become a lawyer. When a man determines to succeed, he indeed can do all things."

At the time Robert Schumann was attending the university, he was also taking piano lessons with a very fine teacher, Frederick

Wieck. Schumann made rapid progress with this teacher, and found it more and more difficult to study his law books. On one of his summer trips, he heard a concert by a famous violinist, Nicolo Paganini. "If I could play the piano as that man plays on the violin, I should be perfectly happy." So he wrote again to his mother, and finally she agreed to allow her son to give up law and study music.

Robert took up piano studies again with Frederick Wieck, and with another teacher he studied harmony and counterpoint. He wanted so much to excel that he practiced even more than his teacher thought best. And then Robert did something that was to change the course of his life. As he practiced, he noticed that the third finger of his right hand seemed weaker than the other fingers. To make it stronger, he fastened it in a strained position and kept it that way for hours at a time. Eventually, instead of his finger becoming stronger, it became crippled.

Of course, Schumann was discouraged, and he knew he could never become a master pianist. He did not, however, give up his dreams to be a musician. "If I cannot perform music," he told his teacher, "then I will compose music."

From then on, Schumann concentrated on composing.

Something else happened at this time to affect Schumann's life. His teacher, Professor Wieck, had a lovely young daughter Clara, who was often at home when Robert went to the house for his lessons. Clara was an exceptionally talented pianist. She was only twelve years old at the time, but already she had appeared many

ROBERT SCHUMANN

times in public concerts. Clara and Robert became close friends. When he was twenty-two years old, and she was thirteen, Clara gave a concert and included on the program a piece that Robert had composed.

Robert and Clara spent more and more time together and grew to love one another. Clara's father, however, did not want Robert and Clara to marry. "You must not see Robert any more," ordered Professor Wieck. "He will ruin your career as a concert pianist."

But the years passed, and finally love won out. Clara and Robert, now both distinguished musicians, were united in a marriage of lasting happiness. He was thirty and she was twenty-one. Some of Robert Schumann's finest music was written for Clara and dedicated to her.

Early in the first year of their marriage, Robert returned to writing songs, something he had not done for twelve years. In the space of less than one year, he composed nearly all the songs that brought him his greatest fame. One of these songs was *Two Grenadiers*.

Robert liked to write about music, too. He was editor of a magazine in which he wrote articles about music that was being composed at that time. He tried to encourage young musicians whom he thought did good work. Once he wrote a kind article about Mendelssohn, who said, "I am quite delighted. Such praise comes from a pure heart. Ten thousand thanks to the man who wrote this."

When Schumann first met Johannes Brahms, he exclaimed,

"Hats off, gentlemen, a genius." He wrote articles in his magazine encouraging Brahms' compositions.

Clara and Robert often left their cozy little home in Leipzig to give concerts all over Europe. Clara was fond of playing her husband's music. In Russia, the royal family honored the couple by inviting them to play at Court.

Robert continued to work hard. Besides the songs, he wrote symphonies and chamber music and many pieces for piano.

To Clara's great sorrow, when her husband was forty-four years old, he complained of a very strong and painful ear malady. His illness required him to be sent to a hospital for his care, where he stayed two and a half years before he died.

After Robert died, Clara took her eight children to Berlin and then to Wiesbaden, where she once again took up her career as a concert pianist. In memory of her husband, she composed some piano pieces using melodies from Robert's own compositions. In this way she helped to keep alive the memory of her husband, Robert Schumann.

b. Zwickau, Saxony, Germany - June 8, 1810
d. Endenich, near Bonn, Germany - July 29, 1856

FREDERICH SEITZ

In the tiny town of Guntersleben, Frederich Seitz was born. His parents called their little son Fritz.

While Fritz was growing up he often heard the music of German composers: Brahms and Schumann, Beethoven and Schubert. His parents enjoyed listening to music and wanted to share their love of music with their son, so they sent him at an early age to study harmony, as well as violin, with Johann Christian Lauterbach, a well-known violinist in Dresden.

Fritz studied conscientiously. Then it came time for him to leave his parents' home and earn his own living. He said to his family, "My teachers have told me of a fine orchestra in the city of Magdeburg. Perhaps I can go there and try to find a place in the orchestra."

Packing a few belongings and his violin, and bidding his family "Auf Wiedersehn", Fritz left on the seventy-five mile journey to Magdeburg.

After his arrival there, he played some violin pieces for the conductor of the orchestra. Imagine his joy when he was told that he would be hired. "Dear mother and father," he wrote to his parents, "I played for the conductor of the Magdeburg orchestra. He asked me to play several pieces. Then he told me to return to the inn where I was staying, and he would send word to me. I waited anxiously, not knowing whether or not he had been pleased by my playing. Finally, the next afternoon, a message came offering me the position of concertmaster of the orchestra. You can imagine how happy I was!

"The trip to Magdeburg was long, and the roads were rough, but I have found a nice inn where I can live for a time. As soon as I can, I will come home for a visit. In the meantime, I send you both much love. Your son, Fritz."

Fritz wrote violin pieces, some concerti for violin and piano, three children's trios, and pieces for cello.

Frederich Seitz stayed in Magdeburg for a number of years and then moved to the city of Dessau, not far away, where he remained as concertmaster until he died at the age of seventy.

b. Guntersleben, near Gotha, Germany - June 12, 1848
d. Dessau, Germany - May 22, 1918

WILLIAM SQUIRE

Evening was coming on, and the light in the music room grew dim. "I can barely see the notes on the page," William said to his father who was giving him a cello lesson.

"Very well, then, I will turn up the gas lamps," William's father said, "but if you had memorized the sonata, you could play it in the dark."

William knew his father was right, and at that moment he decided to have the piece memorized by next week's lesson. He worked hard, and at the next lesson, when the light in the room faded with the setting sun, William went on to play the sonata by memory. His father was pleased to see that his son knew how to practice well.

As he put his cello in the case at the close of the lesson, his father said, "Please sit down for a moment, William. I have something to discuss with you. As you know, I have enjoyed being your teacher. You have been a fine student, but now I think you should study cello with another teacher. Would you like to try to win a scholarship at the Royal Conservatory of Music in London?"

William hesitated a moment. "Yes," he replied, "if you think I am ready, I would like to study in London. Do you think that Edward Howells might teach me?"

"Write a letter," his father suggested. "Ask Mr. Howells if you could have the honor of an audition with him."

William wrote the letter, and soon afterwards he received a reply, inviting him to appear at the Conservatory for an audition. Father and son traveled together to London. Coming from the open countryside of England where the air was clear and cool, it was a strange experience to feel and smell the gray, sooty smog that enveloped them as they walked down the crowded streets.

After asking for directions, William and his father made their way to the Conservatory. "There it is, just ahead," William said.

As they approached the front door, Mr. Squire said, "Just remember, William, play with a beautiful tone, and let Mr. Howells see how much you love to play." Inside the Conservatory, William knocked on the door of the studio marked with Edward Howells' name. The famous cellist greeted them warmly, and invited them into his studio.

"What will you play for me?" Mr. Howells asked William.

"I would like to play the last movement of the Boccherini concerto," he answered. William played for the cello teacher, who listened attentively.

"Thank you, William," Mr. Howells said as the young man finished his performance. "In a few days I will let you know if you have won the scholarship."

Back home once more in Ross, the two waited impatiently for news from the Royal Conservatory. Within a week, a letter arrived from London.

"Good news, good news," William called out when his father came home that evening. "I have great, good news. I have been accepted at the Royal Conservatory. Mr. Howells will give me cello lessons, and I will be admitted to the composition class as well."

At the Conservatory, William was a conscientious student. He practiced diligently many hours a day, and when he was twenty years old, he was ready to give his first public cello recital. He wondered how it would be to play before a large audience.

He went to his sister for advice. She had just given her first song recital, and William thought she would have some helpful suggestions.

"Emily, how was it, singing for all those people?" he asked her.

"Oh", she replied, "I just forgot about all the people in the audience, and pretended I was singing for the composer. Then it was fun and I could do my best," she explained.

William took his sister's advice, and his recital performance was admired very much by the audience. His sister, standing in the lobby after the concert, listened to the comments that people made about her brother's playing.

"They like your warm, full tone," she told William. "They like you, too", she added with a smile. "They like your generous spirit and your congenial nature."

William Squire was encouraged by this success and four

years later he was ready to perform. He played the Saint-Saens *Cello Concerto in a minor* at the famous Crystal Palace in London.

From then on, Squire was offered many different positions. He played in the Queen's Hall orchestra, and was first cellist at London's well-known center of music, Covent Garden. He went on tour, and made recordings. Gabriel Fauré, the great French composer, dedicated his composition, *Sicillienne* to William Squire.

In addition to performing, Squire spent much of his time composing music. He wrote a cello concerto, two operettas, and many short pieces for cello. *Danse Rustique* and *Tarantella* are two of his compositions that are favorites of cellists everywhere.

William Squire's life spanned ninety-two years, and for all that time, he remained an active musician. Think of all the changes in science, art and music that took place during Squire's long musical life!

Ross, Hartfordshire, England, Aug. 8, 1871
London, England, March 17, 1963

SHINICHI SUZUKI

Long ago on the Island of Japan, a new emperor came to the throne to rule his country. He wanted to bring new ideas from other lands to the people of Japan. In his travels, the new emperor had heard music from western countries. Music of such composers as Mozart and Beethoven rarely had been heard in Japan.

"I want the orchestra of my court to play music of western countries," the emperor declared. "We must send for violins and other instruments and train our musicians to play them."

At first, these new instruments and the music they played sounded strange to the Japanese people. But there was a teacher in Nagoya who was interested in this western music. His name was Masakichi Suzuki. As a boy, he had learned from his father and grandfather how to make the shamisen. This three-stringed instrument was used to play Japanese music. Now, he wondered, "Who in Japan will make these violins that are needed for playing western music?"

One day Masakichi Suzuki met a violinist at the Teachers College in Nagoya. "For many generations," he said, "my family has earned its living by making shamisen. Now I have heard music of the violin, and would like to learn to make one. Would you be kind enough to lend me your violin for one night so that I may look at it carefully?"

"Yes, I will be willing to lend it to you," answered the teacher.

So the young man took the violin home and drew exact pictures of the way the violin was put together.

The next day he returned the violin. "Thank you very much," he said to the teacher. "Now I shall go home and try to build an instrument like yours."

Masakichi Suzuki was twenty-nine years old when he made his first violin. Not long after that he decided to build the Suzuki Violin Factory. "Now we will be able to make enough violins for all the people who want to learn to play," he said.

From their lovely home on a cool autumn day in Nagoya, Masakichi Suzuki and his wife announced the birth of a son, Shinichi. During his days in primary school, Shinichi and his brothers and sister liked to go to the factory to play. Sometimes they would get into an argument and hit each other with the pieces of violins stacked in the building. But as Shinichi grew older and became more serious, his father encouraged him to do well in school. "Shinichi," he told his son, "some day when I am old, I want you to become the owner of the violin factory. To prepare yourself, you must go to Nagoya Commercial School and learn to become a good business man."

Obeying his father's wishes, Shinichi studied at the commercial school, but during his vacations he spent time at the violin factory. He enjoyed watching the violin makers work. He listened to their stories and by the light of the lanterns hanging from the ceiling he helped to put the final polish on some of the violins.

Something very special happened in the Suzuki family at this time. Shinichi's father called his children into the house one day and said, "Here is something we have purchased for the whole family to enjoy together." It was a record player — or a gramophone, as it was called then. "Here," he said, "you wind it up by hand. The record goes around, you put the needle on, and the sound comes out of the horn." Everyone was excited. It was a surprise to all the children to hear the sound of music coming from a machine.

"Let us play this recording," Shinichi's father said. "It is a piece by Franz Schubert called *Ave Maria*, and it is played by a violinist named Mischa Elman."

Shinichi listened in amazement. Such a beautiful tone coming from a violin! The music touched his heart. Never before had he thought of a violin as an instrument that could speak so eloquently. He listened often to that recording, and to another of a Haydn minuet.

"Father," Shinichi asked one day, "may I bring a violin home from the factory? I would like to teach myself to play those two pieces."

At first, the sounds that Shinichi made on the violin did not please him. But he kept trying. Gradually, he became fond of the violin and began to develop a love for music.

Now that Shinichi had graduated from commercial school, he became a regular staff member at the violin factory. It was his job to see about sending violins to other parts of the world. For two years he was satisfied with his job. Then one summer he went to a countryside inn to recover from a slight illness. He enjoyed meeting the other guests there. Among them was a man whom he would hear from again very soon.

That Fall, indeed, a letter came from this friend. "Would you like to join us on a geological research expedition?" the letter read. "The trip by boat will be led by Marquis Tokugawa, an important person in the emperor's court."

Shinichi wanted very much to go. His father gave him permission. He packed his bags and took his violin. The ship set out on the journey, and Shinichi, with a pianist who was also a guest on the expedition, enjoyed playing music. The leader of the expedition, Marquis Tokugawa, began to talk to Shinichi about his interest in music. "I love music," Shinichi told him, "but I have no thought of becoming a professional musician. My interest is only in discovering the meaning of art through my violin playing."

But the following autumn, Marquis Tokugawa came to Nagoya and visited the Suzuki family. To Shinichi's father, he said, "What would you think of your son's going to Tokyo to study violin?"

At first, Shinichi's father did not like the idea, but with such an important person asking the question, how could he refuse? Spring came, and Shinichi's father agreed that his son, now twenty-one years old, should go away to take violin lessons. He lived at the fine mansion of the Marquis, where many brilliant and fascinating scholars came to visit. The young man felt extremely honored and fortunate to be in the company of such fine people who shared their thoughts with him.

Suzuki studied violin with Ko Ando in Tokyo for about one and a half years. Then the Marquis suggested a way that the young student could get to Germany to study. "Will you allow your son to go to Germany to study violin?" the Marquis asked Shinichi's father.

"I agree that it would be excellent for my son to study in Germany," Shinichi's father said. "Yes, he may go with you."

So, together, the Marquis and Shinichi left Japan.

When Suzuki arrived in Berlin, Germany, he did not have any idea about a teacher for himself. He listened to the performances of many artists, seeking a teacher whom he felt could speak to his heart as perhaps Mischa Elman had done on that first recording he had heard years ago. For a time he did not find the person he was searching for. Then one day he heard the Klingler Quartet perform music by Mozart. At last, here was music with a spirit that touched him deeply.

He immediately wrote to Professor Karl Klingler asking if he would accept him as his student. The professor listened to Suzuki play and told him, "Yes, I will accept you as my student. You will be my only pupil."

For the first four years, they studied concertos and sonatas; for the second four years, they studied chamber music.

Some of the friends Suzuki made in Germany were as important to him as his music lessons. They were intelligent, sensitive people

SHINICHI SUZUKI

of good will. He always wanted to learn from the people he met. He was curious about new ideas. He was learning about himself and about being a better person. He was learning how art can help people to feel joy and contentment of spirit.

It was at one of the home concerts in Berlin that Shinichi attended that he met the young woman who was to become his wife. Together, Shinichi and Waltraud returned to Japan. In Tokyo, where they lived, students came to their home to study with Suzuki-sensei (pronounced sen-say, meaning teacher). Then, when he was thirty-three years old, he joined the teaching staff at the Imperial Conservatory and the famous Kunitachi Music School. With his three brothers, he formed the Suzuki Quartet.

"Here he comes, here he comes," the little children would call out as Suzuki-sensei came walking down the street toward his home. The small children loved this friendly man, and he loved them. One day, a small four year old boy came to the house with his father. "Can you teach my son to play the violin?" the father asked.

"How will I teach such a young child to play the violin," Suzuki-sensei wondered. He thought and thought about this. Suddenly, the idea came to him. "As soon as a child is born, he hears his parents speaking. Soon he begins to try to speak too. First he makes sounds. Gradually, he begins to say words that he hears his parents use. His parents are happy when he learns to speak. He says the same words over and over again. He learns new words. Then he puts words together. Almost all children can do that. Surely any child can learn to play the violin in that same way if he has patient encouragement from his parents and teachers."

So, putting together all the ideas he thought about through his many experiences, Shinichi Suzuki started the Talent Education Movement in Japan. He composed several songs for young children to play. He hoped that through music children everywhere would grow to have a "noble mind, a high sense of values and splendid ability." Many children the world over are learning to play music following the ideas of Shinichi Suzuki.

b. Nagoya, Japan, October 17, 1898

PETER ILYICH TCHAIKOVSKY

Come on, Sasha," Peter said to his baby sister. "Here is a pencil and some paper. Let's sit down at the table and we can write a song to Mama."

Peter's mother had gone away for a visit to St. Petersburg, and four-year-old Peter missed her very much. Writing a song for her would make it seem that she was not so far away.

Baby Sasha sat down beside her brother, and listened to him sing some tunes and write them on the paper. When he was all finished, Peter said, "What shall we call our song? How about *Our Mama in St. Petersburg*?" Sasha clapped her hands. She thought her brother was wonderful to be able to make up his own songs.

That night, when Ilya Tchaikovsky, Peter's father, came home from work, his son ran to him. "Look what I have made for Mama!" he called out.

When his father saw the song, he picked Peter up in his arms and hugged him. "How dear of you, little son, to make that song for Mama. We will send it with the postman in the morning."

Within the month, Peter's mother came back from her trip. She brought with her a governess, who could be a teacher for Peter's older brother. But four year old Peter cried to be allowed to attend his brother's lessons with Mlle. Fanny, and by the time he was six years old, Peter could read French,

German, and Russian and he spent many hours reading and writing poetry, too.

In the large sitting room of the comfortable Tchaikovsky home, there was a wonderful machine called an orchestrion, a kind of barrel organ that could play music to sound like an orchestra. "Please play the music of Mozart," young Peter begged. He loved to hear the music over and over again. When his four brothers and one sister would run outside to play, Peter would often stay in the house and play on the piano the tunes he had heard on the orchestrion.

Once, when Peter was forbidden to play the piano, he pretended to play by tapping his fingers on the window. The glass broke, and cut his hand. Peter's father said to his wife, "Well, my dear, I can see that music is so very important to Peter. Perhaps we should allow him to have piano lessons."

They found a young girl in the small town who could give lessons to Peter. Within 3 years, he could read music and play as well as she.

Like his father, Peter, too, was warm-hearted and loving. He wanted to protect everything that was weak or unhappy. One day, he heard that someone was going to drown a kitten, and implored him not to do such a cruel thing. When it was agreed, Peter rushed home to his father who was busy in a meeting. He burst into the meeting room. "They will not drown the kitten, they will not drown the kitten," he happily exclaimed again and again!

Mlle. Fanny took care of the Tchaikovsky children, who were with their parents only at mealtime. She encouraged the children in their lessons and in their play and she provided them with loving affection. So when Peter's father decided to move his family away to a new town, and not take Mlle. Fanny with them, Peter was very sad.

In the new town, there was nobody to share Peter's interest in poetry or music. He was unhappy. He wrote a letter to Mlle. Fanny, telling her how much he missed her. "I am sad," he wrote, "but playing the piano comforts me a great deal."

That summer, as a special treat for Peter, his mother took him to St. Petersburg to hear an opera called *A Life for the Tsar* by the Russian composer, Glinka. Peter sat on the edge of his chair, enthralled by the singing and the orchestra. He would always remember this exciting experience.

When Autumn came, and Peter was ten years old, his mother told him, "Now it is time for you to attend school to prepare for a profession. I have made plans for you to go to the School of Jurisprudence in St. Petersburg, where you can study to become a lawyer."

At the school, when the time came for parting from his family, Peter was terrified at the thought of being separated from his mother and father. His mother tried to comfort him, but nothing seemed to help calm his fright. As the carriage started off to take his mother home, Peter ran screaming after her, trying to grab the wheels to stop the carriage. When he was older, Peter remembered that day as one of the most terrible times of his life.

At school, Peter was very lonely. Some of his teachers were kind to the homesick boy, and after a time he became accustomed to his studies and he did well, except for mathematics. He enjoyed being with other students, and liked to play pranks, but most of the time he was so busy with school work that he had little time for music. Every now and then, though, he did take time from his work to play the piano. Whenever there was to be a dance or party in town, Peter would be invited to play piano to entertain his friends.

At last, after nine years at the School of Law, Peter graduated. He was nineteen years old, and he took a job as clerk in the Ministry of Justice. It was not long before he knew that he did not want to spend his life as a clerk. Music was what he truly loved, and more and more, he was thinking about making music his life's work. He studied music theory and spent many evenings in the theatre, listening to opera and ballet. One of his favorite operas was *Der Freischutz* by Carl Maria von Weber.

One evening when Peter's family was gathered around the dinner table, he said, "What do you think, Father? Do you think I am too old to begin my musical studies in a serious way?"

"You are only twenty-one years old, Peter. I do not believe it is too late for you to study to become a professional musician. But how will you begin?"

"There is a new conservatory opening in St. Petersburg," he

replied. "I can apply to become a student." Young Peter was one of the first pupils to enroll in the new school. He continued his job as clerk for a time, but soon the conservatory director, Anton Rubinstein, told him, "Peter, you have so much talent for music, why don't you leave your job as clerk, and spend more time composing?"

"But how will I pay for my lessons, and for my room and food?" he asked.

Rubinstein said, "I can help you find jobs as accompanist in concerts, and pupils for you to teach." Peter also found work arranging parts of operas for short concerts. He gave up his habit of fancy clothes and parties, and saved money by living in a small room. His hair grew long and his clothes were shabby, but now he was more content than he had ever been before.

In a letter to his sister, Sasha, Peter explained how he felt. "Don't think I imagine I'll become a great artist," he wrote. "I simply want to do the work for which I feel I have a calling. Whether I become a famous composer or a poor teacher my conscience will be at peace."

Young Tchaikovsky worked hard. He continued his technical exercises, studied piano and flute and organ, and began composing in a serious way. His teacher, Anton Rubinstein, assigned Peter to write music to a play named *The Storm.* The young composer thought the play had an exciting story, and although he had little experience writing music for an orchestra, he tried to make the instruments describe what was happening in the play. When he had finished writing the music, he showed it to Rubinstein.

"Well, what is this?" Rubinstein shouted. "Who said you could have the violins divide their parts, and play with tremelo? Who ever heard of using a harp and a tuba, or for that matter, who ever heard of using a Russian folk tune in a serious piece of music?"

Peter listened to what his teacher said, but he was not discouraged by Rubinstein's critical comments. In fact, he appreciated Rubinstein's help, and when he graduated from the conservatory, he won the silver medal. The name of Peter Tchaikovsky was being heard in many places.

One person who admired Tchaikovsky's work was Anton Rubinstein's brother, Nicolay, who was opening a new music school in Moscow. "Please come to Moscow," he pleaded with Peter. "I want to offer you a post as teacher of harmony at the new Russian Musical Society."

After thinking it over, Tchaikovsky accepted the job, even though the salary was very low, and he did not really feel qualified to be a teacher. But Nicolay was very helpful to the young musician, and even conducted his orchestra in the first performances of many of Tchaikovsky's compositions.

Although Peter missed St. Petersburg, he did make new friends in Moscow. Life was very different from St. Petersburg. People in Moscow were more willing to accept new ideas, and he joined a group of young composers called The Five who were experimenting with different ways of writing music.

During this time, Nicolay Rubinstein encouraged Tchaikovsky to write a symphony. It proved to be a very difficult task. He would begin to write frantically and then, not liking what he had done, he would tear it all up and start again. "Peter", his teacher would suggest, "write more slowly, and criticize your work as you go along. Then you will not have to throw away so much of your work." But that was not Peter's nature, and when he composed, he became very nervous and excited, and could not sleep. At other times, he was sad and depressed, and had trouble concentrating on his work.

At last after making many changes, he finished the symphony. He asked to have it performed in St. Petersburg but Anton Rubinstein and the newspaper critics and the people of St. Petersburg were not pleased with the symphony. "Never again will I ask to have my work performed here," Tchaikovsky declared.

In Moscow, however, it was different. There, the people cheered for him after the performance of his first symphony. "They are calling you to come to the stage," his friend sitting beside Tchaikovsky said. "Go on!"

Peter, surprised and afraid, went onto the stage, dressed in his old, untidy clothes. Holding his hat in his hand, he made several clumsy bows and stumbled off. The performance that day was a great victory for Peter Tchaikovsky.

Once again Tchaikovsky met The Five, the group of Russian

composers he had known in Moscow. Balakirev was the leader of the group. They encouraged Tchaikovsky to express the Russian spirit in his work, and to use Russian folk tunes in his compositions. "We like your music," Balakirev told Tchaikovsky, "but because you studied at the Conservatory, your compositions are too strict for our taste. We like music to be more free from rules."

Nevertheless, Balakirev continued to help Tchaikovsky with his composing. Even though Tchaikovsky did not like to be criticized, he was willing to take his friend's advice to write a work over and over again until it was right. It was Balakirev who helped Tchaikovsky perservere until he finished his first real masterpiece, *The Romeo and Juliet Overture*.

When Tchaikovsky was thirty-five years old, the Imperial Theatre in Moscow commissioned him to write a ballet. Some years before, he had written a small ballet for his sister's children. He used the themes from that first ballet, expanded it into a longer composition, and called it *Swan Lake*. Tchaikovsky enjoyed writing this piece with its relaxed and charming lyrical melodies. But when he took it to the first rehearsals, he heard nothing but complaints. The orchestra said the music was too difficult to play; the dancers said there were too many dances to learn; the conductor could not understand the complicated music. "You must change the music. Make it simpler," they all insisted. So Tchaikovsky made many changes, and it was not until years later, that the true *Swan Lake* was performed as Tchaikovsky really meant it to be. To this day it is a favorite of ballet dancers all over the world.

That was a good year for Tchaikovsky. He met Camille Saint-Saens, the French composer, who was visiting Moscow. He won an opera competition. He had a successful performance of his first piano concerto and his third symphony, and he took a trip to Paris, where, for the first time, he heard the opera *Carmen* by Bizet, who was one of Tchaikovsky's favorite composers.

One of Tchaikovsky's greatest admirers was a wealthy widow, Nadejda von Meck. She commissioned the young composer to write music for her, and they wrote long letters to one another about their experiences and feelings, their hopes and beliefs. Madame von Meck and Peter Tchaikovsky never met, but through her letters, she gave him great support, both spiritually and financially. With her help, Peter was able to give up his teaching, and devote all his time to composing. In one letter, Madame von Meck wrote, "Your music makes life easier and more pleasant." Tschaikovsky replied, "It is a consolation to think that there are people who sincerely and warmly love our art."

Tchaikovsky's feelings of hope and despair, joy and sorrow, were intensely expressed in his music. He wrote operas, symphonies, a violin concerto, overtures and ballets, and pieces for the piano. His fame spread. He was invited all over Europe to perform his work. Tchaikovsky festivals were established.

He even overcame his shyness, and began to conduct. It was Peter Tchaikovsky who was invited to America to conduct the first concert at the great music center in New York City, Carnegie Hall.

Peter Ilyich Tchaikovsky spent the last years of his life writing music in the peaceful, quiet surroundings of the Russian countryside he loved so much.

PETER ILYCH TCHAIKOVSKY

b. Kamsko-Votkinsk, Russia, May 7, 1840
d. St. Petersburg, Russia, November 6, 1893

GEORG PHILIPP TELEMANN

In a pleasant and comfortable house on Holy Ghost Street in Magdeburg, Germany, Georg Philipp Telemann was born. Georg's father, Heinrich Telemann, was the deacon and preacher in the Magdeburg Lutheran Church. As he sat in his study, or went about the house, he hummed his favorite hymn tunes, and it was not long before little Georg was singing along with his father. When he was just a small child, he tried to teach himself to play those tunes on different musical intruments. He learned to play them on the violin, flute and cittern before he knew that there was such a thing as written notes.

"Listen to little Georg", the neighbors would exclaim. "He must have music in his bones. He can sing and play all the tunes he hears at church!"

When George was only four years old, his father died. His mother expected George to be a preacher and a deacon when he grew up, just as his father and grandfather had been. She could see, though, that Georg loved music more than anything else, but she did not think that earning a living as a musician was proper. "I know there are Court musicians who are well paid," she told her friends, "but I consider musicians to be like those people in the carnivals who entertain with juggling and minstrel shows. I do not want my son to be a musician!"

Of course, Georg's mother took him to church with her. He loved the singing and the organ music that filled every corner of the church. The singing master of his church, Benedict Christiana, directed the choir boys and the town musicians, and when he saw how interested Georg was in singing, he encouraged him.

By the time Georg was ten years old, he was ready to enter the Old City School. He wanted to study music, to learn more than he had already been able to pick up on his own. One of Georg's first music teachers was an organist at the Cathedral. He forced Georg to read music written in numbers and letters instead of notes. This frightened the young boy, and when he was older, he wrote stories about his experience with his teacher. "My teacher," he wrote, "played as stifly as the grandfather from whom he learned it. But happier tunes than these were already hopping around in my head." After two weeks of lessons with this teacher, Georg left. "Since then," he wrote, "I have never learnt from a teacher."

As soon as Georg began to play violin and flute, he started to write his own pieces. He listened to music to figure out for himself the rules of composing. At first, Georg composed in secret, but as he grew more sure of himself, he began to show his music to some friends.

One evening as Georg and his mother were finishing their dinner, there was a loud knock on the front door. Georg jumped up from the table and ran to see who was there. It was one of his friends. "Georg," he shouted, "come down to the town square. The town musicians are playing some of your pieces, and the singing master has announced that he wrote them! Everyone cheers for the music!"

Indeed, it was true. The music masters were performing the music that George has composed and claiming it to be their own. They were being praised for music they had stolen!

One day, as Georg was sitting in the corner of his room, reading by the light of the sun streaming in through the small window, he jumped up in excitement. "Here is a story that I must set to music!" he exclaimed. Although he was only twelve years old, he wrote the music, then gathered together some singers and players. He himself sang the part of the hero in the story. The opera was performed and the audience was enchanted by the work of this young composer. Of course, this success caused his mother a great deal of worry because she still hoped that Georg would become a preacher.

"Georg," she announced, "I forbid you to play and compose or have anything more to do with music. I am sending you to study Latin and Greek with a university friend of your father. His name is Professor Casper Calvör. He is a distinguished scholar of the church, and an historian and mathematician as well. I expect you to do well in your studies."

Georg, now thirteen years old, reluctantly began his studies with the Professor. Soon they both happily discovered that they had a common interest in music. Professor Calvör was especially learned about the relationship between music and mathematics. He rejoiced in his young pupil's musical talents. He encouraged Georg to resume his studies of instruments, but Georg, remembering his experience with the old organist, decided to learn by himself.

He learned to play violin and organ, viola da gamba, double bass, trombone, oboe, transverse flute, schalümo (like a clarinet) and recorder.

During the time that Georg was with Professor Calvör, an incident occurred which brought more attention to the young musician. The local miners were to hold a great festival. They had hired a composer to write the music for the occasion, but he had fallen ill. "What shall we do?" they wondered. "We have nobody to write the music for us."

"Have no worry," one of the miners said. "I know of a young boy who has just written and performed his own opera. His name is Georg Philipp Telemann. I will ask him to write the music for our festival."

Georg was indeed happy to take on the job. He wrote the music, rehearsed the chorus and orchestra, and, standing on a bench because such a small boy could hardly be seen, he conducted the cantata.

Georg's mother, still determined that her son should not be a professional musician, persuaded him to go to the famous Leipzig University to try the study of law. Leaving behind his music and musical instruments and books, Georg left Magdeburg. To get to Leipzig, he traveled through the city of Halle where George Frederick Handel lived. Telemann was twenty years old, and Handel was sixteen. Immediately, the two young musicians struck up a friendship that would last all their lives. Both were intensely interested in music, especially in new musical ideas. When they were apart, they often wrote letters to each other. Many times, their letters contained musical problems which they would solve and then return in the next letter.

Although Georg would have preferred to stay in Halle, he traveled on to Leipzig. He was determined to try to follow his mother's wishes to study at the University. When he arrived, he looked for a place to live, and was directed to a large rooming house where he could share a room with another student.

George knocked at the door. "Welcome," said the young student as he invited him into the room. There, to Georg's amazement, hanging on the walls of the room, were musical instruments belonging to the young man. Georg said nothing. When friends came in to play music together, he pretended to know nothing about music. But one day, when Georg was attending a class, his roommate saw a piece of music in his suitcase. Georg must have forgotten to leave this composition at home with his mother. It was the music he had written to the words of the Sixth Psalm.

Georg's roommate was fascinated with what he saw. He asked Georg if he could have the piece performed in the great St. Thomas Church in Leipzig. "Why didn't you tell me that you are a musician?" he asked in amazement. Of course, Georg had to explain that he was at the University to satisfy his mother's wishes, but that he really wanted nothing more than to study music.

The day of the performance of the Cantata arrived. In the audience was the Burgomaster of Leipzig. He asked to have Georg Telemann come to the City Hall the next day. When Georg arrived, the Burgomaster greeted him enthusiastically.

"Your music is truly beautiful," he said. "I would like to commission you to write a piece twice a month for our Church of St. Thomas."

Georg was happy to accept the commission, and his music brought fame to the Church and to himself as well. When the Cantor of St. Thomas Church died, Georg Telemann was elected to take his place. He had studied the Cantor's work, and learned much from it, but Telemann's style was quite different. He was writing music with simpler melodies and forms. His music could be more easily understood by ordinary people, not just by trained musicians.

This was a time when a big change was taking place all over Europe. The common people in the towns and cities wanted to hear music that they could easily enjoy. They wanted happier, more simple and beautiful tunes that they could hum and sing. In Germany, George Frederick Handel and Georg Philipp Telemann wanted to write music this way. Johann Sebastian Bach, however, continued to write more complicated music of the past, and people were beginning to get tired of that.

Another change was taking place in Europe, too. In earlier times, music was written for people in the Courts and in the Churches. Now, a new group of people — the business people and merchants — were becoming wealthy. They wanted to be as important as the people in the Courts. One way they could achieve this was by giving money to artists and musicians to support them in their work, just as Kings and Popes did in years before. They could build opera houses to show off their riches. And they could ask composers to write operas about their own country, to be sung in their own language.

At the University at Leipzig, students were excited about these new ideas, and Georg Philipp Telemann was caught up in the excitement. He wrote many compositions which the students liked to hear or sing or perform. He wrote operas for them in which they could sing or play, and music which they could perform in coffee houses, or at festivals and public concerts in Leipzig. It seemed that now anyone, not just the rich and noble, could come and enjoy themselves.

Unfortunately, the head of the University and the Deacon of the Church did not approve of what Telemann was doing, because many of the students were leaving the church choirs, prefering instead to sing in Telemann's operas. But the people of Leipzig were enthusiastic and crowded in to hear the concerts.

In addition to everything else Telemann was doing, he accepted a job at the New Church of St. Mathew. "We will offer you the post as Organist and Director of Music," the Dean told Georg, "with the understanding that you will give up your operas, and especially your singing in your own operas." Telemann agreed to this.

At St. Mathew's there was no choir. Women were not permitted to sing in church choirs in those days, and there were no choir boys at St. Mathews Church. What was Telemann to do to perform his music? He invited friends from his groups at the

316

University to sing. To imitate the high voices, he had them sing in falsetto, or high head tones. He organized orchestras to accompany them. In the older times, the church orchestras were made up of special players trained in the courts or guilds. But Telemann liked to hire "beer-fiddlers" from town, and wind players who performed "tower-music" from church balconies.

Although Telemann was enjoying his work, he suddenly decided, when he was 24 years old, to look for a Court patron who would support him as he continued to compose and study to develop his skills. In Poland, Count Erdmann von Promnitz, who was fond of Jean Baptiste Lully's music, said to Telemann, "I will be glad to be your patron if you will oblige me by writing your music in the style of Lully."

Telemann was fond of Lully's music, and agreed to the Count's wishes. Sometimes, when the Count left his Court to travel in his country, he took Telemann with him. They heard Polish folk music played on fiddles and Polish bagpipes made of goatskin, with head, horns and all left intact on the bag. Telemann was so fascinated with the tunes and rhythms of the folk music that he used many of them later in the music that he composed.

While Telemann was in the Count's Court, he met and married Amalie Louise Juliane Eberlin, the daughter of a banker and musician. Although they could have stayed on at the Court, they decided to go to Eisenach, the birthplace of Johann Sebastian Bach. Georg took another Court job, where he was to hire singers and conduct, and to perform as solo violinist in his compositions.

Another musician in the Court was Pantaleon Hebenstat. "Come on," Hebenstadt would say to Telemann. "Let us prepare to play the solo violin parts in a concerto grosso in church this Sunday."

In his diary, Telemann wrote about these occasions, telling about his preparation for the concerts. "I always locked myself in my room, fiddle in hand, shirt sleeves rolled up, with something strong to oil my nerves, and gave myself lessons so that I could measure up to his (Hebenstadt's) dexterity. And mark you! it helped greatly toward my betterment."

Johann Sebastian Bach attended concerts at the Court in Eisenach, and he and Telemann became friends. When Bach and his wife had their second son, Carl Philipp Emanuel, they asked Georg to stand as godfather.

Soon after, a great sadness came to Telemann. His wife died after only 15 months of marriage. In his grief, he wrote a beautiful funeral poem to her. Trying to leave his sadness behind, Telemann left Eisenach. He said to a friend, "I will leave the protection of the Court and go to a free city. People there will not depend on music coming from the Court. The common people can decide their own musical life."

"Where will you go?" the friend asked.

"To Frankfort," he replied, "where I will take a position at the Church of the Barefoot Friars."

In his new job, Telemann immediately plunged into work. "I work hard," he wrote, "owing to a nature that cannot bear idleness." He was to compose music for every feast day, and lead music in the

GEORG PHILIPP TELEMANN

Barefoot Friar's Church. He was also to teach in the city school. He wrote piece after piece for a musical public who wanted music in the modern style. He composed for every church service and every occasion in church or town.

To add to these duties, Telemann took on the job as Director of Music at St. Catherine's Church, and took on a commission for the Duke of Eisenach for writing church and chamber music. True enough, Telemann could not have had an idle moment!

In Telemann's time, there was a law forbidding people to smoke pipes in their own homes. Consequently, the men of Frankfort formed "Smoking Clubs." One such club had members who loved music. "We must find someone," the head of the club suggested, "who can lead us in our musical activities and organize our celebrations, banquets, and tobacco-smoking festivities. He must be able to write our music, care for our finances, and our giving to charities. Who will that person be?" It was agreed by all present that Georg Philipp Telemann should be asked. They invited him to one of their meetings.

Telemann arrived at the fine, imposing mansion where the wealthy club members gathered. It was a spacious building belonging to a wealthy family. Inside, the rooms had great high ceilings and large windows. The members were seated in the heavy-timbered smoking room. Telemann heard their plan, and agreed to accept the job. He organized the musicians to perform his work, and they played concerts to guests invited by the smoking club.

More and more, Telemann was interested in the idea of music being played for anyone who enjoyed hearing it. He planned outdoor concerts, and performed church music in public places, and concert-hall music inside the church. Of course, the Church officials were angry at first, but ordinary people were very happy with Telemann's ideas. They were glad that the church could no longer control even the music that they could hear. Now, if they could pay a small fee, people could hear concerts in many places all over the city. Concerts were becoming so popular, that even the newspapers carried notices to inform everyone about them.

The restless Telemann, after a few years in Frankfort, decided to move to Hamburg, where he took on many new responsibilities. Besides providing the city with many concerts, as he had done in Frankfort, he also became leader of the Goose Market Opera House where he directed his own operas, and the operas of other composers, for 15 years. George Frederick Handel's operas were popular in Hamburg, and Telemann often conducted those.

Meanwhile, many, many people from all over Europe were writing letters to Telemann, telling him of their thoughts and plans. People interested in science and art knew that he had an open mind to new ideas, and they wanted to share them with this great musician.

As Telemann grew older, his eyesight began to fail. One of the hobbies which he had developed over the years proved to be a great comfort to him. He was interested in rare plants. When George Frederick Handel heard about the trouble Telemann was having with his sight, he sent him some rare plants from London, with a letter saying: "If this Passion for exotic plants prolongs your life and preserves your natural vivacity, then I offer with pleasure to contribute to it in as many ways as possible.....You shall have the finest plants of all England."

After Telemann completed composing his last Passion setting, he wrote a poem, writing in his shakey hand, and almost impossible to read because of his poor eyesight. This is the poem, translated from German:

"With ink whose flow is much too thick
With quill pen soft and apt to stick,
With stupid eyes, and gloomy weather,
My lamp these pages barely lighting,
I scratched this tidy piece together
So do be gentle in your chiding."

At the good age of 86 years, after a long life of dedication to music, and to the common people, Georg Philipp Telemann died.

b. Magdeburg, Germany - March 14, 1681
d. Hamburg, Germany - June 25, 1767

ANTONIO VANDINI

Antonio was in no hurry as he strolled down the noisy, bustling main street of Padua, his cello tightly clutched under his arm. He was going to a rehearsal at the Basilica, but on the way he could wander through the market place where the air was filled with the good sweet fragrance of fruits and vegetables. A peddlar standing in his stall saw Antonio come by. He called out, "Friar Vandini, the pears and pomegranates are fresh and ripe today." Another peddlar, not wanting to be outdone, tugged at the Padre's sleeve, insisting, "Try my peaches, good Friar." Vandini stopped, set his cello down, took some coins from his pocket, and bought some fruit to eat with his cheese and bread at lunchtime.

In the years before he had come to live in Padua, Antonio had been cellist and "maestro di violoncello" in the Italian city of Bergamo. Then he had received an invitation from the Church of St. Anthony in Padua to come as principal cellist in their orchestra. He was glad that he had come. Padua was a beautiful city. From the small house where he lived, Vandini could see looming over the city the six great domes of the Church of St. Anthony. On his way to work each day as he walked over the cobbles of the wide plaza in front of the Church, the four huge arches that spanned the entryway seemed to welcome him inside. Today, he opened the heavy decorated door and made his way to the place where the orchestra rehearsed. He stopped in the side chapel for just a moment to gaze at the wall where the bronze, gold, and silver sculpture told the story of St. Anthony healing the young man.

Indeed, Vandini was happy in his new job, and thought he would never leave this splendid, captivating city.

Something happened, though, to change his mind. One evening, just moments before the rehearsal at the Church was about to begin, Vandini rushed in to take his place in the orchestra. His friend, Tartini, who was principal violinist in the orchestra, looked across to the other side of the immense choir section, and noticed Antonio's excitement. As soon as the last note of the rehearsal was played, Tartini hastened over to the cello section. "What has happened, good friend?" he asked. "I can see you are quite excited."

Vandini pulled a letter from his pocket. "Look at this", he said. "It arrived by post just before I left home to come to the Church. It is an invitation from the city of Prague to play in the coronation celebrations for King Charles VI."

"Ah ha", smiled Tartini. "Do you know I have received the same invitation this very day? What do you think? Shall we go?"

"I don't know. I will be sad to leave this city and this Church," Vandini mused. "But, yes, perhaps we should go. We shall meet in Prague, Brother Tartini."

The cellist, Vandini and the violinist, Tartini, met as they had agreed, and took part in the grand festivities honoring the new King Charles VI. Both of them stayed on for 3 years while they held excellent jobs in the Court of Count Ferdinand Kinsky.

By this time, Vandini's fame as a cellist was spreading all over Europe. Invitations to perform came to him from many cities, but as the years passed, he longed to return to Padua. Together, Vandini and Tartini returned to their beloved city, and the magnificent Church of St. Anthony, which was decorated sumptuously on the inside with paintings and almost life-sized sculptures telling the stories of the miracles which St. Anthony performed.

At the entrance to the choir where the orchestra played, were four large organs with pipes framed in richly-carved wood, and so polished that they shone like gleaming silver. On ordinary church days at St. Anthony's, the music was performed by the church orchestra and sixteen singers. The cellists, holding their bows in the old-fashioned way of the viols, with their fingers underneath and thumb on top, played with a rich deep tone that filled every crevice of the large church.

"How beautifully Maestro Vandini plays," people would say. "He can make his cello sing like a human voice."

Vandini composed a cello concerto, as well as sonatas and solos which he oftened performed in Padua, and he and Tartini played together for special occasions. Sometimes the two men travelled together to give concerts in neighboring towns.

"What is that I hear?" said Vandini as they passed by a

church in a small town. Going closer, they could hear the sounds of an organ, and a choir singing. Quietly, they opened the large wooden door of the small, rustic church. A young priest stood in the entry. "Good Father," Vandini said, "what is that heavenly music being performed?"

"It is an oratorio by a young priest from Bologna", was the reply. "His name is Padre Martini, and his music is well loved here."

Both Vandini and Tartini were so inspired by the music that they decided to send a letter to Padre Martini. They wrote, "It was our great good fortune and pleasure last evening, on our way to give a concert at The Marches, to hear an admirable performance of your oratorio. We were greatly impressed with the luxuriant counterpoints and the long flowing lines of your melodies. We look forward to the day when we can play your compositions. With kindest regards and sincere admiration, G. Tartini and A. Vandini, Padua 17." (Jan. 17, 1737)

Vandini and Tartini spent many years working together, and it is likely that Tartini wrote his two cello concerti especially for his good friend. During their life times, the music-loving world appreciated these two muscians, not only for the pieces they composed, but just as much for the beautiful performances they shared with their countrymen.

b. Bologna, Italy 1690
d. Padua, Italy, after 1771

ANTONIO VIVALDI

ho is that young boy with the thick curly red hair?" the old sacristan in the chapel asked.

"Why, that is Giovanni Vivaldi's son Antonio," came the reply. "I understand Antonio has a great talent for playing the violin, just like his father. In fact, when his father is away, the boy takes his place in the chapel service."

Antonio Vivaldi's first violin teacher was his father, Giovanni. The boy did so well and showed such talent that he, too, was employed at an early age as violinist in the chapel where his father played. Father and son often played sonatas together during the solemn church services at the beautiful chapel of St. Mark's in Venice.

One day Giovanni said to his son, "Antonio, I want to arrange to have you study organ at the chapel, and music theory with my good friend Maestro Lagrenzi. You are a fine violinist, but I believe that some day the world will be hearing music that you compose."

Antonio studied diligently and continued to learn everything he could about music. He also wanted to become a priest in the Catholic Church, and he studied for the priesthood. When he was fifteen years old, Antonio took his vows to become a priest; when he was twenty-five, he was ordained. "There goes the red priest," people would say when they saw the red-headed Vivaldi making his way in his long black robe down the cobblestone street.

Antonio had been a frail and sickly boy. Now, soon after he began his duties as priest in the church, he discovered that his poor health made it impossible for him to carry on his church work. Although he would always be called the red priest, Vivaldi turned the rest of his life to music. He wrote a letter of explanation to his bishop, "I must give up my duties as a priest, but I will never forget my church. I will put my music to the service of God."

Venice, the city where Vivaldi lived, was a lively musical place. Music could be heard everywhere — in the theaters, in the churches, and in every nook and cranny throughout the city. Venetians heard music from morning until night. Rich and poor, they loved to sing — at home, on the streets, and in their boats on the canals.

Visitors often came to warm, sunny Venice from the cold northern countries of Europe. The diary of one visitor describes the way he liked to walk in the market place and stand near the church of St. Mark's watching the people go about their business. It amazed him to hear the people sing. In his diary he wrote, "A man from the dregs of the populace — a shoemaker or a smith dressed in his work clothes, starts a tune; other people of his sort join with him and sing this tune in parts." He went on to write that these working people sang with great beauty, each one singing his part perfectly and in a fine style.

The city of Venice celebrated many festivals and holidays during the year. Almost anything could be reason enough to have a celebration. It might be a wedding of an important person, a visit by a foreign prince, the election of an official of the city or church, or the birthday of a famous person. Of course, no celebration would be complete without special music for the occasion. During some festivals, the canals were crowded with processions of hundreds of gondolas, with the voices of the gondoliers filling the night with enchanting songs and serenades.

This was the kind of city where Antonio Vivaldi grew up. The people of his city wanted music, and they liked the composers who tried new ideas in their compositions. So when Vivaldi gave up his work as a priest, he looked for a position in which he could use his musical talents.

Such a position came to him immediately, and he remained in that job for his entire life. In Venice there was a school where poor, orphaned and abandoned girls were sent for an education. It was called the Conservatory of the Pieta. It was a religious school where the girls spent most of their time learning to sing and to play musical instruments. At the time Vivaldi became maestro do coro, there were six thousand girls in the conservatory.

"It will be your duty," Vivaldi was told, "to compose music for all occasions, to teach the girls to play and perform, to direct the orchestra, perform on the violin, and purchase instruments." It was a big job and much was expected of him, but Vivaldi was prepared.

One morning as Vivaldi was working in his study, the priest from the church of St. Mark came to see him. "Antonio Vivaldi," he said, "in one month, the church will be celebrating the feast of

St. Cecelia. We will need an oratorio for the occasion."

"It will be ready, Father," Vivaldi replied. He immediately began preparations. He had everything at the conservatory that he needed to get ready for the celebration. He had the instruments, the people to copy the music that he composed, money to organize the concert. He was training a fine orchestra and a chorus to perform his work, and best of all, Vivaldi always had a mind full of new ideas. He was ready, then, when the feast of St. Cecelia came around.

Frequently an order would come to Vivaldi to prepare some music in a very short time. "In two days the Pope will be coming from Rome to take part in our church service," a messenger told Vivaldi. "We will be in need of special music for the service."

"In two days?" Vivaldi repeated. "I must find a way to work fast." So, pressed for time, he borrowed ideas from music he had composed before. Sometimes he would use a melody he had written for an instrument, and add words to make it a song. When the Pope came for the church service, Vivaldi's orchestra from the conservatory was there. The music they played was a concerto grosso that Vivaldi had completed in that short time.

To countries all over Europe, news spread about Vivaldi's violin playing and his composing. Many musicians traveled to Venice to hear Vivaldi's work and to study with him. Others came just to be in that wonderful musical city. George Frederick Handel visited Venice and charmed the Venetian people with one of his operas. Arcangelo Corelli visited, too. Francesca Veracini paid a call to

ANTONIO VIVALDI

Venice, and while he was there he wrote a sonata.

One of the wealthy aristocratic musical families that lived in Venice at that time was the Mocenigo family. A member of the family studied violin with the famous teacher, Giuseppi Tartini. When he arrived for his lesson one morning he said to his teacher, "At the next concert in our home, Francesco Veracini, a visitor from another city, will play a sonata that he has written. We would be honored if you would come to hear him."

"I would be delighted to come," answered Tartini.

The evening of the concert came. The elegant music room was filled with eager music lovers. They looked forward to hearing this violinist from Florence. Veracini stepped forward. He bowed and announced that he would perform his sonata. His playing was brilliant. Tartini, seated at the back of the room, was astonished at Veracini's skill and musicianship. He was so amazed, in fact, that he decided he should return to his home city to study and practice to try to play as well as Veracini. Eventually, Tartini became one of the greatest violinists and composers of his time.

We cannot say for a fact, but we certainly can imagine that Vivaldi, Veracini, Tartini, and Handel would often meet together for some lively talks about their work.

Vivaldi wrote many operas which were performed in cities all over Europe. It was his custom when he was conducting an opera to entertain the audience during the intermissions. In the audience one evening was a visitor from Germany who wrote a letter to a friend telling about Vivaldi's violin playing. "Vivaldi performed a solo accompaniment admirably, and at the end he added an improvised cadenza that quite confounded me, for such playing has not been heard before and can never be equaled. He placed his fingers a hair's breadth away from the bridge so that there was hardly room for the bow. He played thus on all four strings, with imitations at an unbelievable speed. Everyone was astonished, but I cannot say I was captivated by it, because it was more skillfully executed than it was pleasant to hear."

Violinists were happy to try Vivaldi's new ideas about violin playing. "Vivaldi's music is more exciting to play," an orchestra member said as he left a rehearsal. "It is more dramatic and passionate, and I like the soaring, poetic passages that he writes."

It is difficult to imagine how anyone could write as much music in a lifetime as Vivaldi did. He was well paid for his work, and he enjoyed spending his money. When he died, Vivaldi was penniless and was buried in a cemetery for the poor. Penniless though he was, he left the world with great musical riches. He was a man of great contrasts. He was weak and in poor health, yet he had a fiery, strong nature. He was fast to anger but quick to calm again. He was pious and mystical but persevering and well-organized. Above all, he composed music with furious energy. To all musicians who came after him — to those who wrote music or performed his compositions — Antonio Vivaldi left a bountiful musical treasure.

b. Venice, Italy 1678
d. Vienna, Austria, July 26, (?) 1741

KARL MARIA VON WEBER

Eight children have I," complained Franz Anton Weber, "and not one of them a musician!" More than anything else, Franz, a violinist and conductor himself, wanted a son who would grow up to be famous in the musical world.

It happened that after his first wife died, Franz married again — this time a poor, shy young girl of twenty-one. Their first child was a small frail boy, sickly and lame, but his parents gave him a princely name: Karl Maria Friedrich Ernest von Weber.

"Perhaps this is the child who will be a famous musician," the father wished aloud. "We will start his music lessons soon."

Before little Karl could walk or talk, Father Franz began giving his son lessons. "See what remarkable progress our son is making on the piano," he proudly declared to his young wife. "And listen to him play the violin." So eager was the father to have Karl succeed that he was very strict with the small child. Even Karl's older stepbrother would rap the little boy's fingers with the bow for every mistake he made. Was it this rough treatment that he received from his father and stepbrother that helped him grow up into the tough, wiry and self-confident person who created so much fine music?

During Karl's early years, his family constantly moved from one place to another. "Pack your things, we are leaving today," his father announced to the family. "We are off to the next town."

There was nothing unusual about this announcement for the

Weber family. Karl's father and his mother, a singer, had joined a group of traveling musicians. They performed short operas and plays as they traveled from town to town. They never settled down to a real home. Home for the Webers became one dingy theatre and rooming house after another, but it proved to be an education for the growing boy.

When young Karl had his eighth birthday, his father decided it was time to show off the boy's talents. "We will travel over Germany, Karl. You will be the pianist, and I will be the page turner. You will be a great success."

At first, audiences were not interested. People were heard complaining, "That poor little boy. He is very gifted, but his father is forcing him to be great when he is too young. He should have a good home and go to school like other boys."

But Karl's father thought his son was a genius, and Karl believed it, too. He was teaching himself, learning from experience. He was watching, listening, and feeling the things that went on around him. "Some day I will write an opera," he said to himself, "and I will understand the theatre because I have lived in it these many years."

When Karl was eleven years old he sang in the choir at the cathedral in Salzburg. Michael Haydn was there and gave the boy lessons in composition. In honor of his teacher, Karl dedicated his first six compositions to him. The following year, when he was twelve years old, he composed his first opera, as he had promised himself he would do.

One of Karl Maria's charms was his sense of humor. He enjoyed playing tricks. In Darmstadt, where he lived for a short time, he had a dog named "Miss." When he walked down the street with the dog, he would call out to the dog in a loud voice, "Miss!" All the girls would turn around to look!

At another time Karl carried a joke too far, and it caused him a great deal of trouble. He was angry with the Duke of Wurtenberg, with whom he had had a quarrel. One day an old woman in the court asked Karl where she could find the washerwoman. Karl pointed to the Duke's apartment.

When the duke heard about this insult, he was furious. He had Karl arrested and put in prison. Fortunately, the duke's brother heard what had happened. "My dear brother," he pleaded with the duke, "please free Karl from prison. I want him to be music teacher for my children." And so Karl was freed, and was more careful after that about his jokes.

Now Karl was eighteen years old and settling down to earn his living. In the city of Breslau there was a famous opera house. For many years the finest operas were produced there, but now the opera house was failing. The performances were not good, and people were not coming to hear them. "Have you heard the news?" the people of Breslau were saying. "The opera performances are getting worse. They are a disgrace. And now they have hired that eighteen year old Karl Weber to be the conductor. Surely now it will fail altogether!"

"Ach, it is so," said another. "Why did they not hire an older

336

KARL MARIA VON WEBER

and more experienced director?"

There was a great commotion in Breslau, because the people cared deeply about their opera. Soon, however, they discovered that they had no need to worry. Karl Maria von Weber gave all his energy to make the Breslau Opera House once again one of the finest in all Europe. "I will insist that the musicians follow my instructions. Together we will make magnificent music."

Karl inspired the musicians to do their best for a leader who worked so diligently and with such dedication. In a short time, the fame of the Breslau Opera had been restored. Once more, beautiful music came from the stage of the opera house.

Karl's long working hours began to weaken his health, but he continued to work and compose. As a pianist and a composer, his name was spoken with praise throughout Europe. Many people enjoyed reading the articles he wrote about his musical activities and the work of his fellow musicians.

One of Karl Maria von Weber's most famous operas was *Der Freischutz*, which means in English *The Free Shooter*. The German people loved it. It was a truly German opera, an old story that took place in the Black Forest, about a demon, magic bullets, and a lady in love saved from death by a magic wreath given to her by a holy hermit.

There was excitement at the opera house after the first performance of *Der Freischutz*. In the audience were soldiers just returned from war, proud of their country. "At last we have true German opera. We don't have to imitate the Italian or French music any longer," they said.

Karl Weber used German stories and myths in his opera. Some said, "Did you hear the way he made the instruments in the orchestra create the magic of the demons? You could hear the sounds of the forest. He made the orchestra sounds match the meanings of the words."

"Yes, and he gave the characters in the opera special musical themes, which helped us follow the story," other listeners commented. "We especially liked the *Hunters Chorus.*"

Whenever *Der Freischutz* was played in Germany, it was received with great enthusiasm, but when it was performed in London, it was a different story. A writer at the time told about it. "The London public is unmusical. When *Der Freischutz* was performed, there were cries of 'Cut it short' from the balcony. Nothing but the *Hunters Chorus* saved that fine work from immediate condemnation in England," the writer continued. "I can remember perfectly well the exquisite melodies in it being compared by the English music critics to 'wind through a keyhole'!"

Although Weber was in poor health, he accepted an invitation to travel to London. "It is our wish," the director of the opera house wrote, "to have you come to supervise the performance of your new opera, *Oberon.*

With great courage, but little strength, Weber staged the opera and did everything required of him. But before he could return home, he died, just before he would have been forty years old.

Karl Maria von Weber gave the world many new ideas about

writing music. Before his time, when a composer wanted the orchestra to sound loud, he would write *LOUD* in the part. But Weber had a different way. By starting a few instruments of the orchestra, then adding others one by one, he could build up a loud sound. He also originated the idea of sudden changes fom loud to soft, or from fast to slow. He would use a pause to give the feeling of suspense and excitement.

Sometimes he divided the violin sections to play different parts, to give the feeling of rushing motion, to describe wind or other sounds of nature. Weber was especially fond of the clarinet and liked to use it along with other woodwind instruments to sustain harmonies, and to use brass instruments to give brilliant and full sound for special effects. Weber's new ideas were truly an inspiration for composers of orchestral music who came after him.

b. Eutin, Oldenberg, Germany, November 18, 1786
d. London, England, June 5, 1826

Appendix I

Sources of music by composers in the Suzuki Piano School

Composer	Title	Original Source of composition	Volume
Johann Sebastian Bach	**Minuet 3**	**Second notebook of Anna Magdelene Bach**	Vol. 2
	Minuet 1	**Suite in g minor for Clavier BWV 822** Trio (7th movement) in G major	Vol. 2
	Minuet 2	**Second notebook of Anna Magdelene Bach**	Vol. 2
	Minuet	**Suite** for Clavier BWV 822 Minuet 1	
	Minuet	**Notebook of Anna Magdelene Bach** BWV 115 **Minuet**	Vol. 2
	Musette	**Notebook of Anna Magdelene Bach** BWV anh 126	Vol. 4
	Gavotte	**Suite** for Clavier BWV 822 Gavotte (en Rondeau) Third Movement	Vol. 4
	Minuet I	**Partita** I in B flat BWV 825 from **Six Partitas**	Vol. 4
	Minuet II	**Partita** I in B flat BWV 825 Minuet I da capo	Vol. 4
	Gigue	**Partita** I in B flat BWV 825 Allegro ma expressivo	Vol. 4
	Prelude	**Praeludium** from **Well Tempered Clavier** BWV 846, **Volume I**	Vol. 5
	Invention	**Invention I** (15 Inventions) BWV 772	Vol. 5
	Little Prelude	**Preludes for Lute** BWV 999	Vol. 5
Thomas Haynes Bayly	**Long, Long Ago**	Song for voice and piano	Vol. 1
Ludwig van Beethoven	**Sonatina**	**Sonatina** in G from Two Sonatas for Clavier G.A. nr. 160 Moderato and Romanze	Vol. 2
	Theme	arrangement of **Symphony III "Eroica"** Op. 55 in E flat (4th movement, theme 2)	Vol. 3
	Ecossaise	composition for piano	Vol. 3
	Sonata	**Sonata** for piano Op. 49 No. 2 Allegro ma non troppo Tempo di Minuetto	Vol. 4
	Sonatina in F	**Two Sonatas** for Clavier Anhang 5 Allegro Assai Rondo	Vol. 2
(Johann) Friederick Burgmüller	**Arabesque**	Composition for piano	Vol. 5
	By the Limpid Stream	Composition for piano	Vol. 5

Domenico Scarlatti	Sonata "Pastorale"	Longo 413 in d minor "Pastorale"	Vol. 6
Robert Schumann	A Happy Farmer	Album for the Young Op. 68	Vol. 2
	Melody	Album for the Young Op. 68	Vol. 2
	The Wild Rider	Album for the Young Op. 68	Vol. 3
	Siciliano	Album for the Young Op. 68	Vol. 5
	First Loss	Album for the Young Op. 68	Vol. 5
Shinichi Suzuki	Allegro	Composition for Violin and Piano	Vol. 1
Peter Ilyich Tchaikovsky	Old French Folksong	Album for the Young Op. 39	Vol. 5
Karl Maria von Weber	Cradle Song	Wiegenlied Op. 13 No. 2 Song with text by F.K. Heimer for voice and guitar	Vol. 2

Appendix II

Sources of music by composers in the Suzuki Cello School

Composer	Title	Source	Volume
Johann Christian Bach	Concerto in C	attributed to Bach, probably arranged and edited by Cassadesus	Vol. 8
Johann Sebastian Bach	Minuet 2	Minuet from Notebook of Anna Magdelene Bach Anh 116	Vol. 1
	Minuet in C	from 3 Minuets #1 for Clavier BWV 841	Vol. 1
	Minuet #1	Suite for Clavier in G BWV 822 Minuet (Trio)	Vol. 2
	Minuet	Minuet in G BWV anh 114 from Notebook of Anna Magdelene Bach (entered in A.M. Bach's handwriting, but composer unknown)	Vol. 2
	March in G	from Cantata #207 Soprano part of Chorus August Liebe	Vol. 2
	Gigue	from Cantata #212 Bass Aria, Es nehme zehntausend Ducaten	Vol. 3
	March in D	from Cantata Burlesque (Peasant Cantata) BWV 212 2 duets for Soprano and Base with violin, viola, corno, flauto traverso, continuo	Vol. 3
	Allegro Moderato	Sonata #1 in G BWV 1027 for viola da gamba and clavier (also used in organ sonata-Trio)	Vol. 3
	Gavotte	Suite for Clavier BWV 822 originally in g minor (Gavotte and Rondo)	Vol. 4
	G Major Suite	Minuet I and II BWV 1007	
	Arioso	from Cantata #156 BWV 156 Ich steh mit einem Fuss im Grabe, originally in F	Vol. 5
	Suite #1	Suite #1 for cello Gigue (7th movement)	Vol. 5
	Suite in G	Suite in G BWV 1007 Prelude	
Jean-Baptiste Sebastian Breval	Sonata in C	Sonata in C for cello and piano (Allegro and Rondo Grazioso)	Vol. 4

Pronunciation Guide

andante	ahn-dahn'-tay
basilica	baa-sill'-ih-kah
Beethoven, Ludwig von	Bay-toff-en, Lood'-vick fawn
Breval Jean Baptiste-	Bray-vahle' Jhahg Baa-tee'-steh
Bruch, (Max)	Brookh, Mahx
Buxtehude, (Dietrich)	Boo'-kstah-hoo-deh, Dee'-trikh
Caix d'Hervelois, Louis	Keh d'Ay-veh-lwah' Loo-ee
Casals, (Pablo)	Kah-salls' Pah-blow
Cherubini (Luigi)	Ker-you-bee'-nee, Loo-ee'-gee
Chopin, Frederik François	Shu-panh; Fred-er-ick' Franh-swah'
clavier	clah-veer'
concertstucke	con-sehr-schtook'-ah
Cordelliers	Kor-dell-yay'
Czerny, Karl	Chair'-nee, Karl
Daquin, Louis-Claude	Dahn-kahng', Loo-ee' Clawd
D-Aumont, Duke	D'Oh-mohng', Duke
David, Ferdinand	Dah-veed; Fer-din-anh'
Der Freischutz	Dair Fry'-shootts
Devrient, (Eduard)	Dehv-r-yohng', Edd-wahrd
Dido and Aeneaus	Digh-do and A-nee'-uss
D'Orleans, Duc and Duchess	D'Or-lay-anhng' duck'-ats
ducats	
ein wunderkind	ine voonn'-dehr-kinnt
Eisenach	Eye'-zen-ahkh
Esterhazy, Prince Nicolaus	Esh-tehr-hatz'-ee
Gelenek	Jell'-in-eck
Gewandhaus	Geh-vant'-house
Goethe, Johann Wolfgang von	Gött-tuh, Yo'-hann Voolf'-gong fawn
Golterman, George	Gol'-ter-mahnn
Gossec (Francois Joseph)	Gah-seck', Franh-swah' Jo-seph'
Halle	Hahl'-luh
Hebenstadt	Hay'-ben-shtahtt
Hebrides	Heh-brih-deez'
Hummel, Johann Nepomuk	Hoomm'-ell, Yo'-hann Nep'-oh-moock

Ingres (Jean)	Inng'-gh, Jhahg
Jeanrenaud, Cecile	Zhahn-reh-no', Seh-seel'
Kapellmeister	Kah-pell'-migh-schter
Kieff	Kee-ev'
knacher	knahck'-er (clap, snap)
Kuhlau, Frederik	Koo'-low
Leipzig	Lighp'-tzig
Leipzigerstrasse	Lighp'tzig-strahss-eh
Lichner, Heinrich	Likh'nehr, Hyn'-rikh
Lochner	Lokh'-nehr
Lully, Jean Battiste	Lu-lee', Jhahg Baa-tee'-steh
Marian (Mozart)	Mahr-ee-ahn (Moh'-tzart)
Meck, Najeda von	Meck, Nahj-ya fawn
Monsieur	Mih-s-yuh'
Mosewius	Mosheh-vees'
Neuer Markt	Noyer'-Markt
Paderewski, Ignace Jan	Pad-err-eff'-skee, Ig'-natz Yan
Pergolesi, Giovanni	Pare-go-lay'-see Jee-o-vah'-nee
Prelude	Preh'-lood
Rencaglias, Signore	Renn-cah'-lee-ahs, Seeg-noh'-reh
repertoire	reh-per-twar'
Requiem	Re'-qwee-emm
Rue de Jardinet	Rü dih zhahr-dee-nay'
Reutter	Roy'-tehr
Saint Chapelle	Sangh Shah-pell'
Saint-Martin, Alexis	Sangh-Mahr-tangh' Al-ex-ees'
Saint-Saens, Charles Camille	Sangh-Sohng', Sharrl Kahng-meel'
Salzburg	Zhallts'-boorgh
Sarasate, Pablo	Sah-rah-sah'-teh, Paa'-blow
sensei	senn-say (teacher)
Tchaikovsky	Chy-kovv'-skee, Pee-ay'-torr Ill'-y-ich
Thames River	Temms River
Veracini, Francesca Maria	Verr-a-chee'-nee, Frahn-chess'-kah Mah-ree'-ah
Weimar	Vy'-mar
Weisenstein	Vy'-zenn-schtine
Wieck, Frederick	Veek, Fre-derr-eek'
Zywny	Zjhiv-nee